Saving Suquamish Sources

Southern Puget txʷəlšucid Salish Dictionary

Based on

Southern Puget Sound Salish 2:
Warren A Snyder, PhD
Texts, Suquamish Place Names, and Dictionary
Sacramento Anthropological Society Paper #9 Fall 1968

Digitized by Jay Miller, Ben Barrett
Biography by Jay Miller, PhD
© 2020

Warren Arthur Snyder
(1918–2000)

Raised in Spokane, Warren attended Franklin Grade and Lewis & Clark High Schools. During WWII he served in the 305th bomber group, nicknamed "Can Do" and commanded by Colonel Curtis LeMay, which flew from England on 337 missions in 9,321 sorties, dropped 22,363 tons of bombs, and lost 154 aircraft MIA over Germany. Like many others, he attended UW on the GI bill, working as an archaeologist at Suquamish excavating Chief Seattle's famous OleMan House in 1951 (https://bit.ly/2EV623E, https://bit.ly/35cggHo), then as an anthropologist assembling materials for their land claim, and, turning to linguistics, worked with native speakers to share texts, providing the data for his phonology, grammar, dictionary, and place names, along with cultural autobiography, stories, and family incidents. His 16 audio tapes are in UW Special Collections stored at Ethnomusicology. His ethnographic file cards were given to Jay Miller, who used them for a Suquamish ethnography further informed by living elders and by linguistic work by Vi Hilbert, a fluent speaker and scholar. Warren developed a wide network in the native community and among fellow graduate students. For example, he introduced Pamela Amoss to speakers of Old Nooksack, which became her MA thesis. After a decade in California, he worked with Maidu and Patwin and his notes are at the Bancroft Library at Berkeley. In all, his career at Sacramento State, from 1955 until he became emeritus in 1983, added to a vibrant anthropology community.

As an expert witness, Warren taught the anthropology community an important if painful lesson. While he was under oath in the land claims hearings there was a summer recess. During that time, Warren discovered a map that better illustrated the Suquamish claim, but affected his earlier testimony. When the hearings resumed, Warren, like any good academic, was delighted to provide better evidence for the Suquamish, only to discover that the lawyers and court decided that "he had changed his testimony" invalidating all of it, because, in court, positions are fixed unless extraordinary legal maneuvering and contortions are invoked. Later expert witnesses for tribes, especially Barbara Lane, in treaty-guaranteed fishing rights cases were scrupulous to keep their testimonies for the many tribes consistent. For the same reason, the State of Washington, regardless of the sympathies of the current Attorney General, consistently opposes Federal treaty rights and local tribes despite its continuous defeat in court. More personally, his experience in court encouraged Warren to shift to linguistics as a safer and more specialized academic concern.

As a hobby, he learned stone masonry from a skilled Italian craftsman. Warren and his wife Claire (1920 - 2000) named their daughter LeeAnn in honor of LeRoy Webb, a fellow graduate student trained at Reed College specializing in the Middle East, who died of cancer. Webb's books went to the UW Department of Anthropology to establish a namesake library, since scattered and replaced with computer terminals, except for core reprints and regional titles rescued by then Burke museum director George MacDonald and spirited off to safety in Ontario. Other books joined the library of Alan Bryan & Ruth Gruhn now at the University of Alberta.

Warren's strong anthropology department at Sacramento maintained close ties to the Northwest through its publication series and hires of fellow University of Washington graduates.

Working mostly as an administrator during his later career, Warren's ongoing commitment to linguistics shows in his report published in the Proceedings of the Conference on the Culture of Schools Held at Greystone House:

Statement of Warren A. Snyder

Within the last five years some of my colleagues in education and some teachers have asked me to talk to them about the principles of linguistics as these may be related to the problems of teaching children to read and write English. The 1960's may be identified as the decade in which the linguistic dam broke in the English-speaking part of the world.   Knowledge of linguistic principles is now diffusing rapidly.

No reader of English can arrive at an understanding of basic linguistic principles without experiencing a clearer perception of the structural monstrosity that written English is. This insight has been achieved by Individual scholars many times going far back into the history of written English. For example, several generations of the Pitman family in England have advocated reforms of written English. Benjamin Franklin advocated reforms. There have been many others. Why did these earlier insights have so little effect on culture change as compared to that which linguistic principles now promise to have? One reason is that the earlier insights were isolated insights. They were not assimilated into a traditional pattern of belief about the nature of language. By contrast, the principles of linguistic science have, especially from the 1920's to the present, developed rapidly into a complex belief system, shared, transmitted and changed by specialists working in a number of different applied and academic areas. Anthropological linguists are among these.

Linguistics is contributing to the synthesis of behavioral sciences. There is a rapid development in the area of psycholinguistics. There is the beginning of a sociology of language.

How may these developments affect the teaching of written English in our schools? We may identify two broad areas of possible influence: (1) contributions toward more efficient, effective and realistic methods of teaching traditional written English, and (2) contributions toward reforms in written English.

The first of these is well under way. The second, at some time in the future, may be in part, a result of the first.

The American anthropological linguist Leonard Bloomfield devised a system for teaching children to read in the 1930's. His system emphasized the concept of the phoneme and of classes of words based on spelling. No publisher could be found for his work until 1961, long after the author's death. Only now is a series of experimental readers and workbooks based on Bloomfield's system being published by Clarence L. Barnhart.

A similar system was devised by Frances A. Hall assisted by the linguist Robert A. Hall, Jr. The linguistic principles upon which these systems have been based are sound.

The anthropological linguist Charles F. Hockett has analyzed English graphic monosyllables which represent regularities of spelling patterns in relation to pronunciation. Others have carried this work further through the use of computers. A number of people are now working on dialect differences in relation to the concept of spelling classes. New efforts are being made to clarify the concept of the grapheme especially in its application to written English.

All of this will be useful in teaching beginning reading, spelling, and remedial reading.

Criticisms from some specialists in education and some psychologists point out that linguistic approaches have over-emphasized the formal structural approach and have slighted problems of content, story interest, and perception. Reading material advocated by the linguist Henry Lee Smith, in collaboration with teachers and psychologists, retains the linguistic approach but represents an effort to improve content and avoid some perception problems.

The "Reading in Color" system developed by the educator and psychologist Caleb Gattegno, while it does not come directly from the traditions of structural linguistics, can be related to the concepts of phoneme-grapheme correspondences and of spelling patterns.

In England, Pitman and others have developed the initial teaching alphabet. Graphs used in ITA correspond closely to phonemes of standard English in England. Some efforts are being made in the United States to apply the method here.

The development of all of these methods will accelerate the diffusion of knowledge of linguistic principles. This, in turn, will increase the recognition of need for reform. Within a generation or two we may predict that resistance to reform will be much weaker and less influential than it is today.
Cultural anthropologists and sociologists may contribute to our understanding of the forces of resistance to change in written English. It will be important to have as thorough knowledge as possible of the social and psychological functions involved in maintenance of the present system of written English so that these may be taken into account when efforts are made to bring about reforms at some time in the future.

These studies will be important for theoretical as well as practical purposes. For example, study of written English by behavioral scientists may contribute to our understanding of irrationality or nonrationality in culture.

The following quotation from Kroeber presents the theoretical point:

"Allied to this unawareness or unconsciousness of cultural form and organization is the irrationality of much of the collective in culture. 'Irrationality' is what it is sometimes called." "It covers a variety of happenings in culture which have in common a factor of inconsistency. The totality of a situation or way of doing comes out less regular and less coherent than It might have been under rational planning." "The point, of course, is that such irregularities and inefficiences were

not thought out but are the result of long and complex histories, with quite different factors often impinging successively." "In one sense the outcome is 'irrational' indeed, in that the institution lacks the full reasonableness which its defenders claim for it. Actually, it rather is non-rational, and only partly that. Most strictly, it is that the institutional pattern is irregular, not wholly consistent."

Discussion

It was suggested that the introduction of linguistics as a school subject might well provide an excellent opportunity to study how teachers resist change. Teachers, were defended, however, on the grounds that they are not as irrationally conservative as all that. They are after all in direct contact with the children and thus know what will be accepted and what rejected.

Snyder confessed that the introduction of linguistics in California schools was bound to create much furor deserving of study by anthropologists.

Observers would have to be placed in classrooms because teachers did not always report up the hierarchy what was happening in their classes. There was not just a single educational power structure, but many.

As indicated by his statement above, Warren was a life-long team player, during WWII, at UW, and during his department building at Sacramento. His fieldwork and publications came early in his professional career, but the friendships and networks in which he became involved lasted a life time. He kept in touch with the Northwest, sponsoring visits, research, and publications across the generations.

Publications

Archaeological Sampling at "Old Man House" On Puget Sound. Research Studies of The State College of Washington (WSU) XXIV: 17-37 1956 (tDAR id: 133326)

"Statement of Warren A. Snyder" and "Discussion," Culture of Schools, Final Report, Volume I, by American Anthropological Association for Office of Education (DHEW), Washington, DC (files.eric.ed.gov/fulltext/ED039209.pdf): 51-56 [undated]

Southern Puget Sound Salish 1: Phonology and Morphology, 1968 Sacramento Anthropological Society Paper #8 Spring 1968

Southern Puget Sound Salish 2: Texts, Suquamish Place Names, and Dictionary, Sacramento Anthropological Society Paper #9 Fall 1968

Rose Marie McDuff; Warren A Snyder; Maxwell Owusu, The Ethnohistory of Saint's home church of the Church of God in Christ, Los Angeles, California, MA Anthropology, California State University, Sacramento 1973

Steven F Arvizu, Warren A Snyder, Paul T Espinosa, Demystifying the Concept of Culture: Theoretical and Conceptual Tools, National Dissemination and Assessment Center, California State University 1980

16 sound tape reels at the UW Special Collections, some in Melville Jacobs's papers https://bit.ly/355ntJn: (http://archiveswest.orbiscascade.org/ark:/80444/xv95437)

Linguistic notes on Maidu and Patwin languages, in English, Maidu, and Patwin, BANC MSS 2012/120, Bancroft Library, University of California, Berkeley, Gift of LeeAnn Snyder Martin 2012. Transferred from Dorothea J. Theodoratus papers (BANC MSS 98/103 c).

Warren Snyder recordings

Vi Hilbert Collection
2005-1.143-156
16 tapes UW

#143   64:47 x2 sides Jan 55
Southern Puget Salish 5' reel Irish brand
Amelia Sneatlum
1 what Si'ał said
2 sqlalitut
3-8 vocabulary
9 vocabulary
10-14 vocabulary

#144   64:04 x2   Jan 55
Southern Puget Salish 5' reel Scotch brand
Amelia Sneatlum
1 vocabulary
2-8 vocabulary
9 vocabulary end
10 vocabulary Jerry Kanim
4 hunters ee
5 sqlalitut

#145   64:05 x2
Southern Puget Salish 5' reel Scotch brand
Jerry Kanim Marie & Charles
1 ♀ voice ♂
2 vocabulary Jerry Kanim
3-7 vocabulary Jerry Kanim
8 vocabulary Jerry Kanim
9 Bear & Rabbit in Snoqualmie Jerry Kanim I 6
10-14 end

#146   62:32 x2
Southern Puget Salish 5' reel Scotch brand
1 vocabulary Jerry Kanim
2 vocabulary Jerry Kanim
3 Star Husband Snoqualmie p11
4-5 " "
6 " "
7-12 Star Husband sq

#147   63:36 x2

Southern Puget Salish 5' reel Scotch brand
1 " " Jerry Kanim
2 Transformer sq
3-7 " " '
8 " "
9-13 " "

#148   64:31 x2

Southern Puget Salish 5' reel Scotch brand Jerry Kanim 55
1 " "
2-3 " "
4 " "
5-6 " " volume increase
7 " "
8 " " volume low
9 very low
10 " "
11-15 " "

#149   64:20 x2

Southern Puget Salish 5' reel Scotch brand
1 " "
2-7 " "
8 " "
9-13 " "
14 " "

#150a   63:00 x2

Southern Puget Salish 5' reel Irish brand   Jerry Kanim
1 vocabulary
2 vocabulary
3 low
4 " "
5-7 vocabulary
8 song

#150b   63:16 x2

Southern Puget Salish 5' reel Irish brand Jerry Kanim
1 vocabulary
2-8 vocabulary

#151   35:29 x1

Southern Puget Salish 5' reel Scotch brand
1 Transformer
2-7 "

#152   29:09 x1

Southern Puget Salish 5' reel Scotch brand
1 Transformer < very low
2 "
3 "
4-7

#153   64:18 x2

Southern Puget Salish 5' reel Irish brand   Jerry Kanim
1 Coyote
2-7 "
8 Snow Bird
9-14 "

#154a   39:16 x1

Southern Puget Salish 5' reel Soundcraft brand   Jerry Kanim
1 vocabulary
2-8 vocabulary

#154b   39:24 x2 Jerry Kanim

Southern Puget Salish 5' reel Soundcraft brand
1 vocabulary
2 vocabulary ?
3-8 vocabulary

#155   64:49 x2 Jerry Kanim

Southern Puget Salish 5' reel Irish brand
1 vocabulary
2-7 vocabulary
8 vocabulary
9-14 vocabulary

#156   65:16 x2 Jerry Kanim

Southern Puget Salish 5' reel Irish brand
1 vocabulary
2-7 vocabulary
8 vocabulary
9-14 vocabulary

Duwamish et alia (F-275) was instituted by jurisdictional act of 12 February 1925 (43 Stat 886) to allow suit in the Court of Claims by Washington State Indians and Tribes living west of the Cascade Mountains, an estimated population of 4597 in 1940, for a general accounting of funds ($71,496.45) allegedly still due under treaty stipulations, compensations for lands taken, and hunting and fishing rights. The final report of 933 pages was forwarded to the Department of Justice on 17 November 1931; the court on 4 June 1934 (79 C Cls 530) dismissed this claim, arguing that it was eliminated by financial and service offsets already provided to the plaintiffs. Appeal was denied 27 May 1935 (81 C Cls 976, 295 US 755). Growing outrage at such lack of justice rsulted in the more successful 1950s Land Claims in which Warren Snyder testified, with mixed results, for Suquamish.

Suquamish Traditions

Jay Miller & Warren Snyder

Abstract

Ethnographic sketch of the aboriginal Suquamish on the Kitsap Peninsula across Puget Sound from the city of Seattle is based on 1952-54 notes by Warren Snyder rechecked with elders for Economy, Technology, Society by Rank, Age and Gender, Intertribal Relations, Medicine, Ritual, Folklore, and War Tales. Appendices add another battle and an index to elders and subtopics.

Introduction

As preparation for his book-length overview of Puget Sound ethnography, following up a prior study of its major ritual – the shamanic redeeming from the land of the dead (Miller 1988: 1999), the 1952-54 fieldnotes of Dr Warren Snyder were typed into a computer and edited into this ethnography. Copies of it have been in the keeping of the Suquamish Tribe for over two decades, but this publication now makes it available for peer review and scholarly evaluation. A similar effort was made with the 1927 Chehalis area materials from Thelma Adamson, only there her notes had to be condensed and here his had to be fleshed out and articulated with help from living elders. Strongly motivating these contributions has been increasing despair that anthropologists, especially in the Northwest, have been actively denying their own founders, both women and men, even as local native peoples constantly remind each other not to forget their elders. This growing contrast only adds to the larger sense of loss.

Named for the important leader prior to Chief Seattle, the Kitsap Peninsula is the western edge of the Lushootseed (Puget Sound) peoples. Their language and traditions place them within the southern dialect chain, distinguished from the northern one by some important vocabulary differences and respective accents on the first or second vowel of the basic stem or root of a word.

Throughout Lushootseed territory, each "tribal" group is closely associated with its own river drainage, which provided cohesion and identity to an otherwise diverse collection of autonomous communities and camps. On the east and west sides of Puget Sound, however, were exceptions to this dendritic Y-branching pattern. On the east, the drainage of the Duwamish had a complex outlet with an H or trellis pattern, fostering an important population concentration on the interconnecting Black River, since diverted and filled. On the west, the Suquamish ancestral territory is located between the Sound and Hood Canal, a salt-water hook. Significantly, this homeland lacked any major rivers, so their subsistence adaptation required extensive travel to collect supplies needed for winter, in addition to the harvesting of local foods from sheltered bays and local small streams.

Their usual and accustomed (UNA, U&A) fishery, therefore, was judged by the Federal Court to have extended from the Fraser River mouth and Puget Sound to Hood Canal, of necessity. Barbara Lane (1974: 4) specifically noted "The Suquamish often traveled to Hood Canal and to upper Puget Sound as well as in other directions to harvest natural resources or to visit with relatives in other areas." Local resources, moreover, were also utilized, as these were available. "Shrimp were taken near Indianola and near Holly on the east shore of Hood Canal" (Lane 1974: 20).

Most recently, before aggregating on their present reservation, the people now known as the Suquamish (Riddell 1932), occupied about six winter towns, located on inland bays on the east side of the peninsula. The west side of the peninsula along Hood Canal was too windy, cold, and unprotected to allow for anything but camping during mild weather or for enduring privations necessary for religious devotions. All of their villages and camps represented central locations giving ready access to diverse nearby resources, to Puget Sound, and to interior forests. Those in the inland bays also had the advantage of access to the shores of both the Sound and the Canal via canoes, trails, and game tracks.

Modern elders recall going with parents and grandparents to the Edmonds area to gather blackberries and basketry materials. In alternate years, they camped at Mosier near Mukilteo to take advantage of the biennial run of "pinks" (chum salmon) there.

Suquamish tacitly approved the settlement of Port Gamble (Little Boston) on the northeast side of the Canal by S'Klallams who were working at the Pope and Talbot Mill started there in 1852. A similar situation also applies to the Klallam colony at Seabeck near the Washington Mill.

Important trails across the Kitsap Peninsula included those from Dye Inlet, from the villages at Chico - Erland Point to Seabeck, from Poulsbo (known to Suquamish as Mapleville), from the village at Suquamish to Port Gamble. That from Silverdale on Dye Inlet was so useful it is now paved as the Anderson Hill Road. Martha George (Indian Claims Commission 1952: 44) explicitly testified to the use of these trails.

The occasion for the return of the Snyder note cards to the tribe was a 1982 fishing rights trial requested by the Skokomish, acting as successors in interest to the nine aboriginal Twana winter communities, which were located along the western and the lower portions of Hood Canal. Their request was intended to establish their primary right to fish in the Canal and to exclude other tribes as this became necessary to guarantee profits from commercial salmon fishing. As judicially determined, Skokomish were given exclusive rights to fish the canal, but, to their credit, sent shellfish to the Suquamish museum dedication and allow Suquamish to fish in the canal during good runs.

Since ancient times, Suquamish came to Hood Canal because of signals from nature, not invitations or permission. Many people went there when the basketry materials were ready, or the shrimp, or the oysters, or passed through on their way to hunt in the Olympics. The fall run of dog salmon was announced by the ripening of the salmonberries, much as the spring runs coincided with the blooming of the dogwood.

As they finished the processing of dog salmon for winter use, the guardian spirits of the most inexperienced visionaries came to them while they were still at the Canal. Older, more experienced visionaries knew their spirits well enough to have them arrive after they were safely settled in the winter villages. People helped the new singers, by gathering around to help with these songs while they were still in the camps. Later in the winter villages, shamans and other professionals would give them better help at controlling their powers.

Research

Located close to a major city, much material exists relating to Suquamish, but little of it has been published. Early converts to Catholicism – Chief Seattle was baptized with the name of Noah – much relevant data is located in the Seattle Catholic archives (Buerge 20). Records from the trading post run by William Deshaw [De Shaw], son-in-law to Chief Seattle, are now stored on the campus of the University of Washington.

Active fieldworkers have included Edward S. Curtis (1913), who collected another version of the Lushootseed battle in Canada at ends of these notes and singular materials from Jacob Wahelchu, a famous leader who lived for over a century. In 1910, John Peabody Harrington collected linguistic data and place names from Chief William Rogers, hereditary leader of the Duwamish but living on Miller Bay among the Suquamish, who regarded him as one of their subchiefs. In 1942, Harrington returned to nearby Port Gamble and coastal Washington.

Just before his tragic death, the young Herman Haeberlin worked among the residents of the Tulalip Reservation in 1916-17. After resuming her position at the University of Washington, Erna Gunther edited his notes and translated his 1924 German text to provide the classic summary of Lushootseed tribes, concentrating on the Snohomish, Snoqualmie, and Nisqually.

In 1918, Thomas Talbot Waterman, continuing efforts by Harrington and Haeberlin, worked closely with Arthur Ballard in the collection of folklore and developed close ties at Suquamish, particularly with Jack Adams and family.

During the early 1930s, pleas by Lushootseed and neighboring tribes were heard to demand compensation and recognition for inequities from the loss of their lands and resources. These issues were raised again during the 1950s when the federal government established the Indian Claims Commission allowing tribes to sue for compensation for the loss of land, property, and improvements. Warren Snyder testified for Suquamish (Indian Claims Commission 1952: 94-97), but that fall testified again on the basis of a compelling document and map that clarified his earlier testimony. While this is good academic practice, it is deadly in a court of law, where any change of opinion is ruthlessly discredited, and Dr Snyder became an object lesson for expert witnesses who have come after him.

Some time after her 1935-36 fieldwork among the Puyallup-Nisqually, Marian Smith, a kindly woman crippled by polio, visited on the Port Madison Reservation with Sam Wilson. Her notes (Folder Four), now in London, detail family histories of Wilson, Kitsap, and Seattle; religious and spiritual topics; mythic and personal happenings; and technology (Amoss 1975). Smith remained in correspondence between 1939-47 with an amateur archaeologist named Ernest Bertelson living at Suquamish. Copies of his letters and his artifact collection, particularly from Old Man House, are now respectively in the Archives and the Burke Museum at the University of Washington, or on loan to the Suquamish Tribal Museum.

Before and after his testimony for Suquamish land claims, Dr. Warren Snyder worked in the Suquamish area from 1952-55. He began as an archaeologist testing the site of Old Man House, but, during the claims litigation, he collected ethnographic information to testify on 13, 16 June 1952 and 4, 5 August 1953. Then, at the encouragement of Dr. Melville Jacobs, he turned to linguistics, producing a grammar of Suquamish Lushootseed. While his ethnographic note cards remained in storage, these linguistic materials were published (1968) in two volumes of grammar and of texts, place names, and dictionary that is interesting for its sweeping diversity of camps, resource areas, graveyards, forts, and places mentioned in mythology.

Lastly, according to a late, great Suquamish leader, while the locations of ancestral Suquamish villages are scattered in all prior sources, an important feature for determining residences, whether camp or village, is proximity to fresh water. For example, Blake Island lacked any water source. Overnight campers had to carry water with them, though now that it is a public park, drinkable water is provided by the state.

Lawrence Webster, past tribal chairman and grandson of Jacob Wahelchu, said that good water was only available at a few locations on the Kitsap Peninsula. On the East Side were Grovers Creek and others in Miller Bay, Indianola – a spring in the sand flats to the east, Kingston Bay – at its head, Manzanita, Eagle Harbor at Winslow – a small but good water supply, Liberty Bay near Scandia and Sherman, Dyes Inlet at Clear and Chico Creeks, Gorst Creek on the Port Orchard side, Blackjack Creek, Colby, Ollala, and Wilson Creeks. On the West Side were Creeks on Port Gamble Bay, and Big and Little Beef Creeks near Seabeck on Hood Canal.

Editing

Based on these note cards by Snyder, a basic Suquamish ethnography can be presented. The breath, scope, and purpose of his three field research are rare for the Northwest or anywhere else, making it all the more valuable. The cards which are presented below were given to Jay Miller in September 1982 during a meeting in the Sacramento home of Warren and Grace Snyder. Miller was then preparing to serve as the expert witness for the Suquamish in the case adjudicating Skokomish claims to a primary fishing right in Hood Canal. When the notes reached Seattle, Miller reviewed and edited them in anticipation of this publication, before turning the originals over to the Suquamish Tribal Archives.

The notes consist of 5x8 inch cards, each devoted to a particular topic and elder, with long entries numbered sequentially. They were arranged in a file box according to conventional headings like land, material culture, economy, society, religion, and folklore. Miller undertook to write out the sketchy phrases and sentences, relying on his own fieldwork among Suquamish. Any comments he introduced into the narrative are marked by [brackets]. Topics are arranged from the most to the least voluminous, noting in {curved brackets} the initials of the person who provided the information to facilitate comparative work in the future. Linguistic terms that have not been verified are in *italic* while those confirmed by Vi Hilbert are in **bold**.

Because data from women have been relatively scarce, each topic begins with material supplied by Julia Jacobs {*jj*}, who lived at Indianola until her death. She was the mother of the former tribal chairman, Lawrence Webster (1899-1991, thus 83 in 1982), and the adopted daughter of the long-lived Chief Jacob Wahelchu, who died at the age of 112 in 1911 (cf Miller 1999: 11-13). Other material was provided by Wilson George {*wg*}, living at Tulalip, Ellen Sigo George {*eg*}, his double first cousin (two brothers married sisters) living among the Port Gamble Klallam, and Ed Sigo {*es*}, living at Shelton in 1952 before he moved to Squaxon Island where he died in 1982, and John Adams {*ja*}, about 80 in 1952 and living near Poulsbo (known to the Suquamish as Mapleville), until he died just short of his 90th birthday in July 1961. He was the son of Jack Adams (**hadᶻius**), who died at the age of 75 in 1931 and was a major source for the information collected by John Peabody Harrington about 1910 and by TT Waterman about 1920.

Suquamish Traditions

Economy

Year {jj}

The year was divided into different seasons. There was a time of the year when the wind blew a lot, around March or April. This was called **spopohəgʷd**. There was a time in the fall when the salmon fishing and berry picking first started. It was called paTalos [pəd "time of" + ƚalos = "sliced salmon"]. A cold winter was called sťəs = "cold", while winter in general was called pats [pədtəs = "time of cold"]. Summer had two names, shadab [warmth] and **padhadab** ["time of warmth"].

Drying {jj}

Berries were treated in the same way meat was cooked. They laid fern on sticks and then put the berries (huckle, black, salmon) on top. They turned the berries over every so often until they were thoroughly dry. Then they were stored in hard baskets for winter use. When they wanted to use some dried berries, they soaked them in water and smashed them in a hard basket with a piece of wood used just for this purpose.

Horse Clams were shelled and the inside muscle put on sticks about 2½ feet long, pointed at one end. They made a long fire and put a frame across one or both sides. The clam sticks were leaned against this frame and turned often to dry and cook. When they were done, women strung them on cedar bark strings and dried them further in the sun.

Butter Clams were steamed and dried. They gathered rocks together and made a fire on top of them until the rocks were red hot. Then they took the fire off and made the rocks level. The clams were left in the shells, put on the rocks, and covered with mats. They cooked for about 20 minutes. When they were cooler, they were shelled and put on sticks like horse clams. They were roasted, put on cedar strings, and put in the sun. Butter and horse were the only two kinds of clams that were dried. They were eaten after being soaked in water, boiled, or chewed as they were. Sometimes the clams were slightly smoked to give them a different flavor.

Deer and Elk {jj}

The meat was sliced thin and laid on sticks over a fire to cure and dry.

Salmon {jj}

Soup. Fresh salmon was boiled. It was cut up, put in water, and boiled. Then they added small roots that looked like onions and were called **ċabəd**. They had a sweet taste and used to grow over near Seattle. The Yakama still dig and use them [camas?]. They also put in another plant that looks like macaroni and was called **piyaẋə** [bitter root]. They put the soup in a big, hard basket. They had certain baskets for eating soups, usually round and 3 feet wide. Julia's father had one. Everyone sat around the same basket to eat the soup. They used wooden spoons, big around with a short handle. Each person had their own spoon to dip into the soup.

Smoking. Salmon was butchered with a special bone knife. Julia heard about but never saw them. She can't describe them exactly. They put sharp sticks into the strips of flesh to make it stretch and stiffen. They hung these up, with a fire under them. They used fir bark for the fire, sometimes alder, but fir was best. The fish were left there for a few days, less then a week, until they were dry. They used a smokehouse for this after the whites came. Before that they used their living quarters in a plank house.

They only dried salmon and herring. Julia never heard of them drying sole or halibut [?]. Herring was dried like salmon except that the bodies weren't spread out with sticks. They were strung on sticks and hung over a fire to smoke. Dried fish was eaten boiled or as it was.

Seasons {*eg, wg*}

Ellen remembered that her father had different names for the "moons" of the year, but she didn't recall them. Wilson said that the coldest part of the year was called x̣aʔx̣aʔ. Following was *elsoqwa* [ɫsoq̓ʷa = "has a younger brother"]. It was called this because it wasn't as cold and the weather was milder. The word x̣aʔx̣aʔ means "sacred, forbidden, taboo." It refereed to all the words to live by, like telling someone not to lie, talk back to a parent, or show disrespect for someone older. Or x̣aʔx̣aʔ gʷadsyabukʷ, "Don't ever fight." Early December before x̣aʔx̣aʔ was called šizalwas, meaning "put away [sheath] your paddles." This was the time when they stopped hunting and fishing. Other terms for the seasons included pax̌kolə, meaning the change of weather to the spring time following spopohəgʷəd = "winds inside," and waq̓ʷaq̓us = "frog's face", referring to the frogs that come out in February to sing, following "younger brother time."

Each "moon" or month was devoted to a particular activity, with approximate Western calendar months:

July was spent drying clams, catching early salmon, and picking blackberries, blackcaps, red huckleberries, and red elderberries;

August involved continuing to dry clams, pick salalberries, eat fresh summer dog and humpy salmon (not good for drying), and hunt for fattened deer;

September to October saw much activity with the fall salmon runs, the beginning of duck-hunting, and the picking of huckleberries;

November had things winding down except for taking ducks;

December was the start of the sacred season, the first games and ceremonies, although they still dug some clams and took bottom fish from canoe heated with fires inside;

January to February were spent at ceremonies and visiting;

March was the beginning of the salmon return;

May was for salmonberries and red elderberries, with some camas dug on Smith Island, steamed or kept dry in a basket;

June to July brought salmon trout, with some dried after it was cooked.

Wilson said they started making their canoes in the spring and tried to finish them during the summer. The purpose was to have them done by the time the salmon started to run.

Ellen said a Klallam told her that when you worked on a dugout canoe, it shortened your life unless you washed and kept the cedar smell off your body. Wilson said it only shortened your life if you worked on cedar after dark.

Dog Salmon Eggs {eg, wg}

These fish eggs were dried and smoked in deer guts. The gut was turned inside out, cleaned, blown out, and filled with the eggs. They ate it like cheese and it tasted something like it, too. They ate it mixed with salmonberry sprouts or potatoes. They never dried silver salmon eggs because they had too much fat and soon spoiled.

Potatoes {eg, wg}

Ellen said the Klallam got their first potatoes from the Chehalis. Ellen's Klallam father in law's grandfather got them and planted them at Port Discovery Bay. They were growing there when the first ship came in and the whites bought some of the potatoes for the crew. Ellen believed that the Suquamish got their potatoes from the Chehalis at about the same time.

Salmon Trolling {es}

They gathered and dried kelp, tied strands of it together, and used this for trolling. They made partly curved hooks from a hardwood like ironwood or dogwood and attached them to the kelp ropes. These were baited it with clams, especially cockles, and used it in the Sound where there were salmon for most of the year. The creeks had salmon only during the spawning season. At other times they had to troll for them in the Sound.

Deer {es}

Deer came down to the beach only during the summer (June, July, and August) when the flies were bothering them in the woods. The rest of the year they were back in the forests. After a kill, the animal was butchered and the meat sliced to be dried over hot coals. The deer had regular trails through the woods. Ed had heard of traps being set into these. They tied a rope from a tree with a hoop hanging at head height over the trail. When a deer ran down the trail, it caught its neck in the loop and strangled itself. Hunters used these animal runs to travel back into the woods everywhere. Ed has used them on Squaxin Island. He believed that the underbrush of the past was quite similar to what it is now.

Specialization {ja}

There were special men to do the different tasks, like whites have carpenters, blacksmiths, painters, and so on. Each of them had "something" [power] to help made him or her do that job. A hunter might have Wolf [power]: stəqayo. Specialists could also do other things. A hunter might have "something else" for fishing, but he was not as good at being a fisher as being a hunter. A few men might be good at all of them, depending on what they have.

They had names for the different times of the year: ƙaqʷlab means everything was nice and quiet now, about May; əɬska meant older brother and was December, followed by əɬsoqʷa, younger brother; waq̓ʷaq̓os was when the frogs started in February or March; paƛxʷay was dog salmon time in October; paƛkolə was in the fall when they started to dry salmon and pick huckleberries; and **pədhədəb** was the summer months of June, July, and August when they picked berries.

The yearly cycle by approximate month ran as follows:

June to July = picking and drying blackberries, traveling to the areas where they were found and living in summer camps. There was little fishing then but they hunted. Women went berrying and men went hunting. Women dried the berries and the meat, along with cockles, horse clams, and butter clams.

August = picking and drying salalberries, storing them in deer intestines. Men went hunting, started getting ducks.

September = fall salmon runs, silver and tyee (king). They moved to the streams the salmon were going up to build dams [weirs] across them and spear fish to be sliced and smoke-dried. The body was split and held open with cedar sticks. There were no berries now. Women were busy drying salmon, also getting and drying clams. Men were hunting ducks, eaten fresh, not preserved.

October = ate fresh huckleberries. They worked hard catching and drying dog salmon. Men started fishing for smelt and continued through early December.

December = There was little doing then, cold weather and snow brought the people back to the winter villages for ceremonies.

January to February = herring started to run in late January and continued into early March. They were caught and dried, together with spring salmon, **yubač** when fresh and **ƚalop** when dried.

March to April = no particular fishing, mostly hunting. People still in the permanent winter villages.

May = left the winter villages and went to various camping areas. The salmonberries were ripe, eaten fresh and not dried. Salmonberry sprouts eaten with dried salmon eggs. Only went for bottom fish (flounder, sole, and skate), available year around. It was a bad month for doe because fawns were on the way, so they only killed bucks.

All year long, they took clams, seal, porpoise, and used torchlight fishing for flounder. In the fall and spring, they used to camp near creeks on Port Orchard Bay for the salmon runs. The camping places were located according to what they were after, going to different spots according to the season and what was ready to be caught, dug, or gathered; then prepared, boiled, or smoke-dried it for storage and winter use.

Plants {ja}

Fern roots were dug and warmed on the fire before being eaten. Salmonberry sprouts were pealed and eaten raw. Blackberries were picked, put in deer gut, and placed on a platform over a fire to dry. They kept a long time in this way, and were soaked in water before they were used in food. They did the same thing with cranberries.

Fish {ja}

Herring. When these spawned on seaweed they would collect the eggs and eat them raw. They shook water grass to get the eggs off. Then they washed and ate them. They also took branches and little trees three to four feet high and put them in the water off the beach.

When the tide came in, the herring spawned on the branches, which the Indians collected for the eggs, washed off and eaten raw. They dried some over a fire to preserve them for later use.

Smelt. They split cedar limbs and wove them into a "dip" net [more like a seine] about a foot wide and six feet long. The smelt spawned on the beach. People dug a hole there to hold the smelt after people dipped them up from the shallow water. Someone else then took them from the hole and put them in baskets, usually women and children. They cooked the smelt by sticking them crossways through the middle onto hardwood slats. Each one could hold a lot of fish that way. They placed the slats in the ground leaning toward the fire, turning them several times to cook thoroughly.

Hunting {ja}

John saw some of the original forest when he was young. There wasn't nearly as much underbrush then as there is now that the forests have been cut down and second growth has come up. In the old days it was easy to get through the forest. They had to do this to hunt deer, among other reasons. John said there used to be elk in the Suquamish area, but that was before his time. He knows it was true because he once found some elk horns in the woods. The old people said that the elk used to come into the area [from the Olympics ?].

John never heard of running deer or elk down with dogs. The old way was for several men to spread out and go through the woods. It was easy to detect the trail of a deer by the trampled bushes and grass. When they scared up a deer, they shot it with bows and arrows. They also used traps. John never saw one, but the old people said they were made of wood, but he wasn't sure if it were a deadfall or some other technique.

When the deer was butchered and the meat sliced, it was hung way up over the fire, not close to the heat but in the smoke coming up from the fire. When they wanted to use the dried meat, they hammered it to soften it up. Since it was already cooked, they could also eat it as it was. Their hammer was a stone pestle shaped like an elongated dumb bell. They also used it to break the bones to get the marrow out after the old people had eaten the meat off the bones.

John hunted with his uncle [John] Curly around Poulsbo and Keysport, going back into the timber for grouse, pheasant, deer, and elk. People always considered it a good hunting place. John hunted there in 1896. They also fished in the area. There were no separate fishing grounds that John knew of. They didn't use traps there, but John heard that they had before the whites came.

Technology

Fibers {jj}

Soft Baskets. These were made of dried cattails. They started weaving them at the base. When they had finished a flat bottom, they turned the cattails up and continued the weaving for the walls. The top was finished in a different way, braided around the edge. These over one/under one twill-woven containers were made in different shapes, for different purposes, mostly storage since they did not hold water. They were decorated by dyeing the cattails. Wild Oregon grape gave a yellow color, and wild cherry bark a brown one. These ingredients were boiled to bring out the color.

Clam Baskets. These were made of cedar boughs, with a checkerboard weave on the bottom. The boughs were then brought up the side and two stripes were woven around them, every inch or so, to give the basket shape. It was a very loose weave to let out the water and grit from the clams. Julia made hers with a handle like a shopping basket.

Hard Baskets. These were water proof and made of cedar roots split into long, even stripes. These were the easiest to use. They were dried in the sun to season them. To make the foundation, a number of them were bunched together. An awl or another sharp point was used to make holes in this long bundle to be able to sew on the outside covering and designs. This sewing also held the bundles together to form the basket. In modern times they have used a punch with an iron needle as the point to make the holes. Before this the awl was of bone. The sewing made the bundles coil around to make a flat bottom before they were piled on top of each other to make the sides. The shape of the bottom determined the shape of the basket, oblong or round.

The sewing alternatively went through the bundles and then over them to fasten the basket together. The finished outer coating was a nice, even pattern of stitches. The decoration used colored stitches woven into the exterior. Colors used were red of wild cherry bark, white of a dried mountain grass, and yellow of Oregon grape roots. All these were boiled in water. Designs were usually geometrical and sometimes intricate. These baskets were used to carry and store water, make salmon soup, and stone boil food.

Mats. Cattails [*olal*] were sewn together with a long wooden needle about 2 1/2 feet long and called p̓ač̓ad. It had a hole in one end and was sharp on the other. They were made from the branch of a bush called q̓ʷačarač, ironwood. Julia had the one used by her foster mother. It had a triangular cross section and was slightly bent, 1/2 inch thick in the middle and 3/4 inch wide. [The mat creaser is called x̌ədalusəd = "push over the face of it" + instrument suffix, "something for."]

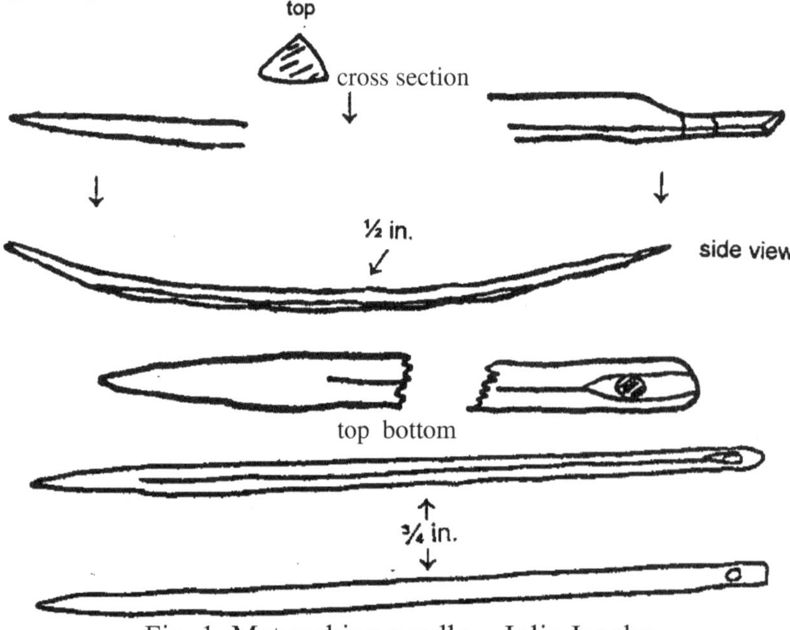

Fig. 1 Mat making needle ~ Julia Jacobs

The cattails were gathered in the fall, about September. They were best then because they were strong and stiff. They grew at Jefferson Head, at Indianola just west of Julia's, at Richmond Beach [stubus], at Edmonds, and at the mouth of the Duwamish where they were best of all. All of these places were also Suquamish territory and they harvested cattails there from their canoes. They were spread and dried in the sun. When dry, they were split into strings. They took a cattail, doubled it, and then rubbed it on the thigh under a hand. This string was tied into the hole in the needle. The other dried cattails were laid side by side on the ground. They used string to tie the ends of the cattails together. When these were secured, they ran the needle through rows of cattails and pulled the thread through. They used several needles to make holes at even intervals along each cattail. When all of the needles were in place, they turned the mat over and sewed it on the other side. They used the mats for beds, piled several layers thick to about six inches. They rolled up mats to make pillows.

Duck Nets {jj}

There were aerial nets made of string, stretched across a narrows, like Agate Pass, with a man on each side. When the ducks were coming, they pulled up the net for the ducks to fly into. They were also put up along shore out in the water or on poles where ducks would be feeding on herring eggs. When the ducks got behind the net, people on shore started making noise to scare them. The ducks flew off in the opposite direction and hit the net. They got their necks caught and couldn't get away, if they didn't break them. As a girl, Julia hunted ducks this way with her parents. There were lots of ducks then, but no more.

Canoes {jj}

They used a small hand adze to dig into a carefully selected cedar log to turn it into a canoe. Julia saw lots of them made, but the adze had an iron blade in her day. It took about half a year to make a canoe. When all carved out, they burned the bottoms, then scraped off the char and rubbed the surface until it was smooth and hard.

Cooking Pits {jj}

There were two cooking pits on the sandspit at Miller Bay. To make one, they gathered rocks and made a fire on top of them. This got the rocks hot. Then they cleaned off the remains of the fire. They leveled out the rocks and put food on top of them. The food was clams, mussels, potatoes, or a root [sčadə] that looked like onion. They covered the food with a cattail mat and left it for hours. When it was cooked, they gathered around the big open pit and ate it.

Dog Yarn {eg}

They used dog hair and the "cotton" from pink fire flowers [fireweed] to make a yarn for blankets. The dog had long hair. Ellen's grandfather said the dog was black with [woolly] long hair. When finished, the yarn looked gray. Ellen did not know how the hair was taken off the dog.

Basketry Hats {eg}

These hats were used for protection from rain or sunshine, woven of cedar root like a hard basket. Women wore them, maybe men, too, but Ellen and Wilson were not sure. The hat had the shape of an hourglass or an X. Ellen's half-sister, a Suquamish, had such a hat.

Combs {eg}

Before the whites, women used combs made of yew wood with long teeth, "like a Chinese comb." Ellen's grandmother had one made by her own father. It was as wide as a hand. Ellen thought that men used them, too, but she wasn't sure.

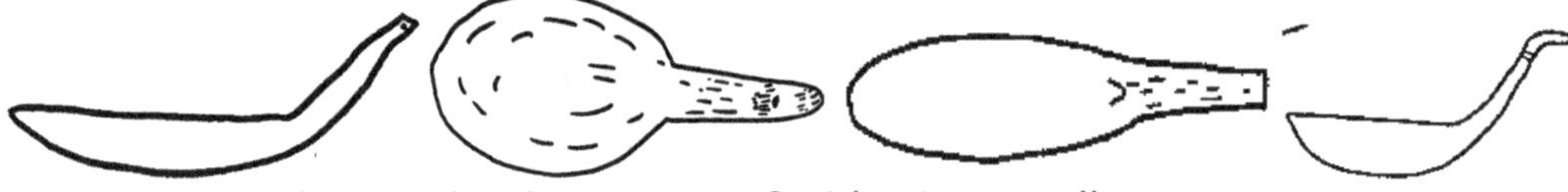

Fig.2 Eating Spoons, top & side views ~ Ellen George

Dishes {eg}

They used to make large spoons out of wood and horn. Ellen had one used by her grandmother, made of horn. The bowl of the spoon was 120 mm long, 75 mm at the widest, and 16 mm deep. The handle was 80 mm long, 30 mm at the widest, and 7 mm thick. Ellen also had an old Klallam spoon. The bowl was 130 mm long, 117 mm wide, 23 mm deep. The handle was 85 mm long, 35 mm wide at the base, and 7 mm thick. It was hooked at the end and perforated.

To make these horn spoons, they took a horn, wrapped it in weeds, and put it in hot water. When it was soft, they split it and opened it out. Whenever it started to get hard, they put it back into the hot water. When it was most soft, they bent it into shape. They kept bending and putting it in hot water until it had the right shape. Then they cut and trimmed it so it had even edges. Ellen didn't know what they used to cut it. When it was finished, they let it harden for good. Then they used dog fish skin to sandpaper the surface smooth. Such spoons were used for eating and for stirring cooking food.

Ellen's grandmother also had wooden spoons made of maple and alder, similar in shape to the horn ones. All of them were plain, no carving or decorations. Her grandmother also had large wooden platters. These were 2 to 2½ feet long, rectangular with four corners, almost square. The ends were 2 or 3 inches high, sloped slightly outward. The inside was a basin, like baking pans. These platters were used for communal meals.

Stone {eg}

Ellen said there was a big rock just south from Johnson's, up from the beach, where people used to go and get stone for making tools.

Weirs {wg}

Wilson never saw these closely. They were made of poles driven into the ground on two sides, with split cedar pounded between them making porous walls. These stretched out into the water from the beach, as far out as the tide went. At low tide fish were caught inside, but they swam out at the high one. Therefore, the fish, herring and cod, were gathered up every low tide when the trap was dry.

Digging Sticks (Dibbles) {wg}

It was used for clams and roots, tapered to a fire tempered and hardened point. Each woman had two or three of different lengths, for different purposes, made of ironwood. All of them were big enough around to be comfortable in her hand, and slightly curved for better thrust. The longer ones were for horse clams and other deep foods, while shorter ones were for little neck clams and anything else requiring shallow or fast digging.

Bone {wg}

Wilson's father worked with bone, cutting and grounding it with a rough stone, mostly to make knitting needles. There was a Duwamish who made bone barbs and put them in a metal point to make salmon spears. He tied two barbs together with a string and put pitch over all of it. This was Henry Moses, a young man about fifty [at Renton].

Sweatlodges (*sxʷcic̓abi̓*) [swuxtəd] {wg}

Wilson saw and used one at Point Glover. They were always built by a stream where there was running fresh water. They were built of fir or cedar saplings, against the wall of a bank. The earthen bank became the back wall, after they dug it out and squared it off. They stood the poles together as close as they could, about three thick, to make the walls and stuffed the cracks with moss, which eventually took hold there and grew on the walls. Split cedar was put across the top for the roof, the split side up and the bark one down. Another row was laid over the cracks with the split side down and the bark up. Then dirt was put over the roof to seal it tight. When done, the lodge had a square shape with an entrance in the middle of the front wall, open to the roof and about 18 inches wide.

The door was made of split cedar, just big enough for a person to get through. Usually, there was room enough for only one or two people. The inside walls also had moss stuffed in the cracks and were about five feet high, so people had to stoop slightly in there. There were no seats, only cedar limbs on the floor.

The fire was built outside to heat the rocks, which were taken inside. If you had dry bark that didn't make much smoke, you could use it to build a fire inside on top of the rocks, but you had to brush the coals off when the rocks were hot. It was cleaner to heat the rocks outside. Once they came inside, a little water was thrown on the rocks to create steam. When the steam got too light, they added more water. They stayed inside for as long as they possibly could.

When you had enough, you went to the creek to throw cold water on yourself. Then you could go back to sweat again. This procedure could be repeated several times during one session. When you were all done, you rubbed yourself with soft, shredded cedar bark. The used rocks were safely stored in the back against the dirt wall.

Wilson never heard that the sweatlodge was used in connection with the guardian spirit quest, any ceremony, nor had any other special meaning. It was just supposed to be good for a person to do this.

Burning Down A Tree {es}

Ed watched his grandfather do this. First his grandfather determined the direction that the tree was leaning and built a fire on the opposite side. After the fire was started, he piled rocks against the place where the fire was burning the tree. The rocks kept the heat focused on that spot. It took three or four days to burn a tree down, though four or five feet thick. He came to tend the fire a couple of times a day and add more fuel.

Wood {*es*}

In the old days, the bow was held horizontally. The end of the arrow was grabbed between the thumb and first joint of the index finger. They grabbed the arrow not the string.

Bows were about four feet long, made of yew. They were flat, not rounded in cross section, and narrowed at the middle for an easier grip. Some were all straight, others curved at the end. He watched his uncle curve the ends once. He wrapped a piece of blanket soaked in water around the end, buried it slightly in the ground, and moved some of the fire to the spot. When it was baked soft, he took it out, scorched it with a heated nail in three places on the inside, convex side, and then bent the end back. He did the same to the other side. Ed did not believe that the Suquamish ever put rawhide on the back of the bow. He felt that only "Eastern" Washington [Plateau] Indians made sinew backed bows.

The fire drill was rubbed between the hands to ignite some fine kindling to start a fire. They didn't use a bow to twirl it.

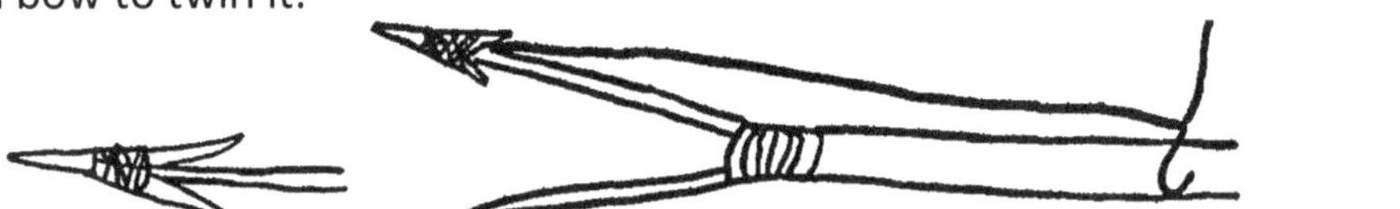

Fig. 4 Salmon spear ~ Ed Sigo

Salmon spears usually had two points, made out of ironwood or of bone barbs rubbed smooth on rough stone. The points were mounted in a Y shape with the barbs held on each tip with wrapping and a covering of pitch. If they had no rawhide for the wrapping, they used wild cherry bark.

The cod lure was used in the San Juans [by Klallam ?], but not in Puget Sound. It was carved of light wood, four inches long, in a pattern of notches along a point. They pushed it down to the bottom on the end of a spear, then pulled up the spear. The lure slowly came up, slowly revolving so cod would follow it up to be speared.

Tools {*es*}

Arrow points were made of bone without barbs. Ed once found a chipped one at Erland Point so he knew that kind was used in the past. Ed never saw the bone points either, but they were described to him as made of two pieces of bone, tied together, and covered with pitch on the shaft. They didn't use feathers very much.

They used flint from Erland Point to make tools like chisels, adzes, and points. The chisels were unhafted and struck with pieces of wood to plane down wood. They used elk horn for wedges. Stones pestles were used to pound meat, break clams, and work wood.

Fibers {*ja*}

Cattail mats. They had a long stick of hardwood with a hole in one end for a needle. It was about 30 inches long. They put a string in it. They had another piece of wood with an angled groove along the bottom to crease the mats along the line of the string to make the mat stronger. The mat creaser was called **kadalwacat** [x̌ədalusəd].

They got cattails and dried them in the sun. They got them from east of John's home near Poulsbo and the spit near Indianola. They used to go over from Point No Point to Edmonds where there were two marshes.

Then they took two stripes off a cattail, rubbed them on the  thigh, and twisted the two strings that resulted into a thread. They pulled this through the hole in the needle q̓laqtəd [oaitəd]. They put the cattails down on a flat place side by side. They made two layers of them by tying the edges together. They took the needle and pushed it through each of the cattails in one of the layers, through as much of the  row as they wanted. When one layer was all threaded, the cattails were turned over and the thread was put through the other layer. Then it was turned over to put another thread through about four inches from the first. This way the thread went back and forth through a series of rows along each cattail.

The mats were used in houses to sleep on or serve food. John used a small one as a boy over his lap when riding in a canoe. Other things were covered with mats during a canoe trip to keep them dry.

Nets *{ja}*

To make the dip or drag net for smelt, they got cedar boughs and bit through them with  the teeth to start splitting them. They held on to one end with the teeth and grabbed the other with the hands to split it. They did the same with cedar roots. The boughs made strips six feet long. They lined them up until they were about a foot wide and then wove the cedar root twine through them to hold the net together. The net was widest in the middle and tapered to the ends where the boughs were all bunched together. They held the net at these ends and pulled it through the water.

Smaller nets were made out of cedar limbs steamed over a fire so they were easy to work. They twisted the limbs together to make a rope and wove this into a net.

Tools *{ja}*

A fire drill was used to start fires with a fine cedar bark kindling. This was placed on a hearth board with notches in it to hold the point of the drill and cause the friction that started the fire. The drill was rotated between the palms of the hands until sparks began to burn the cedar dust. They blew on it until it started to flame and then added the fine bark. When they moved from place to place, they carried fire in the canoe, just like that used for night fishing. They put a board with mud over it into the canoe bottom and moved the fire in on top of it. This kept it safe and contained. They didn't use the fire drill often, just when their fire went out. This fire drill was the only method known to John. They did not strike fire from flint.

Spoons were made of wood, some of cattle horn, after the whites came. They were made locally. One man used to come from the north and bring big plates made out of rock [argillite ?] to trade. That was in the 1860s. John's great grandfather had a wooden plate.

Everyone ate out of this one dish, about two feet long, one foot wide, and five inches deep, made of maple. Such plates varied in size, but all were smooth and undecorated.

John heard that the ancient people had rock mortars to pound food, such as dried horse clams to get the tough skin off, deer meat to soften it to eat, and hazel nuts to crack the shells.

A herring rake was about 12 feet long with sharp pieces of hardwood stuck in along one side about half an inch apart for about two feet or more. Sometimes the points were made of bone. The pole itself was fir or cedar. They used it like a paddle from a canoe. They put the rake in the water in front of them, drew it back, and shook the impaled fish off into the canoe behind them. After whites came they started using nails for the teeth of the rake. They hammered these in, but in the old days they had to drill a hole for each board with a sharp bone rotated between the palms.

Bows were made by John's father out of yew wood. He never put sinew on the back of the bow. His bows were short, about 30 inches and he bent the ends in a curve by steaming them. This gave the bow more power and made it easy to carry. At the middle grip, the bow was rounded but the rest was flat. John watched his father's father make such bows seventy years ago. The bow string was elk sinew. Arrows had two or three eagle feathers attached with a twist to make the arrow spin. They had metal points and cedar shafts. Arrows were used to kill ducks, deer, elk, and men.

Harpoons were used for seal and porpoise. John had seen the outfit of Old Joe. His spear [harpoon] had a back that was cut to fit the fingers and string tied to it. Bladders for air floats were attached way back on this string. The front of the string was tied to the detachable point with barbs to hold it inside the prey. When they speared a mammal, the pole came out but the head stayed in while it ran away with the line. They threw the bladders overboard to slow it down. When the animal tired, they hauled it close and killed it. They got it in the canoe before it sank.

Fish spears [ƛagʷəcəd, ƛakʷ + icəd = insertion instrument] were used for bottom fish like flounder at night. They built a fire in the middle of a canoe upon a mud coated board or gravel and used this to attract fish and game. A rainy night was the best time to catch ducks because they were blinded by the light. These fires burned pitch wood because it gave a bright, clean fire.

The spears were made of hardwood or bone. Later the points were made out of a metal file. The points were tied on with wild cherry bark. Some spears had two prongs like a Y and others had three like a leister. Bone points averaged about 10 inches long, some longer. The plain tapered bone point was a little rounded but sharp, and the other end was flat. There didn't seem to be foreshafts or barbs.

Duck spears were similar to fish spears, except they had a string attached so they could be thrown and retrieved. They were more like harpoons but the head did not detach because ducks were not strong enough to break the pole, which was 10 feet long.

Canoes {ja}

John made canoes with metal tools. In the old days, they used stone and horn. He roughed out the canoe and put water inside. He heated it with rocks to make the walls soft. Then he stretched the canoe to the shape he wanted and held it there with sticks and supports. He started with little sticks, but as he threw hot water around the insides with a clam shell and got it softer, he changed to longer sticks to widen it. If he did this too much, it would all split. Jack made a few small cedar canoes in this way. He made the last one 50 years ago. He didn't make others because there was no good cedar left in the area. He said {Gove Isaac} Stevens promised in the treaty that Indians could always make canoes. He named three styles of canoe: shovel nose [ƛlay], women's [stəwatɬ, all purpose], and racing.

Mat Houses [x̣ix̣qalgʷiɬ] {ja}

John lived in these around Port Orchard when he was little. They were started with four fir poles dug into the ground. Cross poles were added to steady them and roof boards were put over these. The roof had a gradual slope. The boards were made of hollowed out cedar boards about a foot and a half wide. They were laid in alternation so the grooves interlocked because one board was up and the next one was down, forming troughs to drain off the rain. If they weren't traveling with these roof boards from the plank houses, they used bark from a dead cedar tree, because this stripped off wide and hard. These were also laid in alternating overlaps.

Cattail mats were put all along the sides, with the long side parallel to the ground, and tied to the poles. Several were used so they overlapped and kept out the rain. When they wanted light, they pushed boards or mats aside with a pole. There would be as many fires as there were families, arranged down the center. They used mats and boughs as flooring. When they broke camp, the roof boards and mats went in the cargo canoe. If there were a lot of these, the big canoe was towed behind the family one.

Society

Ranks

Leadership {wg}

Status depended to a large extent on ancestry. They would speak of their genealogy and point out the weak spot if they were finding fault with someone. But if someone ran you down, you would point out to them where their own "blood" was weak, according to Ellen. In an argument, they might spit on their little finger, hold it up, and say "That's what you are." [Implying a weak, defiled, and puny ancestry.]

Weak blooded people did not have as much "say" as did a higher ranked person. Low class people were not allowed to mingle with high class ones.

The leader of the high class people only suggested what he wanted done. He let others know so they could help him decide. If the other people decided it was all right to do so, then it would be done. What the majority of them wanted was what they would do.

If a camp was going to move, the chief would suggest it and tell everyone to decide on the date If all agreed, then they would move on the day selected. Wilson told the story of a man who sometimes wouldn't camp among the other people. He would always be going off away from the camp to stay by himself. Once when the group moved camp, the chief said, "He always wants to be alone. He is only one person and we are a group. We'll just leave him here. The man was making a new canoe in the woods. When he finished, he went to his people but they were gone. He followed them to the new camp and from then on he camped right in the midst of the encampment. Wilson said, "He found out it was wrong to act so stubborn."

This was also how Jim Seattle lost the chiefship of the Suquamish when they voted in Chief Jacob Wahelchu. The head chief was always supposed to have the "first say" on things. He did the suggesting and then let the people vote on it. Jim Seattle had inherited the chiefship, but he was quick tempered and easily offended. The people didn't like that, so they voted for Chief Jacob to be the head man. The people would get together, then each man got up and said his part about what would be a good thing to do. Then the people would decide what was the best thing to do. The people did not want Jim Seattle because they didn't want someone who would "go all to pieces like that." Jim Seattle still had some "say," but Chief Jacobs had the "first say." In fact, everybody had a "say."

There would be a headman for the different areas where people were living. For example, Wilson remembered that there was a headman in the Port Washington area. His name was sq̓axʷtəd. This was before the white people came that he was headman there. The people of this area would listen to him. Such positions of leadership had a strong tendency to run in family lines.] As honorary Suquamish chief, Bill Kitsap's father's grandfather had been the old chief Kitsap.

A low class man, if he were very smart and good, could become the headman if the people chose him. Then he would be chief until he died unless he did things that people didn't like. Then they would replace him with someone else. There were headmen in different villages or areas who would have the "first say" in each. They were always chosen by the agreement of all the people. A low class person had the right to get up and make a suggestion. If the others agreed that it was a good idea, they accepted it.

The headman of a band would choose who he wanted to be the leader of a war party. Or he could be the leader of a war party himself if he so chose. Chief Kitsap was like that. He always led the war parties. When a raid was planned, it was necessary to talk it over and for each person to have a "say." They would have to approve or disapprove the whole plan. A headman could not do anything that importantly effected his people before he had their approval.

A village would usually be made up of two or three families. They would always camp close together. Sometimes a family would adopt a person into their kindred. This would be a friend of theirs who didn't have a family or who just wanted to live with them. One man was the head of each family. Age did not matter in this. If he were smart and had good ideas, the family would recognize him as headman. He would suggest to the family what he thought they should do, "if it was all right, they would use his idea." Where there were several families in a village, they would all have to agree on one person to "have the first say" in the community. When the head of a family died, it sometimes happened that a son of his became the head, but this was not always the rule. They wanted someone who was smart and whose ideas were good. This was the most important consideration in selecting a new headman.

The entire tribe would get together under one head when some trouble arose. This would be when they were attacked by someone else, or something like that. Kitsap [q̓c̓ap] was the earliest chief of the tribe that Wilson recalled. They had him for chief because he was such a good war leader. An arrow never got through his skin. It just glanced off and away. It never stuck in his body. {wg}

After Kitsap died, *walak* took over for a short time. He was a good speaker. That was why the people chose him to be headman. He led until treaty times. At the treaty, he was an interpreter. He could talk Chinook Jargon and Seattle couldn't. Wilson didn't know how *walak* was related to Kitsap or to Seattle, Kitsap did not chose anyone when he died to succeed him.

Seattle [syaɫ, siʔaɫ] was chosen headman at the time of the treaty. He was chosen to make the treaty. Ellen believed that Seattle was born among the Duwamish, but she didn't know whom he married. His son was married to the sister of Ellen's grandmother. When Seattle was old, the mother of Ellen and Wilson took care of him until he died. They were living at the old village at Suquamish, at Oldman House. That was where their mother took care of him. She was related to him, but not closely. She called him sapa [tsapa = grand father-uncle]. She used to cook his food and take it over to him. His mother used to say, "Chief siʔaɫ has got lots of relations, but here I am taking care of him until he dies." Sam Snyder used to carry water to the old chief when Sam was a little boy. Seattle remained a chief until his death.

Jim Seattle was chief then for a little while. He was something like old Kitsap. He was good in war. The people listened to him for a time. But he got so that he talked rough to the people. So they told him they were going to replace him. They chose Jacob then to be the chief. In those days, the whole tribe moved together so they didn't have to send for anyone to come in for the meeting to ask their opinion about changing the chief. They were all together. [Jacob Wahelchu was chief until he died 2 October 1911, at the age of 112.]

Kitsap was only chief of the Suquamish. It was only after Chief Seattle that the Suquamish and Duwamish had the same chief. Seattle could be the chief over both tribes because he was related over there.

After the treaty, the Duwamish had a head chief named kabsəd. After Seattle signed the treaty, William, the brother of kabsəd, wanted a separate treaty so that they wouldn't have to move away from the Duwamish River. They didn't get it because of trouble with other Indians [the 1855-56 Treaty War]. The government moved Governor Stevens [he went back to fight and die in the Civil War Between the States] so he didn't settle with the Duwamish. After that, the Duwamish were moved all over.

One of Seattle's parents [his mother] was Duwamish, but Wilson was not sure which. This was what made it possible for him to speak for both peoples. As Kitsap was just chief of the Suquamish, Wilson thought that before the time of Seattle the two tribes had separate chiefs.

Sometimes a chief might name his successor. If he didn't, the people had to choose one. He was not necessarily from the family of the old chief. But the people had to agree on the person selected by the dying chief, at least for a time. If he were not acceptable, they chose someone else. The head chief never owned any hunting or fishing grounds for his exclusive use.

If a hunter killed more than he needed, he might take some of it to the head chief, but this was nothing special. A hunter always cut up his meat and distributed it to other people. He just kept as much as he could use for his own family. A hunter or fisher would give part of what he got to the chief first. If it were the village chief, he was given his portion first of all. Often the whole village would eat together and share what they had. They always gave the chief a piece of whatever they caught, no matter how little it was [to show their appreciation for his looking out for their welfare.]

But if a family had very little, the chief would also share what he had with that family. That was how a good chief looked after his people. A family might have a good hunter or more than one, but no good fishers. Another family might have good fishers but no good hunters. So they would share the various types of food that they had so everyone got a range of things to eat.

For example, one family might have caught a porpoise and another a seal. They would cook them on different fires and, which ever one was done first, everyone in the village gathered there to share in it. The man that caught the animal would give portions to each person. If a young man caught it, his parents were the ones to pass it out, showing what their boy could do. Sometimes, someone was chosen to hand out the meat. This person was selected by the head of the family. After the feast, if any was left, it was divided among the people to take home.

Sometimes a family lost a child or adult member to death. The hunters and fishers would bring the family food to eat because they could not get their own meals during mourning. The head of the family would choose someone to butcher the deer or fix the fish. What was left over after the family and everyone had eaten was divided by the head of the family, or someone he selected, to give to people outside of the family. The family that lost a child would not keep what was left of the food. People who received the food were then supposed to take it home and divide it with others who could not make it to the wake and feast. Wilson saw this happen in his family when he was about 20.

Once Wilson was at a feast in La Conner [Swinomish]. He had some fish of his own. When he left he took his fish back without dividing it among the people there. That night he dreamed. Someone asked him, "Why didn't you divide those fish with some of the people there?" Someone else said to the first voice, "Why didn't you tell him when he was still up there?" The next morning, Wilson's wife said he had talked all night long in his sleep. That day they went to eat with the Sneatlams, some of his relations in Tulalip. He took some of his fish there to give to them so as to clear himself of his trouble. He was not feeling well and kept shouting out on the way there. His wife told him to pray for help. He took his rosary and did so. He couldn't eat much, but later he did feel better.

That was the first time he found out that there was a spirit, like those in the smokehouse, following him wherever he went. One of his old people had had this spirit and so he had inherited it. It followed him like a dog wherever he went. Wilson was not sure just what kind of a power it was. Its song kept ringing in his ears, even while he was in the Sneatlam house. Yet he did not know what it was. He did not want the power, so he refused to sing it. By giving this salmon to others, he was able to clear himself partly. Also, he thought his prayers to God kept it away from him. Whatever the cause, he has not been sick because of this spirit any more.

When Warren Snyder asked him if a chief could demand food from others or what would happen if a chief had more food than he needed and still demanded food from others who did not have much, Wilson said that if the chief had a lot of food and the others did not, the chief always divided it among the people. By the same token, people "naturally" gave part of their food to the chief first. If a person did have food and refused to divide it with others, the likelihood was that he would become sick, or anything bad could happen to him [for he was offending spirits as well as neighbors.]

The chief usually did not go out to hunt and fish. His wives went out gathering berries and clams. His slaves went out to fish and hunt. Only young slaves went hunting. The chief directed his slaves and told them what to do. He would tell his slaves when to go hunting and where. He told them what to do to the game after they got it. Sometimes, it was divided among the people, either cooked or uncooked depending on his "say." Most chiefs also had slaves make their canoes and other utensils. The chief was expected to spend his time directing the activities of his slaves and advising the community. This was equally true of the high blooded people as well as the chief.

If a chief sent for a relative and gave him something, such as a canoe, the relative brought back something to give to the chief in exchange, such as a blanket. If what he gave was less than the relative thought the canoe was worth, then, at some later time, when the relative gave a potlatch, he would give this chief something more to make up for the value of the canoe. The speaker would announce that this was in payment for the gift of a canoe. [Then their sharing was balanced and even.]

Some people had only one or two slaves. Chiefs always had more than two. People who had few slaves had to do a lot of work themselves. But the slaves always had to do as much work as their masters were doing, so these slaves worked long and hard. The master and slave sometimes worked together, like hunting and fishing as a pair. The master was the boss, though, and the slave did somewhat more work than the master, usually, in these cases.

When they lived in the big plank smokehouses, the slaves had a certain section of the house where they stayed [usually nearest the door, the most vulnerable spot.] The slaves did all of the cleaning, and they got the water and wood. When people were camping, however, and using the smaller mat houses, the slaves had a separate mat house of their own to stay in.

For very important meetings, women were not allowed to speak, only at less important ones could they personally voice an opinion. A woman could not become a chief. If she were smart, she might be allowed to speak informally. Women could not speak at a war meeting either. That was strictly men's business. Only those going into the fight could speak at such meetings. Mostly, women spoke at meetings where their own marriage or something else of keen interest to them was under discussion. Even then only very smart women were listened to. A woman had to be older and more experienced before she was heard. A woman who had gone through the change of life did not have any more right to speak than any other female. As in the case of a headman, the important consideration was the level of intelligence, ability, experience, and oratorical fluency

Chiefs {eg}

People took their troubles to the chief. He had two or three others, subchiefs, under him. They would straighten out family troubles or whatever came before them. The chief was the head of the tribe and he had to be smart. If anyone wanted to know anything, they would go to him for the answer or for advice. A man who became chief had to be high blooded. He couldn't be a commoner or ordinary. Usually the chiefship was inherited.

Speakers {ja}

John's grandfather was a speaker. He was a spokesman. During a potlatch, he would do the talking until he was hoarse. He spoke for Chief Kitsap. They used a long potlatch house that stood where the light house is now. His job was to forward what the chief said. The chief told him what to talk about, but not exactly what to say. Mostly he described what was going on, especially when the chief was passing things out. He gave away to and fed the people. It was called cgʷəgʷə [sgʷigʷi] (potlatching or inviting).

Slavery {*eg, wg*}

High class people had slaves who did work for them like getting wood, digging clams, and so forth. Ellen's grandmother had slaves. When the slaves were freed in 1865, she tried to get them to leave her, but they didn't want to go. Finally, they did leave her, but when they went picking berries or digging clams, they would always bring some to her. They continued to help her even after they were free. {eg}

Most of the slaves were good so they didn't have to be punished. The master would beat them if they were not dutiful and good. Some masters might be mean to their slaves, but others would advise him not to punish his slave too much. Scolding was usually considered to be enough to get a slave back into line. But if a slave were very bad, he'd be punished by making him work longer and harder. Most people knew that slaves worked harder and minded better when they were well treated.

A slave might ask a man who was good to his own slaves to buy him because his present master was too harsh. Wilson said that his own grandfather got more than one slave in this way. His uncle helped to buy one of them.

Slaves ate after the others were through. They ate by themselves. People ate off a mat and there was a separate one for slaves. Slaves could marry, but any children belonged to the master of the [slave] parents. They were allowed to be present at a meeting to discuss important matters. A master might even allow a good, smart slave to talk at such a gathering and to give his opinion on some question.

When the cousin of Wilson's grandfather died, they killed one of his slaves and buried him underneath his master. It was not done outright, but by trickery. They were taking the body in a canoe to the burial place. Wilson's father's father pulled a knot out of the bottom of the canoe so the water started to leak in. The slave had a knife so the man asked to use it to stop the leak. When they got to shore, Wilson's relative kicked the slave in the shin and then stabbed him when he bent over. They buried him under the body.

Wilson never heard of burying a slave in a post hole when building a house or of killing slaves at a potlatch. They might give them away, but more often they sold them at such large gatherings. When a boy got married, his father might give him a slave. His own grandfather bought a young slave about 14 or 16 to care for Wilson while he was young. His name was **saya** and he was supposed to help Wilson's mother take care of the boy. He used to carry wood, get water, and perform other duties around the house. He was from Alaska. His own uncle, his father's brother, sold him. He was from high blood, but still his uncle sold him. He died while Wilson was yet a baby.

The West Coast Indians around Fort Rupert used to sell slaves a lot cheaper than did the people around Olympia and the southern part of the Sound. They used to get them cheap from the yəłuiłtx̣ [Ucluelet] across from Neah Bay on Vancouver Island. That was where John Kettle's wife came from. John and his wife were the last slaves left around Suquamish. Kettle was first owned by Chief Jacob, then by Alfred, who was the son of Chief Jacob's brother and that way inherited the slave.

They bought most of their slaves from the north, but they did buy some in the area of Puget Sound. In the generation of Kitsap, they used to go out and raid for slaves, but Wilson wasn't sure where they went for them. {*eg*}

The grandmother of Curly way back was captured by people from the north. They took her and made her a slave. That is why people around here look down on John, because he had slave ancestry. Yet Curly became a great man, a speaker, any way.

They had slaves right here in Suquamish. John Kettle was one. He was from the north. Slaves got wood, clams, and packed water. The owner didn't do this. Anybody could capture someone and then make them work. The slave lived with the person who captured him. They had to marry other slaves. A free man could marry a slave, but the people looked down on such a person afterward. The children were considered as slaves and the people would look down on them too. When they traveled in a canoe, the slave did the paddling. Slaves could have power if they trained for it, then went out and got it. [Like Simon, a Snohomish enslaved at Minter, and ransomed at Fr Nisqually.]

The master could kill his slave if he got mad enough. Kitsap had a slave who had a daughter Kitsap went after. His wife said "Don't do it," but Kitsap persisted anyway. The daughter scratched his face, so he took a weapon and split open her head. The mother of the girl used to go into the woods to sit and cry. She must have had something [power] because shortly afterwards Kitsap died. It must have been she who did it. She had something.

There was a Suquamish who was a kidnapper. He made slaves of children. An old man here who died about 50 years ago was kidnapped by that man and taken to Skokomish where he was used as a bet on the outcome of a horse race and thus the boy was lost.

John never heard of killing a slave at a ceremony or anything similar. They were pretty much well treated, it was just that they were slaves. If Suquamish were kidnapped by northern Indians but came back later, they were still considered slaves. *{ja}*

Age And Gender

M1 (First Menstruation) *{jj}*

A girl was not allowed to stay in the house at this time. They made a little tent [hut] for her up in the woods somewhere near their home. This was a great disgrace [concern ?] for the family. [Good families were especially determined to seclude their daughters at this time to protect others from the great power she was soon to learn to control.] They didn't want the girl to look at anybody. If she did, the person would become sick. They didn't visit her, except for one old woman who attended her. This might be her great grandmother or her grandmother. If they were not alive, then it was some other old woman who was a relative. She told the girl what she was supposed to do.

She couldn't eat for a few days. She was away from her folks for a month, but it was only for a few days of this that they starved her. They starved her for the first few days that she went out. She had to clean herself every morning. She had a certain place to go to clean herself. This would be at a stream but not in the Sound. This was a special place for her. Others were not supposed to go there. Then they took her back home.

While she was there, she worked on baskets and other tasks. If she didn't do this during the change in her life, she would always be lazy and not want to work. The tent she was in was a hut made of branches from fir trees. They also made her a bed in the inside from a special type of fir tree branches because they smelled so sweet. The girl was also given a dry weed like nettle to rub over her body to clean and toughen it.

They were told they could not use their fingernails to scratch themselves with. If they itched, they had to use the dried nettles. Their fingernails were like a poison to them if they used them to scratch their own bodies [short-circuiting their raw power].

Girls were allowed to eat only special foods, none associated with men. She could not eat salmon because if she did, salmon would disappear from the Sound. It was a long time after she had left the hut that she was finally allowed to eat salmon again. Also, during her later monthly periods a woman was not allowed to eat salmon.

A girl ate roots from the forest, such as fern root. She also could eat clams. She couldn't eat meat such as deer or elk while she was in the hut because then these animals would become scarce. Julia was not sure if they could eat berries. There were no other ceremonies or public events. There were no feasts.

Marriage {jj}

When a boy was interested in a girl, his parents gave belongings to the girl's folks. After that, half a year to a year later, the girl's parents would bring presents back to those of the boy. They would return as much as they had received. Julia saw this done when she was a girl. There was just this one exchange of presents. If a boy were the son of a chief, then he had to look for the daughter of a chief to marry so his children would be high born. If he married a lower girl, his children would not be high blooded.

A long way back it was a little different. There would be a dance. The girls would be standing around. One boy would dance around. He would have long strings tied around his waist. If a girl wanted to marry him, she would grab hold of a string. Then the boy had to marry her. Several girls could grab the string of one boy and he would have to marry them. They didn't exchange gifts at the dance. [This practice was diffused from the Plateau Prophet Cults active almost two centuries ago.]

A man could have several wives if he could support them. This was done before the time of buying a wife. The boy took the girl to his home. The girl was supposed to work for the boy's parents. She was supposed to do the housekeeping for them. If she didn't, she was lazy and the boy's parents might take her back to her home.

A person could never marry relatives, unless they were at least five times removed in the genealogy. He wasn't allowed to marry any closer than this, otherwise all of his children would die.

Wife buying involved marrying someone outside of the tribe or community. The Suquamish married into any tribe around the area: Port Gamble, Muckleshoot, Snohomish, and so on. Marrying outside of the tribe was thought to be the best kind of marriage. When the granddaughter [Agatha] of Julia's foster father [Jacob Wahalchu] got married, they had a feast afterwards. They invited lots of people and had dances. Chief Jacob gave away clothes, food, and dishes at the feast. They used to do it this way before the whites came. They did not feast when the gifts were exchanged before the marriage.

The couple could go to live with either set of folks, those of the boy or of the girl. When they went to live with the boy's folks, the girl had to help the boy's parents and be good to them. The boy's parents could send the girl back if she were not acceptable. Nothing was done about the gifts already exchanged if that happened.

They were most likely to go to live with the boy's parents, unless there were more than one wife. Before the whites came, they could have more than one wife. People said that the wives used to fight, though. Julia knew a man in Port Gamble who had two wives.

If a man's wife died and she had a younger sister who was not married, then this girl had to marry the man and take her sister's place. This practice was called *balocit* [sbalotsid]. In English this would mean something like sister-in-law [more accurately, potential wife according to the sororate]. It meant more than just that. All of the deceased wife's relatives would be balocid to the husband after her death, but not before. The wife was ?? *łaha* [sx̣aʔx̣aʔ] to the boy's parents.

If the man died, his wife went home to her parents. It was expected that the deceased's brother would marry her, but he did not have to unless his parents wanted him to do so. Also, a cousin of the dead husband could marry her if he wanted to, but the brother had first preference. A man had a choice in this kind of marriage, but a woman did not if the man wanted her.

In either of these cases, there would be no gift exchanges after the initial alliance. If a boy from Suquamish married a girl from another tribe like the Snohomish and the boy brought the girl home to live with his parents, they would give a feast for the new couple, inviting a lot of people to come. If they went to live with the girl's parents, then the boy was supposed to help his inlaws. If he did not hunt and fish for them, he was called lazy, but the girl's parents couldn't send the boy home. The girl's parents could only criticize him and try to make him work.

Parents always wanted their children to marry as high blooded a person as they possibly could because the social position of the children depended on this. Rank was inherited. When lower blooded children grew up and had children, others would say to these children that they were low down people. So the parents always wanted their children to marry high up, so others couldn't later call their grandchildren low class. This was important because grandparents had special rights and duties in the training of their grandchildren.

Julia's foster father was young when his parents negotiated with another family to arrange his marriage. He was about 13 and so was the girl. He and the girl had played together. So when they got older, they were well acquainted with each other and willingly married. It was common for important marriages to be arranged when the children were this age. Sometime, the boy and girl were even younger, about 5 or 6, when the parents made the arrangements for a later marriage. They didn't do this when the children were the first born because "they didn't know whether they would live or die. [See the tale of Five Brothers by John Adams for the mythic justification for this.]

Child Care {jj}

When a baby was born, they cut off the afterbirth and wrapped it up, took it into the woods, and buried it. They washed the baby in the Sound as soon as it was born, placed it on a thin board, and wrapped it up. As the baby grew, they made longer boards for it. They packed the baby on the board, hanging down the back, when they went any where. They held it on the back with a blanket wrapped around the shoulders. Now younger Indians use shawls.

A new mother cooked [heated] her breasts before nursing to increase the flow of milk. She warmed white shells and placed them against her breasts. This made good, plentiful milk.

They had a hammock to put the baby on when they were busy. The hammock swayed and kept the baby happy. They used cedar skin [cambium] like a diaper.   Cedar skin was found underneath the bark. It came off in sheets and dried nice and crisp. Some sheets were big enough to use as a hammock.

Babies were weaned when they were about three or four years old. Julia saw older ones, big kids, playing around when all of a sudden they would run to their mother to nurse. To help with weaning, women put something on the nipple to make it taste bad. They started feeding babies solid food when they had teeth to chew with.

Children were punished by whipping them with a little stick, not the hand, just enough to make them learn they had done wrong. Sometimes, they would make them go without food for a while.

When children were old enough to help, the parents gave them small tasks, saying "Go, get me this." If a child said he was tired and didn't want to go, they would call him lazy and give him a slight whipping. Children were not supposed to talk back to grown ups. If the adult said something mean, and the child answered back, he or she would still be whipped.

Once, years ago there was a famine for three or four years. They wouldn't clean the heads of the children and they had lice. So did their parents. When they got hungry, they would pick their heads and eat the lice. They gave each child one louse. If the child cried for more, they said "You've had one, that's enough."

A child was not allowed to play with any part of a salmon. Julia used to do this but they stopped her. They said she would get sick from this and that the salmon would take her back home with them to teach her a lesson.

Death {*jj*}

If anyone died in a family, the survivors gave the dead's belongings away after the funeral. They gave them to people who came to the funeral. They gave everything away. Then other people had to give them things to use for a while because all that they had was given away. They did this in memory of the dead and because they did not want to see things that belonged to the dead person. It reminded everyone of the loss. They had to start all over getting things to use.

After a person died, it was a disgrace [disrespectful] to mention their name again. They did not want to talk about or mention people who had died. Women cried when a close relative died. They wailed just like singing. The men may cry but not loudly.

Burial {*jj*}

When a person died, they would get a good canoe and split it on the bottom. Then they put the body in it. They took all of this back into the thick brush and trees, where they hung up the canoe. The body was inside covered with blankets. They put favorite belongings, tools and utensils, in with the body. Sometimes, they laid it on the ground and put boards over it like an A-frame tent. When this got old and worn, they made another one for the body. They called this tent *selawtx* [silaltx̌ʷ = cloth house]. There was a burial ground with these at the place where Suquamish is now. Another one was at the end of Bainbridge Island.

Division of Labor {eg}

Men and women had different ways of dressing and different tasks to do. Women parted their hair in the middle and braided it on both sides. Men had long hair but they didn't braid it. It was allowed to hang around the shoulders.
The different jobs included the following:

drying = women did all berries, meat, and fish
cooking = women did it all
weaving = women made the blankets of dog wool and the mats, cutting the cattails for them
baskets = women made them and got their own material like cedar boughs, bark, grasses, and
    roots [men made the open work clamming baskets]
canoes = made by men
clams = women dug them and dried them, but men sometimes watched the clams drying over
    a fire to see they did not burn
berries = picked and dried by women
fishing = men did it
hunting = men
paddling canoes = both men and women

In addition, men put up houses for curing meat and fish, built fire places for cooking, made cradle boards, speared ducks, woodworked planks and carvings, got fire wood, made long wooden needles for mats, and prepared ironwood stakes for cooking salmon and clams.

Ellen said the Neah Bay [Makah] people made the women get the fire wood. Ellen's father wouldn't let her marry a man from Neah Bay because he didn't want his daughter going out and hauling wood in a basket while her husband sat around a warm fire. The Neah Bay people were not very good to their women.

Training {eg}

Boys were made to swim when they were young. They made them fast for a certain number of days. The grandfather would give them a token or a marker, a board, stick, or something. He'd tell the boy where to take it and tell him how to place it. Then the boy did this and came back. As he got older, he was sent further and further away up a mountain or to a lake. This was what they did when boys were seeking their Tamanamus [tahmanawas, Chinook Jargon word for spirit or supernatural, from tah, power]. Some of them used to use this to doctor sick people.

During these cures, they used to get down in the middle of the floor and all the other people would sit around the edges and hit on boards with little sticks to sing with the doctor. Some had little men carved with faces on them. When they were singing, these cedar figures would come out of a corner and dance around and then go back to sit in the corner again. These cedar men had spirits in them.

Ellen said that when she was young these carvings would bump and make a noise if anyone tried to take anything in the house. This happened to her when she was a little girl.

Very few girls had spirits, but they all went out to seek them. They were sent to a creek to bathe. They had to rub themselves with rotten pieces of wood [to remove their human odor.] Some said it was to smooth their skin. [Girls were trained for work that did not require strong spirits.] They would show girls how to make yarn from dog wool and duck down. Then they would show them how to weave. Such finished material was used for girl's skirts. They taught girls how to cut fish, dry it, and cure it. They learned how to make baskets and mats. They went with older women to dig roots.

Mostly men got power. As soon as a man was 14 or 16, he would get married. They would start training boys to hunt and fish when they were four or five. They gave them little bows and arrows, also slings. These were like toys but, at the same time, they were meant to teach the boys how to use such things. The men showed them how to care for and use them. Boys went out hunting in earnest, able to get food for the people when they were older. By the time they were ready for marriage, they were skillful at hunting and fishing.

M1 First Menstruation {*eg*}

They put a girl out of sight when this happened. At night they took her to a creek and made her bathe and scrub with a sponge made of rotten cedar to clean herself. During the day, she was given something to work on like weaving mats, blankets, making yarn, or doing baskets. This was to make her familiar with constant activity so she would be a good wife later.

The second night they would make her bathe again. She was put on a strict diet. They cooked the food, but they waited until it was cold to feed it to her. They gave her very little to eat, no fruit, nothing warm. She could eat roots. Toward the end of the seclusion, the grandmother would invite other old women to join them. They would gather to sing, dance, and eat, although the girl could not join in this, [yet it lifted her spirits.]

The girl was not allowed to touch her own hair. Someone else had to comb and braid it for her. They braided it tightly in two braids and tied them on either side of her ears. Then they wrapped her head up so that none of her hair showed. Ellen believed the cedar bark was used to wrap it, but she was not sure. They gave her a piece of ironwood sharp on one end and flat on the other. She was supposed to use it to scratch herself if she had an itch.

The girl had to eat and drink from her own dishes. She couldn't go picking berries, nor was she allowed on the beach. If a hunter came down with a deer, she must never look at it.

During this period, the girl was instructed in how to conduct herself when she was married. She was given instructions in drying fish, picking berries, digging clams, and keeping a household. If she married a man with a family, she was told to be good to her mother-in-law and other inlaws. She was told not to talk back to them even if they abused her verbally.

Children were not to talk back to anyone older than themselves. They were told to help anyone who was in trouble and needed a hand. This sort of instruction came down to Ellen and her sisters from their own grandmother. Ellen said she went through seclusion but it was hard. She also had a hard time with her mother-in-law, who was mean.

Ordinarily, it was permitted to talk to parents in law, but if they were mad at you or mean, you were not supposed to say anything back.

When the girl was well, the grandmother would give each woman there part of the cloth or mat that the girl was secluded behind. Then she was ready to be married. An unmarried girl was not allowed to speak to any man, not even her cousins. She was to be quiet around men, even her own brother(s). She was not to talk foolishly or play or act rowdy. There were no men nor male kin that a girl could joke with.

Marriage {eg}

Usually a girl married an old man first. When he died, then she married a younger man. Ellen's grandmother married an old man, but he didn't last long. He died. She did not marry any relative of his. She married into another family. After her second husband died, she married her stepson. In those days, a woman could even marry her brother-in-law. She was expected to. Her second husband told his son to marry his stepmother. This was an acceptable form of marriage.

In the old days there was something called a marriage dance. An unmarried man's people would announce the dance. This was his father or grandfather. They invited lots of people. The boy tied some string, probably buckskin, around his waist. Then his relatives started a song. The boy sang too. The others joined in. Any girl who wanted to marry the boy would come up to him while he was dancing and take hold of the string. Several girls might grab hold of the string. The son of a chief got lots of girls. The boy married all the girls who held on to his string. The girls held on to the string and followed him dancing until he was through. Ellen said that the end of the dance marked the marriage. Ellen did not know whether any gifts were given to the girl's parents in this kind of marriage. They did have a big feast, but she didn't know if gifts were exchanged.

The gift exchange was another form of marriage. The boy's parents took him along when they went to see the parents of the girl about a marriage. He was left outside sitting by the door, saying nothing, until he was called in. The girl could not be around during the discussions. When he was called in, then he was considered married to the girl and they ate together. The boy's parents had brought the food for a feast to the girl's home and they ate there. The boy's parents also brought gifts, but these were left in the canoe. If the boy were accepted, they went to the canoe and unloaded the food and gifts.

Sometimes boys would sit at the door a long time. At night he would come just inside the doorway and lie there to get warm. The boy had to be silent. If he were in the way, the members of the household just stepped over him, ignoring him. He might have to sit there for days before they finally accepted [or rejected] him.

They used to have valuable shell beads that they gave to the girl as a necklace. Abalone shells were used, broken up into pieces, and rubbed [abraded] into the shape of beads with a stone. Then they were strung into a necklace. Other pretty shells were also used. Dentalia was a favorite ornament. Anyone with any shell ornaments was looked up to because these were considered very valuable. They would use these shells to trade for other goods, such as blankets and shawls. Chiefs used them to decorate their clothing.

In most cases, the young married couple would go to live with his parents. They would go to visit hers, but mostly they lived with his. When a man got game, such as a deer, he might take part of it to his inlaws. He would treat them first of all. Even when a girl's parents had lots of food, they treated their in laws first. If a man wanted to go and live with his wife's people, this was acceptable, but it was not done usually. [Among tribes of Northern California, this was called half-marriage when a groom lived with his inlaws.]

They preferred to marry into other tribes. There were low class and high class people. So a high class person from the Suquamish would rather marry a high class person from another tribe than marry someone from the low class of his own tribe. Low class people married others of the low class, so they were much more likely to marry into their own tribe. So, marrying into your own tribe was not considered desirable.

As soon after a marriage as they could, the parents of the girl would take presents to the boy's parents. They also brought food to hold a feast there. There was no other marriage ceremony outside of these constant feasts and gift exchanges.

After the Catholic priests came in, they tried to make the men with many wives give up all of them but one. Ellen said that even then some women stayed. Ellen knew a man with two wives, who were sisters, as recently as 1919, when he died. The last of his wives died in 1942.

If a woman did not like her husband, she could leave him. Also, if a man did not want his wife, he could tell her to leave. The girl's parents would take her back and tried to get her married again. Ellen said that this usually didn't take too long.

Child Care {eg}

When a man and wife were expecting a baby, the man would go out and get some cedar bark. He took off the outside bark and went for the thin underbark or cambium skin. He brought it home and they rubbed it between their hands to make it soft. Then they cut it into sizes large enough for diapers. They rendered dog fish livers and stored the oil. They cooked it over a fire to get the oil out. Then they strained it through some cedar skin. Sometimes they made the oil from ratfish liver.

When the woman was six months along, they got some medicine, some leaves, for her to chew and swallow or boil like a tea to shortened her labor. She chewed a plant called squirrel tail, sk"ək"azohop, or made a tea out of wild cherry bark.

When a woman got sick, she wasn't supposed to tell anyone, not even her husband that she was ready to deliver. She was not to groan or cry or make any noise. She had the baby by herself. She went away from the others when she knew the time was close and had the child by herself. When it came, the others would hear it cry. Her mother, grandmother, mother-in-law, or other older woman would go and help her then. Only a woman could help because it was a disgrace for a man to be around when a baby was born.

When the baby was first born, they rubbed it with this fish oil all over the body. Then they put dogfish, never ratfish, oil in a clam shell and warmed it by the fire. They dipped a feather in the warm oil and let it drop into the mouth of the baby to feed it. They fed the baby only this oil for seven days directly after it was born before a mother started nursing.

Ellen was brought up this way by her grandmother, who claimed they fed babies dogfish oil because it kept them well – it cleaned them out so they didn't get sick as easily. This oil was used as a medicine for adults as well as children. It was used for fevers, colds, burns, purges, and almost anything else.

The afterbirth was wrapped up. It was taken into the woods and put up in a tree. People said that if it were put in a maple, the child would be good-natured.

The baby had to be seven to ten days old before it got a first bath. When they bathed it, the mother laid it on her thighs and bathed it with soft cedar bark like a sponge. They did not wash it in the Sound. In the summer, they warmed the bath water in the sunshine. In the winter, they dropped hot rocks in water held in a hollowed out cedar log and bathed the baby with that.

Mothers made a little fire and heated rocks. Ellen saw her own mother do this. They got some weeds growing in clusters on logs out on the beach. These snap when you squeeze them. They are brown and called sⱡoċ [ⱡoċ, ⱡots means "to shoot"). The weeds were put in a basket and the hot rocks were placed on top, so as not to scorch the basket. Then the woman bend over it with a blanket around her neck to keep the steam out of her face. They sprinkled water on the rocks. This was the way she cooked or steamed her breasts for about an hour to increase milk production. Ellen's mother did this twice to cook her milk for a new baby. If this weren't done, the baby would have colic all of the time. Another way of cooking the breasts was to rub them with warmed clam shells. Because the shell was white, it was emblematic of a wish for thick milk.

Nursing could go on until the child was three or four. Even if she had a tiny baby, she still nursed an older one along with the baby. Ellen knows one case where a boy nursed until he was old enough to play ball with the other boys. She never heard of a mother who was unable to nurse. A baby nursed on demand or when the mother thought it was time. If the baby cried from hunger, it was always nursed then.

They ate solid foods along with the nursing. When babies were about a year old, they used to give them bear or seal fat to suck on. Also, they took dried clams, soaked them in water, and let the baby suck on them. Gradually, they went from this to solid food.

To wean them some mothers took flounder gall, which was bitter, and put it on the nipples to discourage the baby.

When a baby soiled its cedar skin diapers, they weren't thrown away. They were wrapped up and saved until the child was old enough to chew and eat, only then were they thrown away. If they threw them away before the baby stopped nursing, the baby would have loose bowels. A baby that was passing all of the time was considered to be "no good." The urine of little children was gathered and put away where the rain would never touch it. When it thickened up, it was used as a shampoo. Men and women both used it to wash their hair in the creek.

The cradle boards for a child were made by the father. He took a piece of cedar about eight to ten inches wide and two feet long and bored holes along each side. Then he took soft buckskin and sewed it onto the board through these holes. He put the inner bark or skin of cedar inside. These were blankets just big enough to cover the baby, made especially for it of dog hair wool and fern cotton, twisted into a string and woven.

The baby was wrapped in cedar skin first, then in a blanket. It was laced into the buckskin on the board with leather strips. A stick was put over the cradle at night to hold the baby in.

They had a way of making a baby rocker. Two pieces of yew wood six feet long were planted in the ground. The cradle board [sxaltəd] was suspended from these by thongs. A string was tied to the top of the poles and the mother made them bob up and down by pushing on the string with her foot. She could sit and do her own work while also rocking the baby.

In the old days, they used to flatten the baby's head in the cradle board. They used to take a small board and place it with paddling on the baby's forehead and lace it down on each side. A baby used a cradle board for a year, but it didn't learn to walk or crawl until out of it. They were not walking as early as children do now a days.

The board was carried on the back by the mother. A strap came over each shoulder and was attached to a strap around the upper part of her chest. When not being carried, or in the rocker hammock, they leaned the cradle board against a wall, post, or tree.

Naming

Children were named at about 12 years of age. The father or uncle would suggest a name; then the family had to decide on it. If the family objected, they picked out another name. If it were accepted and agreed upon, the child was given the name. After they got older they might change this name for another one. Names "went down in" a family, they passing through the generations.

When a person died, there would be a period of time when they couldn't speak the name for a year or so. But the name would stay in the family and it would used again afterward. The family had to agree that the time was right to bring it out again. A family could never use the names of another one, except under exceptional circumstances of friendship.

A name could come from either the family of the father or of the mother. As a person got older, they remained entitled to names from each side. Some people of high blood had several names. If the family could afford it, a potlatch was given when the name was passed on. The quantity of gifts distributed reflected on the prestige that went with the name. At a big potlatch, people announced they were going to take another name, but they also kept their previous names.

When the name of a dead ancestor was given to a child or an adult took a new name, they would show to the public something that used to belong to the dead person who had the name previously. They announced that from now on the name could be mentioned and used. Then they destroyed the article of clothing from the last holder of the name. A "high" name would be known to all around because so many people would have heard it used at the potlatch.

Training {wg}

Boys and girls of 10 to 14 were sent out when it was hailing to run naked facing into the storm. This made them able to face anything when they grew up, and not be afraid, nervous, or excited. They would not be upset or afraid when someone talked rough to them.

Divorce {wg}

Wilson said that Angeline [daughter of Chief Seattle] was lazy when she was married to her first husband. She would lay in bed until late in the morning. Finally, her Skagit husband daxʷsəb told her "There is a canoe. Take it and go home to your people." He didn't want her because he was ashamed she slept too much.

Ghosts {wg}

The land where the spirits of the dead live was far away. Wilson and Ellen did not have a clear idea where it was supposed to be. The dead lived in houses, just like the old plank smokehouses. They slept in them and the shamans visiting on the Soul Redeeming Odyssey were careful when looking around not to wake them.

When evening came, children were told to come inside because the ghosts of the dead might steal them at night. Dark nights were the most dangerous. Moonlit nights were not as bad. Clothes were never left out at night, otherwise the spirits would steal the warmth-spirit from them. If this happened, the owner sickened or died. If any leftover food was thrown outside at night, the ghosts might eat it and make someone in the house sick.

There were two roads to this afterworld. One was short. Anyone who went on this one could not come back. This happened if a person died suddenly by accident or being killed. The long way was more leisurely. It was taken by the odyssey shamans when visiting the ghost land. A person's soul could start along this way and they would still be alive.

Wilson told of his uncle Sam Snyder who was not feeling well. Later a shaman found his soul along the way to the afterworld. He just happened on it on the way to redeem another soul during one of the annual winter trips. The leader heard someone singing, so he repeated the song. This was the song given to Sam by his spirit ally. When they began to sing the song, Sam started to cry. The shaman turned the soul back. The reason that the soul was on the long road was that someone had badly hurt Sam's feelings. He got to feeling that he wished he were dead. That's why his soul started to drift down the road to the afterworld.

When someone in the family died, close relatives might be hurt so badly that they wished they were dead, too. Their souls might go astray like that of Sam. If a person was accused of something they didn't do, they might be hurt badly and their soul would start on its way. Every year the souls of such people were found on the way to the land of the dead.

When someone died, the rest of the family was afraid that if any belongings were left around, the dead would come back for them. Thus, when people were buried in canoes, their favorite things were put into the wrapping of the body. The other stuff was given to people who came to the wake, burial, and feast and who were not closely related. Sometimes pieces of cloth were torn into sections large enough for a shawl and these were given to visiting women. Anything that might attract the dead back was given away. They did not want the dead to return and take other members of the family back with them.

Marriage {ja}

When someone married out of the tribe, the parents of the boy would take presents to those of the girl. Then later the girl's family would reciprocate and pay them back. When John was young, his parents tried to make an arrangement like this with a Skokomish family, but she died before they could be married. This gift exchange at marriage was called oloɬ.

When a man's wife died, her unmarried sisters were considered *balocid* to him and they called each other by this term. If he decided that he wanted to marry one of them, he had an option to **obalocidəb**, to take her as his new wife. While the wife was living, these same unmarried sisters were called **čabas** and they used this term for each other. The families of a married pair were siuxsiaya [**sixʷsyaya**] to each other. This included all of the families except the parents. The fathers and mothers were sxaʔxaʔ to the young couple.

Most couples lived with his family, but even if they went to live with the family of the bride this was still called *okʼʷiɬyoʔ* [ʔokʼʷiɬiw]. The same term is used for living with either family. They used the same word for both without distinction. The boy or the girl belonged to the tribe of the other one as a result of their marriage [cemented by the birth of children]. When living with the boy's parents, the girl was supposed to work for her parents-in-law and be good to them. If the girl had to be sent home for being lazy, it might cause hard feelings and start a feud between the families. It was considered an insult to the girl.

If a man had a brother and the man's wife or both of them died, then the children they had together were *sklazotał* [sqəladzutał] to the brother. When neither parent was dead, then the children were **stalał** (singular) or **staltalał** (plural) to the brother.

When the husband died, his brother or other close male relative had a claim on the widow. Her family decided which of these men would be the new husband based on his abilities. If they could not decide, then the woman could make up her own mind. Once her family had selected someone, however, she was obligated to go through with the marriage. If none of the male relatives wanted to marry her, they did not have to.

If a man were forced to marry her by his family, he might run away. They might not get along or start quarreling and fighting. Such fighting between a man and his wife was called **x̌acab**. A girl might also run away from such a marriage. The exchange presents were not returned. Although they were lost to the givers, this was never the cause of a fight.

Sometimes, in the case of a fight between two tribes, the chief might give a daughter to the chief or a member of his family in the other tribe. This brought a halt to the fighting. Then the tribes were connected through marriage and children. The daughter was treated as an important wife, not a slave.

In the old days, they would sometimes get married when the couple were still young, about 12 or 13 years old. This was not usual. Usually, a first marriage happened about 15 or 16. A boy could not get spirit power after he was married for then he wasn't clean [and innocent]. He had to get it before he married; although, even if a boy were married, he could still inherit power from a relative. Anyone who died could leave power for him. Then the boy would get sick and have to have the power "fixed" in him by a shaman so he could handle it. If he did not have it "fixed," it might follow him around and even give him help, but he would not know how to handle it. Once a person had three sets of power, no one could do anything to harm him.

Difficult Childbirth {*ja*}

A white woman was having a baby assisted by white doctors. The woman was suffering but they couldn't do anything. Someone told her husband, "We have an Indian man who could make the child come out all right." His name was **x̌akəytəd**. The husband said to go and get him. The Indian doctor arrived and explained that the Indian custom was to give the healer what you wanted to pay him in advance and tell him "This is what I am calling you for." The shaman was given money and accepted it.

He came close and looked at the woman. He just looked and said, "The reason that the child hasn't come is that he is tangled up." He told them the sex of the child and what was wrong. Then he went through the motions of untangling the child in front of the woman. He told the white doctors, "Now watch the child come safely." He went outside. The child was born just as he said. The husband went out to thank the shaman and asked "What do I owe you." The doctor said "Nothing". The man made him take a horse, anyway. This happened in the 1850s. Later the other Indians killed that doctor. John didn't know why. {See Asher 1995}

Burial {*ja*}

A long time ago they wrapped the body in mats and put it up in a tree. Later they put what [bones] remained in the ground. Those high born were put into canoes.

One man died here, was wrapped in a mat, and put in a tree. His wife used to go and cry to him. One day she was crying and she heard him say "Is that you? Is that you? Take me down from here. Take me down." She said, "I'm going home to tell the people my husband is talking to me." This happened long before John's grandfather was born. She told her people and they got him down and unwrapped him. He was still alive. He lived for four generations [?] after that.

They only started to bury people in the ground after whites arrived and insisted on it. When they buried in trees, they put tools and other things with them. They wrapped up their favorites in the mat. They buried all over. John has found skulls a quarter of a mile from his place and they found a skeleton at Keyport wrapped in cattail mats when they were building the torpedo station there. In the 1850s a man died at Chico and was buried with all of his gold in his coffin. A boy dug up his body and took the money.

Games {*ja*}

There was a gambling game played with two bones. It was called <u>slahal</u>. One bone was plain and the other had two stripes, one around each end of the bone. There were two teams. The two leaders chose who they wanted on their team. A leader passed the bones to the men [or women] he wanted to hide them. Each team had two men who did this, each with a pair of bones. They would put their hand beneath a covering, like a blanket, and mix up the bones. When they brought their hands out, they might move them around or switch the bones from one hand to another so fast that they couldn't be seen.

The leader on the other side was supposed to guess which hand held the plain bone. If you looked into the eyes of the man holding the bones, you could sometimes tell which hand the bone was in [because his eyes darted in that direction]. Score was kept with pointed sticks of equal number stuck in the ground in front of each team. There were usually a couple dozen sticks, but the numbers varied. If the hand was correctly guessed, the winning side got one of the sticks from in front of the other side. If he guessed the marked bone, his side had to give up both a stick and a set of bones if they had them.

They guessed only one bone holder at a time, or, if he saw a pattern to the two pairs, he used hand signals to guess both sets. To indicate that he thought that the plain bones were on the outside, he pointed outward. To guess they were both in the middle, he pointed straight and down. To guess they were on the left or the right ends, he pointed in the appropriate direction. [These were the basic moves, but actually there was a great range of personal variation and style during the games.] When a side lost all of their sticks, they lost the game.

Sometimes a player would cheat by switching the bones after the other side had guessed. If he were caught, he was warned to stop. This was a very hard thing to accomplish because so many people were always watching. If a person ever cheated, other people would discover it eventually and watch him ever more closely.

Another game was called <u>slahaləb</u>. It was played with a number of different colored wooden disks about two or three inches in diameter. John's father had a set of these, but, even so, he doesn't remember the exact colors used. There were two teams. One of them had two piles of these disks. They were put inside a big ball of shredded cedar bark. Cattail mats were placed on the ground between the two teams. A roll of mats was placed in the center. One of the disks was marked with grooves. John did not recall the nature of the markings.

One player put his hands inside the shredded bark ball and mixed up the disks. He kept track of which pile had the marked disk. The other side guessed one of the piles. The disk holder then threw all of the disks in that pile, one by one, against the rolled up mat. If the marked disk came out, his side lost and he had to give the disks and one stick to the other side. If the marked disk did not come out, his side kept the disks and got a stick from the other side. When all of the sticks from one team were gone, that side lost.

In this game, the sticks were not pointed. They were just plain and laid side by side on the ground. The sticks had different names that indicated how much of the pile had gone. Women danced and sang behind the players. Sometimes the players tried to cheat by slipping the marked disk beneath the mats.

There was a hockey or shinny game called q̓ʷaq̓ʷtəlc. Curly was a good player of it. It was played on the beach with two sides. Many men made up each team; there were no set numbers. Each player had a crooked stick made like a long wooden spoon about 3 feet long. At one end it was flat and bent like a spoon. The handle was round. They were used to hit a round wooden sphere, called sbkʷ, the size of a golf ball.

Two players started the game, standing on either side of the ball. Each tried to hit the ball to one of the players on his own team. The other side tried to block. The field was half a mile or more along the beach. One side tried to get the ball across the goal line of the other. This goal was just a line drawn in the beach sand. Hitting the ball involved scooping it up, not striking it. The other side tried to prevent this by hooking the stick of the ball carrier. Sometimes they hit each other with these sticks, but it was considered accidental. The game ended with the first goal. Different tribes would visit each other and play this game. Suquamish and Snohomish played it a lot. Told 8/2/52.

Intertribal Relations

Because of intertribal marriages, families could go back and forth between different tribes where they had relations. The Suquamish and Duwamish did not feel they were separate tribes, while the Snohomish was a different one, although the Snohomish and Suquamish were always good friends. The Suquamish married as far north as Lummi and throughout Puget Sound. The Skykomish fought with the Suquamish all of the time.

There was never any trouble with the Snohomish. The Skokomish were not always friendly, but the Snohomish were welcome. {ja}

Ed's mother, who was about 83 in 1925, could remember a white man coming to the beach somewhere near Suquamish to talk about the treaty. He filled a plug hat with gravel and put it in front of the people to try and show them that each was to get a lot of gold. She recalled that people were scared of the first ship to come into the harbor near Suquamish. {es}

Medicine

Plants {jj}

The root of hemlock stopped diarrhea. The roots were smashed, put in water, and warmed. They did not boil it because then it got too strong. They drank the warm tea.

Cedar bark healed cuts. It was boiled in water, strained, and used to wash the cut.

A fern root [saẋolč] smashed, boiled, strained, and drunk was good to heal any soreness inside someone.

Rickrish [sƛowilxʷ, licorice root, sqaycq] was used to get sick people to eat, to restore their appetite. It grew on the moss of a tree, was green, and looked like little roots about the size of fingers. If anyone was sick and wouldn't eat, they made them chew this so they would get hungry and eat.

Wild cherry [plilac, playlaʔac] was good for sore eyes. The second skin was peeled off, mashed, and soaked in water. They wrapped the bark in a rag and put it on the eyes. {*jj*}

In her father's house when she was young, the whole place got smallpox. One of his slaves told him that when his people got smallpox, they used skunk as a cure. They would bring a skunk into the house and tease it until it put out juice. So her father had them go out and get some skunks. They got a couple and tied them to the house posts before teasing them. Ellen's grandmother said the stink was terrible, but it worked. None of the family died of smallpox. Other families who didn't use skunks died. The Suquamish hadn't used skunk before this, but this started them doing so. Ellen didn't recall where the slave was from. {*eg*}

Boiled salt water was used to induce vomiting. Willow bark steeped in water and drunk was good for anything wrong inside and to wash sores. John once skinned a toe during a canoe race and they used this as a wash. It cleared it right up. For sore eyes and cuts they used a plant about a foot high with white flowers on top that looked like cauliflower and with droopy leaves like a squirrel tail. In 1947, a man gave John some to chew and wrap on a cut. Sometimes it was steeped and put on the eyes. {*ja*}

Ritual

Salmon Ceremony {*eg*}
The ceremony was held in honor of a dog salmon with a deformed jaw, called **yabos**. They'd gather little sticks and cook pieces of it on the sticks. Then each little kid was supposed to go and swim. They had to gather up all the bones of the salmon and put them in one place in the water where they were swimming. This was to let the salmon know they wanted them to come back again the next year. This salmon was higher than the other salmon. It was like a chief. It was any salmon with a crooked face. Usually, though, it was a dog salmon.

Each one of the children would be given one of the sticks with salmon on it. Then one of the children took the bones out and dumped them in one place in the water. Then all of the children went out there to that place with the empty sticks in their hands. They throw the sticks away before they start to dive, swim, and have a good time.

Ellen has never heard that this was done when the first salmon of the season was caught. This would happen whenever they caught a salmon with a deformed head.

It was only the children who ate these fish. When the children swam this way, they wore mats around the waist.

This was the custom. Ellen doesn't know why they used these mats, but she says that they also put the fish on these mats. This was a special way of eating. Usually, they used large wooden bowls.

Both Ellen and Wilson know about the [First Salmon] ceremony held at La Conner [Swinomish] and among the Lummi, but they have never heard it mentioned or heard any old people talk about a ceremony like this for the Suquamish. However, Wilson confirmed the rite as described by Ellen above. He says you could always get some salmon in the Sound, so it wasn't like the river people who had to wait for the runs of salmon to arrive.

John Adams did not know of any first salmon ceremony. {ja}

Power, Questing, and Spirit Allies {wg}

At a certain time in the fall of the year (about November), when all of the dog salmon were gone and what had been caught was dried, the spirit powers of some of the young men would return for the first time since they had found them. People would be invited. The father of the person who received the Power would do the inviting. The man hit by the power would be repeating the spirit song he received, but otherwise he couldn't talk. The father placed guests in the house where they belonged, according to locales and status. This was in a regular home, not in a big potlatch house. They invited just what the house could hold.

The power only comes at this time of the year. When the power comes, the man has to sing it. The first time the power comes the people are not specifically invited, but anyone comes who wants to hear the song and learn it. Certain people, who know the power and are able to do it, would come and sing to help out. This would help the boy who was sick. The young man could not start singing until someone else sang the song to open his mouth. Wilson says there was one man that had a song no one could sing correctly. The power he had came to him. But no one could hit the song that would start off the sick man singing. They tried but all of them failed. This was a young man who came from up near Shelton [Skokomish Reservation]. He was married to a Suquamish. This man was having a hard time since no one could start his song for him.

There was a young man from Up Sound who could understand the power, yet he couldn't get out and start the song before someone announced that if anyone in the crowd knew the power, he should come out of the crowd to help. [It was not polite or "high class" to volunteer help unless it was asked for.] Finally the man from Up Sound was asked by one of the sick man's parents and he agreed. He started, got up and talked. Afterward, he started to repeat this man's power song.

The sick man was in bed. When the Up Sound man started to sing, he got up, repeated his song and started to dance. Then everyone joined in. The sick man was out on the floor dancing then. He went around the house just as if he hadn't been sick. He was strong again.

There was another young man named šəgʷap, according to a story told to Wilson by Jim dapsotał. It happened long before Wilson's time. A young man was going from house to house in the village. He was singing. They were just "playing and singing for fun." While he was doing this, his power hit him. He became "helpless," like fainting. Some of the people went to the father of the boy and told him to clean up his house. They wanted him to take everything out of the house to make room for a crowd to come and see his son sing and dance the power.

This man didn't want to do this. He thought that his son was just acting foolish. He said, "Why don't you have him in you're house?" He was told, "No, you have to do it because you are his father." Finally, he agreed and prepared his house for the gathering. The people were to sit around the house on the sleeping benches. Sometimes the spectators would sleep there if events went on for a long time. Often, a new singer like this one sang all night. The minimum first time was about four days.

They brought him to the house and his father invited certain of the people inside. In addition to these, others came in just to watch without an invitation. The people invited by the father were the ones the father thought could help sing for his son. It was up to the father to find someone to help his son sing when the boy got sick in this way.

The father appointed someone to take care of the guests and to show them where they were to sit in the house. For four or five nights, they helped this young man. He didn't go to bed to sleep during the entire time. He just went to sit in a corner for awhile and remain quiet. This is how he rested after he started singing and dancing. He quit dancing for a while and sat in a corner every so often. He might sing to himself while sitting there, but it was just for his own benefit. Nobody repeated the song after him, like they did in public.

When he started to sing the song, a man chosen by his father, someone who understood the power, repeated the song as the young man sang it. When the song ended, the repeater started it over again and then the rest all joined in. When they all started singing, the young man did his dance for the first time.

When he was ready to quit, he made a sign. Then he changed his song to other words. The repeater copied this and the same routine as above was followed. The second dance might be different from the first. There might be two or three of these songs and dances. If he changed three times, when the third verse ended, he'd sing the first one again. He would go through each one of them three times during the four days that he was singing.

After he was through with the three songs sung three times, he might start another, different song. He might even go on to a fifth or sixth. When morning came, it was time for him to rest. He sat in the corner and might sing for himself, but he didn't sleep. The other people ate and then slept. But the singer never ate. Some of them lasted as long as 8 days without eating or sleeping. This was the longest they could go. Most of them go for four days.

At the end of all of these activities, the gathering broke up. Some went home, some stayed on a little longer because some of the older people started to sing after the young boy was done. An elder got out on the floor to sing and dance his song. This was to "clear himself [or herself] from getting sick."

When the full series of days was completed, a boy could, eat, sleep, and rest. Then he had to go back to work: fishing, hunting, making canoes, or whatever he did with his power.

The next year about this same time, the spirit would come back for the second time. The next year, the father was prepared for it, as the father of šəgʷap. Sometimes, the father himself got a spirit. Then it was up to the son to take care of him. He chose a repeater to get him started. The second year the same repeater might come back or the father or son might select another one. That time, the repeater did not have to actually sing to start the boy off. The boy sang the same song as the year before and now he understood it better. The entire process of the previous year was repeated again. After the second year, they could sing for themselves. They might have a repeater to help out, but they could sing for themselves. The older a person got, the more he had to do for himself in the singing. Whoever happened to be near when the power hit helped a singer through the sickness.

[Power was conveyed by many different kinds of spirits. Many more than can be named here.] There was a particular spirit which made it necessary for a person to give things away in order to "get clear of it." This power was called **sqayap.**

Another type of spirit power was q̓ʷax̌ʷq̓. When it hit a person, he'd sing it. Then he'll ask for the poles and someone else used them to keep time by bouncing them against the roof while he sang. Others would beat with sticks on boards laid flat. Some people asked for these poles to be used and also for cedar bark to be tied around the pole near the top. When they used it, the cedar bark flopped in time with the song. Not everyone used this cedar bark. It wasn't a helping (curing) power, but it was a "help" to the person who has it. [In other words, it brought benefits to the human ally, but he didn't use it to help others.]

The power called sgʷədiləč did not occur among the Suquamish, but they knew about it for other tribes. Wilson's mother had this power and sang it at Suquamish. She was a Lower Skagit. She was the only one here who had this kind of power. This happened before Wilson was born. She inherited it from some of her people. Wilson says that no Suquamish tried to get it. It belonged Up Sound way. If anyone here got it, they would have a hard time getting it started for it was unknown to the local repeaters. Wilson's father was the repeater for his wife. He had a special power that helped him understand strange powers. He was good as a repeater. He helped lots of people. The name of the power that helped him be a good repeater was sx̌alkəb [monster]

[Power could be used both to hurt and to help, the human ally had to decide.] The whites put a stop to Indian doctoring and that gave a clear path to the bad doctors [shamans]. They started killing all the Indians. The good doctors couldn't do anything about it because the whites had stopped them from doctoring, but they did not stop the bad ones, so they had a free hand and they killed off a lot of the Indians.

Questing {ja}

As soon as the boys were old enough, they started training. They were told to go into the salt water every morning and night. They had to stay in it until their bodies didn't steam when they came out. There was a fire ready for them to warm themselves beside when they got out. John does not know of any restrictions on conduct or the eating of certain foods during this period of training. The boys were not sent out to get power right a way for they had first to train for a long time. They were told when and where to go at the time when they were ready. They were sent to places where the spirits were known to be [for that family].

This might be up on top of a mountain. There was a mountain over by Mission Lake named babdət (Mt Green ?). Some of them were sent there. When a boy was sent there, he was given some sticks to take up to the top of the mountain. He was supposed to leave them there to show that he had actually been up there. Later, older men would go up to see whether the sticks were really there. If they weren't, the boy would be punished.

They might be told to walk all the way around Bainbridge Island along the beach. They would find power there, like John Bull. It was a rock so he was very strong. They used to hit him and beat him and shoot him, but they couldn't kill him. He was hard to kill. He was shot once, but it didn't kill him. While he was in bed, they shot him with a shotgun and blew him in two. This was how they finally killed him.

Some were sent to Point No Point. There were a lot of snakes there, and they would get Snake power. It isn't very strong, though.

When the boys were sent out to seek their power, they had to be clean or the powers wouldn't come to them. They were given physics [emetics] to clean them out. Their finger and toe nails had to be clean. While they were out, they were not supposed to eat or drink. John thinks that sometimes they did not eat or drink for as long as 30 days.

John related that one time when he was a boy, he was running home on the beach after sundown when it was dark. Suddenly, he saw an old, stooped-over woman with a blanket over her shoulders walking on the beach and leaning on a wooden staff. He looked at her and said, "What is that? There's nothing in camp like that." He was young then and didn't know about such encounters and so he ran on. The old people told him that she was a power. If he had grabbed her, she would have knocked him out, and both of them would have fallen on the beach and lain side by side for a long time – maybe as long as 10 hours. This old woman represented a number of powers. You couldn't tell which one you would get. She represented a group of powers called *cǝyod* [siyod]. John did not recall the specifics of these powers.

Instead, his thoughts turned to the story of how his grand uncle Tom or **wǝlpǝkad** tried to cure a little girl. The girl had been eating bread when her mother hit her on the back and made some of the bread go up her nose. She got sick and her parents called Tom to cure her. But they had waited too long. Tom told the father that it was too late, but the father told him to go ahead because she was going to die anyway. So Tom sucked out the bread, but she died just as he had told them she would. He should have been called sooner. This grand uncle was later killed by a Suquamish, but John did not want to talk about the details.

Another time, John said that this man was John Curly, his maternal uncle. Curly was born a Duwamish and lived there most of his life, although he did visit Suquamish often. At the time when Leschi (a Duwamish [Nisqually-Puyallup] whose grandmother was part Yakama) was going to attack the whites at Seattle (1856), Curly went to the whites and warned them about it. Leschi had threatened anyone who would tell the whites, but nothing ever happened to Curly because he told. John and Curly often hunted together. {Curly's daughter had a daughter by pioneer Henry Yesler}

Curly had Rattlesnake power. When he was a boy, he had been in the Okanogan country. His mother had spanked him and he went out into the mountains to cry. Snake appeared to him there. John said that this was like stealing it from the Okanogan. Curly gave it to John, who had the Indian name of **satabsoq** [sk̓idk̓ʷ] meaning "little devil, or rattlesnake." This spirit followed John around all over, but he never had a doctor [shaman] "fix it to him." Eventually, he had it taken way because he was afraid that he might be accidentally responsible for killing someone with it.

Power was sometimes inherited in this way. For example, a father might pass his power(s) on to his son. After the father died, the son would get sick because he had inherited the power(s). Then a doctor would have to "fix" the power in him. That means he would "straighten it out". But the son would not be able to use the power for a long time – maybe 10 or 15 years. Sometimes, one man could steal another man's power, but if it was too strong for him, he would die [because it would overpower him to death].

John says that when he was a boy, a lot of children who were sent to government schools got sick and died. Some of the people thought that the teachers were doing it, but John says it was bad doctors at home who were sending the sickness to them. People who had Bear power could do this. One of his people way back [long ago] killed lots of people with this power.

Someone was working on John when he was a boy in mission school. It hurt him on his left side at the bottom of his chest and made him stop growing. He didn't know who was doing it to him. Another Indian doctor came to work on him. This doctor wasn't called. He just knew about it. He sucked at the place where it hurt. His power was Loon. It isn't a very strong power and he couldn't get it all out. John's parents took him to Dr Morgan at Port Madison, who gave him cod liver oil mixed with port wine. His parents gave this white doctor the credit for helping him, but John says it was the Indian doctor who really helped him the most. It was because of him that he grew up. Even so, he didn't grow as strong as he should have been. The pain came back again later in the same place. John says that it has really been there all the time and that that is what is wrong with him now, late in life.

The general name for all power(s) is **sqəlalitut**. A shaman doctor had to have three sets of them to be any good. If he had three sets, no one could do anything to him. John says that that is why his father could stand up and talk and no one could do anything to him. He was a very good speaker.

Chief Kitsap had lots of powers. Eagle was one of them. The snow is called the "lice of the eagle." If an arrow was shot at him, it would go right through his hair and not hurt him, no matter where you aimed at him. A little red canoe was another of his powers.

John knew a woman called Julia Nappie, **sləqalca**, who had Dog Salmon for a power. She would never eat dog salmon. From this and other cases, John thinks there was a general taboo against anyone eating members of the species of their own power.

People who had the Blackfish (Killerwhale, Orca) for power were good fishers because the Blackfish eats other fish. Anyone who had Thunderbird for power could make it thunder whenever they wanted to. John knew a man who had Cloud for a power. This was Wind who could blow away anything that bothered him. John also remembered Seal, Sea Lion, and Porpoise as power(s). He said anything could be a power. All living things could have power.

Girls could get power too. They could get the same kinds of power that men got. There were many different kinds in all.

John says that a place called Devil's Hole by the whites is located near a sandspit between Bangor and Vinland on the eastern side of Hood Canal. It is a pool of water. The Klallam got power there, but the Suquamish knew there were bad, mean spirits there. If they got too near it, they would back away to make sure it did not get them from behind. They always backed away.

Half way between Charleston and Gorst at the head of Port Orchard Bay there was a rocky place that was used for meetings and sports that included gambling, jumping, and other games. The gambling used two bone pieces and was part of the ancient traditions, long before the whites came. There were smokehouses and camps there on different sides of the bay. Everyone would come there from all over to play games when there was plenty of food. John didn't associate it with any particular time, just whenever there was enough food to get them all together. There was no big potlatch house there. They just had cedar bark houses. The bark was in strips with cattail mats around the whole house.

John was born near Charleston. Indians used to camp there where the Navy is now. That was in 1872 when John was born. He knows this is right because Pete Fowler was born the same year in September and John was born in October. He felt this was important because some places have recorded his birth date in error. The allotment patent has him two years older and this is wrong. His mother was from the Duwamish and named Mary. The father of his father was from the Skokomish, but his father went to live at Mapleville (in the Poulsbo-

Keysport area) after marriage because it was a good place to hunt. Because of his marriage, he could go back and forth between Skokomish and Suquamish. His wife was a Suquamish so "This was his home too."

He used to hunt around that area, way back in the timber. Deer were all he hunted there. He used a bow and arrows when small, but a gun when he was older. There were no camps back in the timber because they were always along the shore. They just traveled into the woods to hunt.

Before the whites came, there was a man and his wife who lived back on Mission Creek. His name was sxʷatkadə and he was the father of Steve Wilson. He was a Suquamish. He didn't know why he lived way back there [as a holy caretaker]. He lived on the southwest side of the mountain where the stream is. Boys in training had to take sticks up to the top of this mountain. Later this old man or others would go up to see if the sticks were there. If they weren't, the boy was punished.

A smokehouse was near the head of Mission Creek, at Mission Lake near the mountain. The man just went into the timber in the fall when the salmon were running in the creek. He'd catch them there and cure them in the smokehouse. Then he would bring them back for storage in the main camp on the shore.

East of the mountain where the sticks were taken, there was a swamp. Once, Jack's father, John Bull, and several others were hunting deer there. They camped there at night. Vapor rose from the pond. When it got high up, thunder started. A young man could go there and get this power. Then he could make it thunder any time he wanted to. A white man asked several Indian doctors around Yakama if any of them could make it thunder. One of the Yakama doctors did it.

Some whites believed in Indian doctors and used them to cure diseases. The whites used to have one Duwamish doctor come to the back of a store and work on them there by sucking out diseases. He had Mosquito for power. It was part of Thunder and showed up in the Rainbow.

Bluejay was a power that allowed a person to talk any language. John says it was here long ago, before the whites. He does not know of any power used to locate the bodies of drowned people.

The Suquamish did not use the "boom, boom" (drum) like the Yakama do. When they were singing in a house, they would take a long pole and hit it on the roof to keep time with the singing. Anyone could keep time with the pole.

This was a long pole about 8 or 10 feet tall. John saw one when he was about 10 years old about 70 years ago. The pole was painted red. These poles were always kept out in the woods. You couldn't keep them in the house because they were part of what a doctor had, and, thus, too powerful for encounters with ordinary mortals. Some doctors did not have them, it depended on what the spirit told his ally at the first meeting. They were kept out in the woods up in a tree or in the hollow of a cedar. The sticks belonged to the doctor, but anyone could beat time with them while the doctor sang.

John says that at certain times, during certain parts of the song, the pole would come to life. Once an Indian doubted this. So they told him to hold a cedar man. It was a figurine, not a pole, a man made of cedar about four-foot high [cf Chehalis]. These figures had handles on the back to hold them. They held them up in front of them when they danced. At a certain point in the song, the figure would come to life. This represented part of the power of a doctor. So they gave this man the carved man of cedar. He danced with it. When they got to that certain part, the carving came to life and took the person through the roof and drowned him in the water. These figures were given up a long time ago. John never saw one, but the old people told him about them.

Near the end of some of the poles, a two foot piece of cedar bark was sometimes tied. Just a single piece. The pole itself was cedar, about as thick as a baseball bat, 3 inches in diameter. Because it was cedar it wasn't heavy. This power of the pole was called təstəd, a sibling of the power boards.

Curly saw some of these poles come out of the water at the southern end of Bainbridge Island. This was a place where this power could be gotten. You would keep going into the water to get this one. When the poles came up, you would build a raft and go out to get them. When you got hold of one, it would take you down into the water. You would stay down there for 3 days and nights. You could do this because you were with the power. This power could be used to kill with, also to cure people. After you understood it, you came up and floated on the water, drifting to shore. You would be weak. Sometimes they came home on their hands and knees they were so exhausted.

While in the water, the thing told you what you're going to be. It gave you songs to sing. It also gave you a dance different from that of anyone else. It would be as long as 30 years before the power could be used. You couldn't doctor with it when you were still a boy. You had to grow up first. It had to be "fixed" in a person only when it was inherited. A person who inherited power would get sick. Then an Indian doctor would be called to "fix" it on him or her. If a man went out and got power himself, it wouldn't have to be "fixed" on him. Sometimes after a person had gotten power, he became sick. This was because the power did not stay with you all of the time. When you called it back, you might get sick. Then a doctor would have to help you.

John's father was hunting near Bainbridge Island at night. Doctor Peters was coming along, half drunk, and saying "He thinks he's a big Indian doctor, but he'll find out. Just watch!" Curly was there, too, and he heard someone singing way off, like crying. It turned out to signify that Dr Peters had got Dr Bob. Dr Peters got the power of Dr Bob and that killed him. Dr Bob was the person who received the poles at Sandy Hook. Dr Peters was a bad man. Forty-seven years ago, Indians were burying three and four people every week. Dr Peters was doing that.

Secret Society ~ Guild {wg}

The secret society of Dog Eaters [sx̌ədx̌ədəb, sx̌idx̌idəb] had certain songs they used to sing. It was a kind of secret power. When they sang the song and got under the influence of the power, they acted silly [crazy]. If a dog were around them, they got it and tore it to pieces with their teeth. They were supposed to eat it, but they really didn't. They made the people believe that they did, though.

They used to make people not belonging to it think that they were doing things that they weren't. They would take a young person, lay him down, put him to sleep, and then one of them sucked on his body. Then he spit out blood supposedly from the young man. Actually, the man had cut his tongue underneath. This was not part of the initiation into the group. It was only part of what they showed others, their showing off to other people what they could do.

Once, Wilson's mother was sick and supposed to be asleep. A couple of members were planning something and she overheard them. It was only in the middle of winter when they would perform. In the performance they made people believe that they could make something move without anyone doing this. They used to make noise with a rattle, a piece of wood hollowed out to hold stones. It was the size and shape of a duck. They would shake it in time with the singing. It was made of two pieces of wood tied together, made in the shape of a bird, and tied around the small end. It was called **yobax̌ʷačatab**.

While they were singing they made the people believe they could make the rattle move without someone doing it. While singing the song, they'd lay it on the ground. But first, they scattered some feather down [q̓ʷəq̓ʷalc] on the ground. This covered the string tied to the rattle. There were two people in the middle of the smokehouse. They were opposite each other. First one pulled it toward him in a jerking way. He had a blanket over himself, covering his head. He could not be seen clearly. This made the bird rattle look as if it were alive. Then the other man pulled it the other way. All of the time, they were singing a song that were supposed to make the bird move. If the down should get thin or become pulled away, they kept watch and ran out to pick up the rattle. They started to use it as a rattle again before anyone could see the string.

The well-to-do people were entitled to join this society. The group itself had a choice as to who was to become a member. If anyone overheard any of the secrets, they had to join. Even a low class person would be taken in if they learned any of the secrets. This forced membership kept everything secret. Women of the high class were also taken in.

When a young man was about 14 years old, he "kind of felt big." Teenagers felt that they knew it all. To keep them modest, they made them join the society because there he had to listen and learn from the older people. They would take a young man away to where the others could not see the initiation. They worked over the initiate and put a spirit power into him. This would put him to sleep. He was helpless then. To wake him up, two people went on either side of him to raise him. Then they let him down again. They did this three or four times, probably three. At first, he was face down. After lifting him, they turned him over on his back and lifted him up and down again, three or four times. When they let him down the last time, they sat him up. That was when they woke him. When he was able, they stood him upright.

Then they take him to a special room where they start him singing. They tell him what power he was to have by singing it to him first. He was in a special room from which he could emerge into the public. They also taught him a dance. When he was trained and ready, he came out before the people at a public gathering to sing and dance. He had a special repeater to help him get started and to followed him around the smokehouse. The boy sang part of the song and then stopped while the repeater echoed it. Then the boy started again, stopped, and the repeater followed. This continued until the song was finished.

Then they had another boy come out and sing. The second boy would have a different power with a slightly different song and dance. The same procedure was pretty much followed in every case. No one else was allowed to sing exactly the same song. The tune might even be the same, but then the words were different. There are many powers that have almost the same song, but each remains distinct within about eight kinds of music.

The public gathering was attended by anyone who wanted to come. They were not told any stories or anything else about what was happening to the initiates when they were training in the special room. Other tribes had the same society so their initiates could join in during rites at other tribes. Wilson was never able to see an initiation because in his day the Catholics were very strong and they forbid these ceremonies.

When a boy received a song, it was his until death. Then the song might be inherited by someone else, but it stayed within the family. When someone died, the spirit ally was "just like a dog" and went to another member of the family who was familiar to it. It could go to any member, not necessarily the son. Membership in the society tended to pass along family lines, so when a boy was initiated, he might be given the song that belonged to some deceased member of his family. A person outside of the family was not allowed to take such a song, unless the family approved it under very unusually circumstances.

These inherited powers or the ones from the secret society did not require a power quest. They helped the boy, however, to get other powers for himself. Thus, once a boy had joined the secret society, he often went out to seek power for himself. They only went out in the winter, never in the summer.

A low class person who didn't belong to the society could go out in quest of power for him/herself. This power then could be passed on in this family at death [but it was almost never a strong one].

Power that was passed on by the secret society was not the property of the society as such. The members of the society decided what power belonged to the family of a boy (or girl) so it could be passed on to him. It was the family members already in the society who decided this.

The instruction in the special room also included what to do if you meet a power at any time. Sometimes, an animal would be a power. Should you meet it, you were supposed to act in a certain way toward it until it talked to you in your language and gave you its power. Sometimes it was in dreams that you saw the animal. The secret society told what to do in a dream of this kind. When the animal spoke to a boy in his own language, then that was his power for life.

Besides an animal, you might meet a person who was not human. These powers will show up as a living person or animal, yet it wasn't what it seemed. After they spoke, then the animal or person disappeared. Then you were to go home, tell no one, and keep it to yourself until it hit as a power and you became ill. When it hit, it was a day during the fall of the year. If you couldn't sing it, it was the place of your father to call for help. The voice of the spirit sank into your body. When it came back, you needed a repeater to help sing it out initially.

In dreams when a person met a spirit, it said "My father sent me to tell you to come out and meet me." Yet the animal or person talking was the power itself. The power told you to meet his father at a certain place. This place might be a spring, or a big stream. Then you must go and swim in this certain place early in the morning until you meet the power there. While the power spoke of "its father," it was really the power itself that was doing this. It really didn't have a father.

If a boy kept clean enough, he finally got power. If he had courage enough to go there and swim every day early in the morning, he eventually got power. After a boy received power, the spring of water might go dry, but break out in some place else, or go dry entirely. Wilson denied that the boy was required to dive a certain number of times, although people often went to lakes and mountains to get power and diving was a practice during quests. {wg}

Ellen said they used to go to Island Lake near Silverdale to get power. The common people who didn't belong to the society could also go out and look for power. Women also sought power. They usually just got common things like birds, and so forth. They usually didn't get any strong power like those that came to men, but they could. Ellen remembers hearing of a woman who got a strong power just like a man's. {eg}

Wilson believed that slaves could get power too. There were many possible ways and kinds of power. Wilson said his family on the side of his father did not have to go out searching for power the way most others did. They could get power even if they never left home, provided that they were clean.

Wilson provided an example of one of his dreams. He saw a bear coming down the creek on all four feet. When it got close, it stood up and its hair [fur] was gone. It was like a human. It told Wilson that its father wanted to see him. But Wilson decided not to go up to that creek. He was afraid. So he wouldn't go to this creek unless someone else went with him for then the spirit would never come. You had to be alone at such meetings to get power.

John Adams didn't know much about the secret society. His father told him that it was a lot of faking. Anyway, it was before his time and he hadn't heard much about it. *{ja}*

Redeeming Odyssey Ceremony *{wg}*

Wilson actually saw this done. It required shamans, generally known as **daxʷdaʔab**, who had a special kind of power. We are out here alive and when the dead come here they look for sick people. Then the dead person's spirit will find the clothes of the sick person lying outside. What they find from these clothes, they take back with them. It was the warmth of that sick person's body that had soaked into the clothes. The dead took this out of the clothes and took it with them to the spirit land. Every time they did this, it weakened the sick person. Then the shaman needed to get over into the spirit land to get the warmth away from the power of the dead people. In that way, he helped the sick person and sometimes this enabled him to get well.

The first shaman asked to cure the sick person chooses another shaman or two to help him. When they were doctoring, they use the verb **opəgʷəd [spigʷəd]**. This was when they performed, singing and dancing to fulfill their power to help the sick. Each shaman had a cedar board representing a power. The Suquamish called this **sptadax̣ [spəɬtədaq]** and the Duwamish called it **spəgʷəd [spigʷəd]**. Each shaman had only one. Sometimes they were in the shape of a human. On the board they would mark their power: Lizard, Snake, some kind of beast, and so on. They painted on the board a picture of the power. Such boards were from six to eight inches wide, and four to five feet high. They were carved and painted. The background was painted white with the other colors over the white.

When they worked on a sick person, they could either use the boards by themselves or they could use a simulated canoe outlined in cedar bark, with the boards set up inside. When they used the boards alone, they would shake when handled, but in the canoe they stood steady and did not move.

The canoe was made of strands of inner cedar bark pounded so that they were soft and pliable, about 10 to 12 feet long. The boards were put in the canoe, but they were dug down into the ground so that they stood up straight. The shamans would be in the canoe making dancing motions, but keeping their feet on the ground so as not to tip the imaginary canoe.

Many shamans made the trip to the spirit land. Usually three was the minimum. When they got out of the canoe, they were supposed to be there. They danced around very carefully, looking for the spirits. They lifted their feet up high and crossed their legs as they walked, moving slowly and carefully. [In this way they were imitating the motions of the dead so as not to attract undo attention to themselves.] All this time, they were looking for the spirit. Sometimes they would find the warm stuff on the clothing of some of the dead.

One or two of the shamans might have a piece of cedar bark draped around his shoulders like a scarf reaching to about the waist. When they found the spirit, they put it on this cedar bark to take it back safely. If they were not using cedar bark, they put the warmth to the breast. When they had the spirit-warmth, they brought it back to the sick person. The shaman pulled off the warmth with two hands and held it toward the patient. Then he put it back on that body with a motion of the two hands brushing the person with the palms out.

If the sick person got well, he might start singing his own spirit song, getting up to dance and sing after only half an hour. If he did not get well, the shamans may have had to repeat the trip because, "There was something else they did not get." While they were doing this, they were all singing constantly.

They usually started for the spirit land in the morning. The trip took from 6 to 12 hours. If the sick person did not get better, then they made another trip, this one their third. If the patient then showed signs of getting well, they don't make any more trips. If he didn't show any improvement, there was nothing left to do. It was seldom that even two trips were necessary.

If they didn't use the canoe, they just stood their boards up on the plain ground so they were straight. When they were coming home from the spirit land, they shook the boards, to speed up the trip back, in time with their singing, moving them forward and back instead of side to side for that might tip the canoe. The people sitting around the house kept time with the music, singing during the trip out and the return. While the shamans were in the spirit land all noise stopped. It had to be very quiet. Even the shamans spoke only in whispers. Everyone was afraid of being heard by the spirits.

The actual trip involved building the outline of a canoe in cedar bark strips big enough to surround all the shamans going along. At the beginning, they got down on their knees and started to sing. The spectators beat time to the song, hitting sticks on boards about a foot long. Usually, it was a cedar board from a house. That sounded the loudest.

Later they stood up and danced, but they never moved their feet around to keep from tipping over. Going, they had poles that they used like paddles. The stroke was long and slow. When they came to a stream of water in the spirit land, they left the canoe to cross a bridge. They go one at a time. The leader at the bow went first. Then all of them entered the camp of the spirit people.

On the trip back, they did not pass the bridge because they took another way back, depending on where they found the spirit. Then they wanted to travel very fast and they shook the boards. In the canoe, they used the poles to make paddling motions that were faster than they used going. They sang and beat time a little faster, also. When they got back, they sank down on their knees in the canoe until they landed and got out.

Then they knelt again and sang some more. Each doctor sang his song. When all of them were done, the leader delivered "what they brought back" to the sick person. The leader went first, but then the others went in turn, each singing and delivering some part of the spirit. They were singing then because the personal power of each of them was coming to them from the place were they initially encountered it. When all had given their parts, the patient sang his own song if he felt revived or cured. They might be working on more than one sick person at a time, if so, they repeated this procedure separately for each one.

Potlatch {*wg*}

Wilson said the smoke house [plank dwelling] was divided into sections for groups coming from different areas. When a man gave a potlatch, he would send word to the headmen of different areas, so that what was given away went to the leaders of these different bands.

Wilson went to many potlatches as a boy. The last one he went to was given by John Seattle at Green River. John was not related to the old chief, he just took the name.

When a leader came, he brought some of his family. This group was seated in a special part of the gathering. The man giving the potlatch would announce the names as people came in. Or he might have a speaker do this. They would have men like ushers who showed each group where to sit and whom to stay with. The people brought gift food with them when they came.

When all the people were there, the leader started, singing his power song. Then he spoke to the people, saying "so and so has come in. That is the last of the people I have invited." Then he changed to another tune of his song and kept singing until he got to the end. Then he started to give away what he had collected together, saying "The first person invited was so and so." Then that tribal leader was given presents, and so on until they got to the last one to come in. Then his helper started his own song, finished it, and gave out his own gifts in the same order. The giver usually called on his relatives to help him. He gave only to the leading members of other communities.

After the gifts had been given to the chiefs, and the feasting was over, there was a Scramble. Everyone was allowed in this event [but the high class thought it too crass to behave in so undignified a manner]. A platform was made on the roof and blankets were piled on it. Then the people would crowd around below it. A man would throw the blankets down at them, one at a time. Everyone tried to get ahold of one of these. They didn't pull or tear it. One of them who had a firm grip would claim it. Then he had to pay the others also hanging on to it for their share. Sometimes an old man would get hold of a blanket and a strong young man would pull it away from the others until he could give it to the old man for his own. [This showed respect and regard for the elders.] Poles were also thrown down and people would try to take hold of them for each represented one canoe. The person left holding the stick had to pay the others for their share.

During the first part of a potlatch, when the gifts were given out to the invited leaders, these headmen could either keep all that they received or they could give some of it to members of their group. It was up to them, but a wise leader shared what he had.

The reasons for holding a potlatch included 1) Naming – this was the most important, whether giving a name to a child or changing one later in life; 2) Remove Stigma – for a daughter sent home by her husband, the father would announce what had happened and say he didn't know why his daughter had been sent home, this cleared her name so she could marry honorably again; 3) Status Changes – mark the death of one chief and the elevation of his heir.

John Adams said they would invite people from all over, tribes friendly to them. They wouldn't invite enemies. It was always a chief who gave the potlatch, but he had other men go out and do the inviting. The name for a potlatch gʷəgʷə [gʷigʷi] means "to gather people from all over, to invite [call, ask]."

The guests arrived singing their own songs. Chief Seattle had a potlatch at Old Man House around the 1850s. He went to Victoria for some blankets. When he left, he told the people, "When I leave Victoria, you will hear Thunder and then you will know I am on my way back." This happened. Curly was the speaker for Chief Seattle at this potlatch.

Sometimes a chief would deliberately stigmatize himself to have an excuse for a potlatch. salq̓b, the second chief after Kitsap and the one ahead of young Seattle, was fixing the fire in his hearth. He wanted his blanket to catch on fire. He went slowly around the flames until his blanket ignited.. Then he held a potlatch. Having his clothing catch fire gave him the excuse he needed to hold a potlatch.

Folklore[1]

The Changer [dokʷibəɬ] {jj}

Around Squaxin Island towards Olympia, the Changer was going there. He wanted to change this land into something else, but the land would throw itself to one side every time he tried to change it. It would say, "I am old land, I'm old land, I'll stay the way I want." Then the Changer left it. Now this land is very hilly. It is up and down all over. This was from the way it was throwing itself to one side.

There is a rock with lots of little rocks around it south of Sandy Hook. This was a person, a man. He and his dogs were chasing a elk. The dogs were barking [too loudly]. All at once, the Changer came along and turned them all into rocks. The little rocks are the dogs. The big rocks are the elk and the man.

The Changer was always going around turning things into something else. One rock at Poulsbo was a person. He was filing a bone to make it into a knife. He was singing about cutting up the Changer when he came along. The Changer heard this and sneaked up behind him. All at once he said: "What are you singing now, Deer?" He called him Deer to turn him into a deer. The Changer took the knife and put it on the back part of his leg above the hoof. Then the deer turned into the rock. They call the rock halils. It has a white mark like a collar around it.

Dog Husband {jj}

There was a girl who had a little puppy. The puppy always slept with her. It began to grow up and it still slept with her. Pretty soon the girl gave birth to a lot of little puppies. The father of the girl was so ashamed of her he left her with her puppies. The father, mother, and all the people left the girl alone.

The puppies got older and older. All she gave them to eat was clams. There was one little girl and four boys. The girl was half and half, a person on one side and a dog on the other.

All at once, they were getting older and she [the mother] used to hear lots of noise in her home when she was out on the beach digging clams. She decided to see what they were doing. So she sneaked up on the house. She peeped through a little hole. She saw them. They

---

[1] Actual stories are in the story section titled 'texts'.

had taken off their dog skins and they were handsome looking boys. She went to the little girl. The little girl was always with her. She went back to the beach to dig. She made a plan and told it to her daughter. They took their clamming sticks and stuck them in the sand and put some of their clothes on them. Then they sneaked up to the house because they heard a noise.

(Before she had gone down to the beach again, she had made a big fire in the house, but the boys did not know what she made the fire for.)

She told her daughter they would grab the furs (hides) and throw them into the fire. Her little girl and she went in quickly. They grabbed the hide coats and threw them into the fire. Then the boys were ashamed and became still. The mother said "Why didn't you be like this before. You have made me ashamed. My family left because you wore clothes like a dog."

The boys grew up to be big, handsome hunters. Two went up to hunt for deer and elk; two went out into the Sound to fish. The mother went picking berries. The boys got all kinds of nice meat and fish. They dried the meats, salmon, and berries. They did this every day and were getting lots to eat.

The father and mother could see the smoke when they were drying all the time and they said, "What are they doing over there?" So they said, "We'd better go over and see." So they went, got there, and saw that there was lots to eat. So the girl was good to her folks. She gave them bundles of meat and other things she had.

They went back to their new home and told the people. The father was so proud of his daughter. She told her father, when he came, about her boys and how they really were.

Then he told his people, "Get ready, we're going back to our old home, my daughter's children are hunters." So they all went back. The boys hunted and fed these people that came back to them. The people were sorry for what they had done before. The father and mother asked for forgiveness. They said that she and her boys would be the leaders of the tribe from then on.

The daughter got married and had other children. They weren't too bad. The grandchildren were better. They didn't show so much hair on the face, just a little brown where it had been in the previous generation.

Star Story (Star Husband) {*jj*}

This is a story the Suquamish got from the Snoqualmie.

Two girls used to go camping. They would be lying on their bed facing the sky. They were sisters.

One of the girls said, "Oh, that is a nice white star. I would like to have it for a boy friend." The other girl said, "I'd like to have that pink star for my boy friend." They went to sleep.

When they woke up, they both had men lying with them. They were afraid of the men, but one of them said, "You wanted me when you saw me up in the sky."

Then these men put the girls to sleep so they wouldn't know which way they were going. They took them up into the sky, the girls didn't know where they were going. They took them to their home.

The girls went out camping again in their new home and dug some fern roots to eat. They did this every day.

Not long after, the older girl had a baby boy by her husband, the white star who had matter in his eyes. The pink star, though, was a handsome young fellow.

The baby was getting older. They went digging fern roots every day and came home every evening. One night they came home and didn't have any fern roots. Their husbands asked, "Why don't you get any anymore." They answered, "Oh, the baby cries so much we can't do anything else but take care of him. The baby didn't actually cry. They just fooled their husbands.

Instead, when they were out every day, they kept digging deeper until all at once wind came up through the hole. They said, "This wind acts like where we came from." So they blocked up the hole. They started to plan what they would do.

They gathered cedar boughs. Then they wove the cedar boughs, warmed them and twisted them to make them soft. When they got home, they'd have no fern roots. They'd tell their husbands the same story, "The baby cries and we can't dig roots." All of the time, they were working these cedar boughs to make a rope. They tied them together until they thought they were long enough.

Then they opened the hole and put the rope through to see if it would touch the land where they had come up from. They let it down, down, down – until it stopped. They thought, "Well, I guess it has gotten to where we came from. They pulled it up. They tied it around the waist of the younger one. They tied the other end to a tree. Then they made the hole big enough for her body to go through.

The younger sister said, "If I get to the bottom, I'll pull on the rope and then you'll know I'm down. When she got down she did this. Then her sister pulled the rope up. She tied her baby next and let him down. At the bottom, his aunt untied the baby and pulled on the rope to let her sister know it was ready to go up again.

Then she pulled the rope up and tied herself. Then she let herself down. When she left, she fixed the hole so that their husbands wouldn't find it. She got down all right. Then they pulled the rope down. She let it come down and pile up there. This is still at Snoqualmie. It looks like a little mountain.

They went home. Their mothers told them they had been looking for them. The girls told their mother the story.

The baby grew up to be a big, nice looking boy. He got married and had children. Their children got big and got married. This was the beginning of the Snoqualmie. They are descended from the stars.

[The mother of Chief Jacob was part Snoqualmie, but even so this story is very different from the way it was told there. The older sister was killed on the way down and the rope remained affixed to the sky so everyone could use it as a swing until mouse gnawed through it and it fell into a rocky heap near Mount Si.]

Responses {*eg, wg*}

The people listening to a story were supposed to say **haboki** occasionally while they were listening to show their continued attention and to keep from getting hunchbacked.

Little Wild Men [ċyatko] {eg}

These little wild men were like animals. They weren't as big as real men. Ellen's grandmother told a story about them.

She was a little girl at the mouth of the Duwamish. One night they were sleeping in their house. One of the woman who had a small baby woke up when her baby started to cry. She saw some men standing inside the house while the residents were asleep. They had a fire right in the middle of the house and they were sleeping on both sides of the house on wooden platforms along the edges.

The next morning she told about what she saw. They looked around and saw that some of the smoked fish were missing. The grandfather of my grandmother said, "They'll be back. We can catch them when they do because they are not very big men."

The next night, they came back and the men were waiting for them. They came in and started stealing more dried salmon. The men jumped them but they all got away except for one. This one they kept. He used to go hunting and in a short time he would come back with a deer with its neck broken. He didn't have any weapons.

They kept him for a while and then they let him go. After that, they would, every once in a while, find a deer or two with broken necks lying in front of their door in the morning. Then they would hang dried fish outside and the wild man would take it at night. So they never had to worry about their coming back to rob them again.

The Wolf and The Winter Salmon {wg}

There were five Wolves and they were brothers. The Wolves and Salmon were friends, but the Wolves killed a King Salmon near a creek. One of the scales of the Salmon got away from them and fell into a crack of a stone. The Wolves tried to get it out with their tongues, but they couldn't reach it. The oldest Wolf failed. The second one tried it and failed. The third also failed. The fourth and fifth ones also failed. So they quit trying to get the scale and went out hunting.

When they got back, they came to the creek to get a drink. The scale had grown into another King Salmon. He waited for the Wolves at the head of that creek. The Wolves came down to take a drink. The oldest one smelled the Salmon in the creek. He stooped down once and the smell was too strong – he got up without drinking. He stooped three times to drink and each time the smell was too strong. The fourth time, he took a drink. When he got up from drinking, Mr King Salmon hit him through the heart with an arrow and killed him.

His second brother came down to drink. He also smelled the Salmon. He got scared during each of the three times he stooped to drink. He always got scared. The fourth time he drank. When he got up, he was also shot through the heart and died.

The third brother did the same. He stooped three times and didn't drink. The fourth time, he drank and, when he got up, he was shot and killed.

The fourth Wolf did the same. He did the same thing, and was finally killed when he drank the fourth time.

The fifth one, the youngest, knew his brothers were all killed but he had to have a drink. He also stooped three times to drink. He would sip a little water and bound back to try to keep from being killed. But he finally drank and then he was also killed like the others. The End

Star Husband {ja}

Two girls were sleeping. They were lying down to sleep. They were looking up at the sky. One said, "I wish that bright star belonged to my sister, and that that red one would be mine." The other sister said, "What else are you going to say? You say everything [and are likely to get us into trouble with your talk.]"

They woke up and didn't know where they were. One of the girls found out that the bright star was an old, old man with matter all over his eyes. The red star they found out was a nice looking young man.

It came to pass that the one talking all the time had a baby. Each day they went and dug fern roots. These men, the Stars, told them "Don't follow any of the roots that go deep into the soil," but the girls asked themselves, "Why did they tell us that about not following a root that goes deep?" So they followed one that went way down. Air came up out of the hole they dug. "Oh, so that's why they didn't want us to follow that root down. We're up in the sky, that's where we are."

So they decided to make a ladder out of cedar limbs, a rope. The Star men asked them, "Why is it you don't get anymore fern roots and you are gone all day?" They said, "Oh, the baby cries too much. We're taking care of the baby all of the time we are out. We can't dig fern roots any more. The baby cries all of the time." This was not so, they were just busy making the rope ladder. When they thought it was long enough to make it to the ground, they opened the hole and put the ladder down. They used a digging stick to put across the opening and hold the ladder up.

They went down, the three of them, on the rope ladder. They got home and the people gathered around. They used the ladder now as a swing. The people would swing back and forth on the rope. They gave the baby to their old, blind grandfather to take care of. They were having a lot of fun swinging on the ladder. Then they noticed that the baby was not crying any more. They asked, "What's the matter that the baby isn't crying any more?" They went to the old man and he was singing "My grandchild is a piece of wood now." Sure enough, it was true. They went to see what the grandfather was singing about and the real baby was gone now. The father of the child had come down and taken the child with him up to the sky again.

In the meantime, Rat chewed the ladder off of the stick. It came down, all piled up in one place. The people wanted to find out where that child went but now nobody could go up to the sky. Bluejay was the only one that could fly up there. But he couldn't get through the hole, he got caught in the opening. That is why the head of bluejay is flat now.

There is a rock over in Snoqualmie that looks just like the ladder piled up. That is where the ladder came down [and it shows the eternal truth of this story.]

Mink and Devilfish (Octopus) *{ja}*

The people were all gathered in one place, meeting. There was a Devilfish (Octopus) lying by the door. Mink said, "What is this thing here lying in the way? I'll take you and throw you out in the bay." Devilfish said, "Who's stopping you from throwing me out in the bay? Go ahead !" "Do you think I can't do it?," said Mink, and he took the Devilfish by the head and dragged him into the water.

The Devilfish said, "Take me out in the deep. Don't throw me here close to the beach. Take me way out." When they were deep enough, he grabbed hold of Mr. Mink, who said, "I was just playing with you. I don't mean anything, I don't mean anything." The Devilfish took him down into the water and didn't let him go until he was almost drowned.

Mink

A child was born and the people gathered around to see who was the father of it. The baby looked at the people and said, "No, my dad isn't here."

Mink told his grandmother, "I'm going over there where the people are gathered. That baby might say. "That's my dad now." His grandmother told him, "You don't want to go there. What do you want to go for?" He went anyhow for Mink was full of tricks.

He got to where the people were gathered and stood outside on one side of the door. He crossed over to the other side of the door. The baby said, "There's dad!" The people looked around to see who the person was that the baby called dad.

He crossed by the door again. This time he walked slowly. So, again, the baby called, "That's Dad! Daddy, Daddy, Daddy, Daddy!" So he took his baby and the woman home with him.

One day they went out riding in a canoe, all three of them. While they were out, the woman saw sea eggs (sea urchins) down on the bottom. He told his wife, "I'll go down and get you some." He went down, gathered some up for his wife, and took them up. She opened them and started to eat them. Each time he went down, he'd be gone longer. The last time, he was gone a very long time. His wife looked down and there he was busy eating all of the eggs by himself down there.

She got mad and threw the baby overboard. Then she went home. When Mink came up, his wife was gone and his baby was swimming around on the water. He told his son, "You swim to those roots over there, to that stump on the beach." That is the reason we still find minks around those stumps on the beaches [and the underside of sea urchins look as they do].

Wolf and Elk *{ja}*

There are two rocks on Bolen's Point that used to be people, Wolf and Elk. Wolf was chasing Elk and they landed on that point. This was during the universal change and flood. Now there are two rocks where they were at that moment. One is a Wolf and one an Elk. They were turned to stone.

Steelhead and Rainbow Trout {ja}

Steelhead and Rainbow were coming down the river. A big Jack Salmon was going upstream. They met. The big Salmon said, "How is the river? How deep is the river?" There was no answer. Salmon repeated his question. Then Steelhead said, "Oh, it's high enough now for a big-headed fish to go up." In reply to this insult, the Salmon went to the Steelhead and the Rainbow and took away all of their paddles. He gave them yew wood ones instead. That is why the bones of steelhead and rainbow trout are now so hard. [The implication is that these modern fish began as humanoids in canoes. At the change, everything (body, canoe, and paddles) became a distinct species and King Salmon benefited from the fat and bones (as paddles) he took from Steelhead and Rainbow Trout.]

Raccoon {ja}

The Coon and his family lived out in the woods. The old man stayed home all of the time. The children always went down on the beach, singing like the Chipmunk about what they were going to get. Instead, a thing would catch them and eat their hearts. This kept on until a girl had a baby coming and the father begged her "Don't go down on the beach! Your brothers and sisters went down and never came back."

She went down anyway. They liked little crabs and she went for some. That thing killed her. The old man went down and said, "I told that girl not to go down but she must have gone anyway for she has disappeared." He found his girl on the beach and he took out of her body the baby that was coming. He took it home and raised it.

When the baby was grown up, he was running around the cedar trees. He said, "Grandpa, you had better make me a bow and arrows because that one with big ears and big eyes (Rabbit) is close by. Better make me a bow and arrows so I can shoot that." The little Raccoon was getting bigger. His grandfather said, "Don't go down to the beach. Your people all died, were killed, when they went down there. Don't go! Don't go!"

The boy got curious. "Why doesn't Grandpa want me to go down on the beach?" He got curious, so he went down and his old grandpa didn't know anything about it. He sang the song his family always used when they were going out for a particular food. Here came that thing! Little coon took his bow and arrows and shot him. He killed the monster.

When the old man missed his grandson, he said, "Where did that boy go. I told him not to go down to the beach, but he must have gone down there." On his way to the beach, he met his grandson returning. The boy had gathered a lot of little crabs and packed them up to his grandfather. He laid them down in front of the old man, who said, "I told you not to go down there." The boy said, "I know you told me not to go down there, but I killed him. He is dead now."

They slept well that night. They had a good feed of crabs and went to sleep. The next morning, the boy went out to the cedar trees he played around. There were lots of people there, relatives of the thing he had killed down on the beach. He was ready and took a something he had made of wood [a club ?]. When he swung it at them, all his enemies on one side died. Then he did the same on the other side. The same thing happened.

He went back home and told his grandfather. "Come out now and take all of the blankets they left. I've killed them now." The old fellow went out and took all the blankets. (A long time ago, the old Indians had a blanket over them instead of a coat.)

The old man, when the grandson got to be a man, went away with him to find a wife for him. People started to sing, "Old man Raccoon must be traveling now. The land is foggy now. It's a nice quiet day but its foggy." [The implication is the Raccoon had such great power he could affect the weather, taking it out of the ordinary to let everyone know he was on the move.]

Five Brothers {*ja*}

There were five brothers. One went out some place and never came back. He got to a cedar tree at night and had to camp there. Something hollered then, "Are you awake?" He said, "Yes, I'm awake." The voice kept this up until there was no answer and the voice knew he was asleep now. It came down and took out his heart, ate it, and threw the body away.

The next brother came. It kept up like that, for all five of the brothers. He'd ask them the same question every night when they camped by that tree.

When the fifth and youngest came, he said, "What kind of thing is killing my brothers?" He took his bow and arrows, following the way they went. He came to the same tree and laid down at the foot of it. The thing up in it asked, "Are you awake yet?" He said, "Yes, I'm awake yet." He made a dummy to look like himself lying down there and he got to one side. The thing asked, "Are you asleep now?" But he did not answer. So the thing came down to take out his heart. The boy shot it with an arrow and killed it.

Then he opened it up and took out the fourth brother's heart and put it back into his body. Then he jumped over his brother back and forth until his brother came back to life and got up. He did the same for the third brother, and for the second one. Finally he got to the oldest brother, but he could only briefly hold up his head before it fell back again. The youngest kept stepping back and forth, but he could never get the oldest one back. He was too far gone. He said, "The oldest brother of the people to come will always die."

The Girl With Long Sharp Fingernails {*ja*}

A girl had long, sharp fingernails. When she got mad at other children, she hooked them in the stomach and killed them. So they decided to take her away.

The Crows were going to take her away in a canoe. They put her on board it. They were paddling with the edge instead of the flat of the paddles so the canoe wasn't going very fast. Someone turned a paddle sideways and then the canoe started to go quickly. All of them started to paddle that way and they went fast now. When they got way out, the Crows flew away and left her alone in the canoe. She drifted and landed where a young man and his grandmother were. He was away. The Grandma took the girl ashore and hid her.

When the young man (his wife was made of wood) came back and started to fight with his wife, the grandmother motioned for the girl not to laugh. She had warned her before, "Don't laugh. It's comical what you are going to see."

The next day, the grandmother and girl went out digging roots. The young man came down after fighting with his wooden wife, and said, "Grandmother, there's someone here." She asked him, "What makes you think so?" He said, "Because the roots you're getting now are good ones. You couldn't get those deep ones by yourself before. There has to be someone here with you now." She said, "No, there's no one here. You know I'm here alone all the time." They left it at that.

So, one day, he went up to hunt in the woods. He came back in the evening and started to fight with his wooden wife. They fought and talked. The young girl couldn't stand it anymore and she started to laugh. The boy looked over and saw the girl. He left the house to throw his wooden wife in the water and came back to take this girl for his real wife. [Cowichan on Vancouver Island regard this as an origin epic.]

Chipmunk and the Basket Ogress {ja}

A Chipmunk went out to pick berries and his grandmother warned him, "When you go berry picking, don't sing." But when he got to the blackberries, he started to sing anyway, "The ripe ones I'm going to eat here and the unripe ones I'm going to save for my grandmother."

The Basket Ogress [skalə] was a wild woman who used to chase children. She heard Chipmunk and chased him. (If you go where there are black berries, you'll still hear the chipmunks singing this song, going chunk, chunk, and so on.) She was going to eat the boy. Before he knew anyone was around, she grabbed and got him at the back of the head. But he ran up a tree and slipped out of her hands. She scratched him from head to tail and that is why chipmunks now have those stripes along the back.

She was at the foot of the tree watching for him when he came down. So, he took a cone from the tree and threw it a ways from the tree. She went after this and Chipmunk got away. When she realized she had gone the wrong way, she looked for traces and saw him going. She chased him.

He got home to his grandmother all tired out. He pleaded, "You hide me. Hide me! She is right behind me!" Grandmother covered him with a clam shell. She scolded him, "I told you not to sing when you go berry picking. Now she's come after you."

When she came, she too was tired and said, "I can smell that boy. He's here! He's here!" But the grandmother said, "He's not here." So the Ogress went away.

Little Wild Men {ja}

The little wild men came from the Fraser River. They were people but wild ones. When the berries are ripe, they come down this way. They were men, but they were wild. There are two tribes of them. The stətaɬ and the ćyətko. They were the same kind of people, but different tribes. They were wild men. They stayed in the woods all of the time. Both kinds of these stole food from Indians. John Adams knows a story about the stətaɬ stealing a girl from the Snohomish. But they were usually good to people and didn't harm them.

There was a girl picking cranberries in a marsh. She heard the ċyatko talking. They didn't talk like other Indians. They were wild. She saw two men coming after her. (A long time ago, the girls were trained, like the boys, to go out, swim and run, to make them strong.) They caught up to her. One of them took the girl. The other said, "No, you can't have her." And they started fighting over her. The girl got away. They ran after her and got her again. Then they started fighting again. This time they fought for good, to settle it. The second man decided that if he couldn't have her, then he wouldn't let the other one have her. So he kept fighting the other one until the girl got away completely.

In another story, a woman was out in the woods seeking power. She heard ċyatko talking, making noise. She found a hollow cedar. She crawled in backwards and pulled in a block of wood behind her. They were looking for her all over. They had long sticks. They poked into the hollow log, and felt the sticks stop. They said, "No, she's not there. There's a block in there. The pole doesn't go in very far." That's the way she got away.

When she thought they were gone, she came out. She was good and hungry. She had been there for days with nothing to eat. But she found the bones of deer and elk killed by a cougar. So, she split them and ate the marrow. She would take a rock and crack them, then eat the marrow inside. Marrow is called dadawšəd. Finally, she got home.

If a person looked at one of these ċyatko, it was like taking a drug. You went to sleep. Sometimes you would know what was going on, but you couldn't do anything. Once, they captured some ċyatko who said, "What we put on our face so we can see in the night, you can't stand. That's what makes you unconscious when you look at us."

A young man was going from the Duwamish to Snoqualmie to see a girl there. Night overtook him half way. He built a big fire. He had his bow and arrows. While at the fire, some ċyatko came. He was lying there. He couldn't move but he knew they were there with him before he passed out. They were laughing at him, tying him up, and playing tricks on him. They took his clothes off. When he came to, there was one going into the brush. The Indian shot him in the back. He went back toward the Duwamish again. On the way, he heard them crying when they found the dead one. They were people, but they were wild.

Another time on the Duwamish River, they weren't getting any salmon at night from the place where they had a dam. What was happening to the salmon, they wondered? So, they wandered along the bank and found human tracks. They followed them. They found him. He was an old man. He lived in a hollow cedar. He was drying salmon there. He was sound asleep just then. He awoke and got scared. He wanted to feed the people who had come there. Instead, they took him down to their homes. They didn't harm him. He would go with them when they were spearing fish at night in the river. He would always take a small salmon and cook it. They kept him a long time until they finally let him go. They gave him back all the possessions he had, but they didn't give him back his fire drill. He would not leave and they wondered why he wouldn't go. Finally, they understood he wanted his fire making equipment. They gave it to him and then he went away. He had to have it to make fire. He was a human being just like anyone, but he was wild.

The uncle of John Adam's father was hunting around Keysport and Poulsbo. He heard these things around so he called his dogs. The dogs wouldn't sleep. He heard them all around his log house. They shoved a stick in from the outside and hit him. Next day he got out of there. On the way, he found where they had their fires and cooked fish.

A white logger was going into the woods one morning while it was still dark. He stumbled over someone lying on the skid road, and the logger fell asleep right there. Another man came along and asked the sleeping logger what the matter with him was. He stood up and told what had happened. After that, he wouldn't go into the woods by himself. It was a ċyatko, but he never knew what it was.

They go around at night better than in the day because of their special paint. Sam Wilson, cousin to John Adams, was on a creek in Port Orchard Bay waiting for bear to come and eat salmon. It was getting dark. He pointed his gun toward a place still lighted to see if he could see things through his sights. He proved that he could. Then he turned them on a dark place. Suddenly, a feeling came over his face. It worked down his body to his knees. He jumped down off the log and almost fell right there. He took off his clothes and went into the creek. He had Bullhead for his power. That's why he went into the bay. At night, when the tide was out, he'd use a torch – you could hear the dog salmon going up the creek – and go down to the shore and hook them in with a gaff. He knew those waters.

Another time, he heard a run of fish coming. He was lying by the fire, but he didn't go and get the fish. He let it go. A dog salmon did not go far before someone else hooked it. While he was lying there, somebody started to open the mat door. His mother whispered to him, "Someone is opening that mat to shoot you." He took his rifle and shot right through the mat, but, even so, he missed the wild man. He heard someone trip on a cedar rail in their hurry to get away. The next day, his whole family got out of there. There were too many wild men.

From their tracks it is known they have long feet, longer than those of most people.

An old Suquamish who was a boy in the 1840s was sent one night to another tribe to deliver a message. He went along a little trail with a small mat as a rain hat over his head to keep himself dry. On the way, he stepped on someone lying across the trail. He immediately fell asleep right there. There were other wild men. They played tricks on him and tied him up. It was raining. When he came to, he got up and started to go on his way. He didn't get far before he found his mat hanging beside the trail. He went a little further and found more of his things hanging along the way. This was how they played. They would never harm you unless you did something mean to them. Usually, they were only interested in coming into the smokehouse at night to steal prepared fish.

There aren't any left now. They weren't killed off, it's just that they all became civilized. Some of our own people had them as ancestors. One cousin of John Adams had a sharp face and was a terrible man; that was because he was part wild man.

War Tales

The Suquamish did not take heads when they raided. Kitsap didn't believe in hanging the heads of enemies in front of the village or camp. That was too much like showing off. They knew that the northern tribes did it, but the Suquamish thought it too crass and didn't believe in it.

There were special men who did the fighting. The leader was especially selected. He was not usually the same as the chief in peace time. The leader had the right to order his men about, to tell them what to do. {*wg*} [He was in charge of all their lives.]

When an enemy tribe would attack, the women and children would go back into the woods for safely, away from the beach and camp. {*ja*}

Kitsap In Battle {*ja*}

Curly told this story about the Puget Sound tribes attacking northern peoples about 1840 or maybe before. There were several leaders, but Kitsap [q̓c̓ap] was Suquamish chief and war leader both. The tribes involved included those from Oakville [staq̓ɫabš, "Inland/Upland People") [Chehalis] from the other side of Tacoma, who got in trouble because they didn't know how to handle a canoe in war, the Nisqually [sqʷali] from near Tacoma and the other side of Steilacoom, and the Mud Bay [sqʷaqcət, Squaxin Island] from near Olympia. These three groups planned the raid before coming to Kitsap to ask the Suquamish to go. Kitsap took 10 canoe loads, with 30 to 40 men in each canoe. The Duwamish weren't asked and didn't go. The reason for the raid is not known now, probably someone was killed, as always went on.

They met these enemies on a sandspit. They were Canadians always coming down to fight with the Skagits on Whidbey Island. They wanted to clean up the Skagits, but they met the tribes from the Sound going the other way. The Canadian leader said "If you call off the fight, we'll give you as many women as you want as wives." They started negotiating, but, meanwhile, people from Up Sound started taking stray arrow shots into the air above the Canadians and managed to hit one of them. So, before Kitsap had a chance to say anything, the battle was on. The arrow shooters got what they wanted.

The sandspit was up on the other side of Victoria. Canadians tried to tip over the American canoes. This was a deliberate strategy of theirs. They tried to do this to the canoe with Kitsap, but he took a spear and tipped them over. Then he speared them like fish in the water. The Suquamish knew how to fight from canoes. The warriors at the bow and stern did all of the shooting, while the others paddled and protected the canoe. Kitsap and his brother [**talibot**] did the shooting from their canoe. The other tribes from Tacoma did not do this. Everyone in a canoe would drop their paddles and shoot. They got the worst of it because the Canadians were able to come along side and shove them over. The Suquamish were always able to out maneuver the Canadians.

Talibot fought bravely. A Canadian came at him from one side, but he plucked his bow string and the Canadian ducked down in a canoe. When he came up again, Talibot had an arrow ready and shot him. The Canadian pulled it out, saying he was a great man, but the point was barbed so it stayed in the body when the shaft came out. Pretty soon, the man dropped dead. Later Talibot was shot in the eye. He pulled the arrow out, but the eye came with it. He continued fighting with one eye until Kitsap said he was asking to be killed. Then Talibot got down into the bottom of the canoe and stayed there.

Sam Wilson heard that the Canadians had Kitsap surrounded with their canoes, yet he came out without a scratch. He had great power from Eagle. After the battle, all of the arrows shot at him shook out of his hair. He had several sets of powers and they all helped him.

A man from Mud Bay had great power, but he had been forewarned that he would be great but his bones would be way off. He fought well at the battle, but his canoe capsized. He came out of the water with his bow at the ready, but he was killed. That was what was meant by the phrase his bones would be far off.

After everyone else in the canoe was dead, another man from Mud Bay spread out his arms and said "kahk" and flew like a bird to another canoe. His power was Raven, probably.

One Suquamish had a coonskin sack full of arrows but he never used them. When they asked him for arrows, he said, "No, you might waste them." When the battle was over, he had the only arrows left. The warriors only had spears, but they were too far apart. Kitsap and the leader of the Canadians were going to fight it out and were coming toward each other. Someone in the canoe with Kitsap handed him a long spear on the sly. The Canadian saw it and backed away. Kitsap was the stronger and so never lost a man.

Four men from Up Sound were left on shore after the battle. Their canoe was tipped over by the Canadians but they had Fish power and swam under water safely to shore, walking to Victoria. When Canadian Indians came along, they hid in trees with tops flat due to the heavy winds. They found some drift logs and made a raft tied together with twisted cedar branches rope. They drifted around until they asked each other to identify their power, but the first three were of no help. The fourth only said, "I've got nothing, but watch those clouds moving." As soon as he finished speaking, the wind came up and blew them to the American side around Port Angeles.

While they were in Canadian waters, they stayed flat and tried to look like some floating logs. That last foggy morning, the Americans looked out and said to one another, "Those look like logs, leave them alone." The four men started jumping around on the raft and the Americans said, "Those are seals, let them alone." Finally, they stuck the sticks they were using for paddles into knot holes and the people on shore said, "That didn't have limbs a while ago. Now it has." So they went out, captured them, and brought them to shore. They locked them up in a house.

People decided to go across the straits because they thought there was trouble on the other side. The village was mostly deserted. A woman visiting from somewhere else started to talk to the prisoners. She spoke their language and maybe was a relative. That night she went around to all the houses and stole one bow and one arrow from each. She gave them to the prisoners and said, "Here's your equipment." She gave them a clam stick because it was sharp on one end. She gave them a big clam shell and said, "Now you crawl under the bench beds when you think all are asleep and dig out a hole with the clam shell." They did this and when the hole was big enough, they crawled out and ran. They came along the shores of Hood Canal to their homes.

One man was crying because his son was lost at the battle. He kept saying, "I thought my son was well brought up and trained. Sometimes I see his face." One day they were out in the sun talking and saw someone coming up the beach over a log. It was the missing boy, so they all finally got home safely.

Because of this, people felt confident and a boy from Duwamish wandered to Victoria. He wanted to get home and asked some Canadian Indians to take him back when they left to pick hops in the Sound. They went toward Port Townsend and half way across the straits, they threw the boy over. That was how they got their revenge, but it was a long time later in the 1870s.

Sometime around 1850 there was a big potlatch at Mud Bay and John's father went. Canadian Indians came to it and asked to see the man who flew during the battle. They took the visitors to him. He was old then. They agreed they had seen him fly like a bird, but the Canadians didn't show off any of their stunts.

Kitsap was a good general. He had men posted at each point to warn if anyone came. No one could get in if they were dangerous. It was after Kitsap was gone that Klallams made a raid on a Suquamish group, but didn't do much damage. The chief at that time was named ċalqəb. The Suquamish got together a party to revenge the raid but the chief found out and asked where they were going. They wanted to get even with the Klallams, but the chief would not let them. He wasn't afraid of the Klallam, he just didn't want any more trouble. They obeyed the chief; he was good and didn't want trouble.

Klallam Attack {ja}

John heard of the raid from his parents, but it happened in the days of his grandparents. Several times, Klallams raided a small group in the bay where Keyport is now. They killed the people by catching them asleep. The chief was ċalqəb, the one after Kitsap and before Seattle. He made the Suquamish raiders stay home to prevent even more trouble.

Skykomish Raids {ja}

The Skykomish [sqayhabš] were mean. They wanted to fight all of the time, and thought they were better than everyone else. Now there are hardly any left. John did not know why they wanted to fight so much.

The Suquamish were camping at Point No Point, probably in the 1850s or 60s. They were there all of the time because it was a good fishing place. The Skykomish had muskets then and attacked the Suquamish. They fought on the beach in the day time. A man named qəlaywap was sent to fight them, but he was a lesser warrior. The main ones stayed in camp eating dried clams because they didn't consider the enemy very strong.

The warrior took some men and hid behind rocks on the beach to shoot at the enemy. A Suquamish was hit in the knee by a glancing bullet, but he was the only one hurt. They drove back the Skykomish, who gave up and left in their canoes. John didn't know if any enemy were killed or hurt.

The Skykomish came to Point No Point another time, saying they were going to take [steal] some canoes. "Instead of making them, we're going to get them from the Suquamish.

They came to the beach and were sizing up the canoes. An old man had a pole stuck in the beach and was sitting in his canoe. Meanwhile, the enemy were shaking canoes and deciding which were the good ones. When they shook the canoe of the old man and said it was a good one, he replied "Will you please get off." He repeated it louder a few more times and said, "Did you hear me." Then the old man took his pole and hit them over the head. The Skykomish couldn't do anything because they were on the beach and were an easy musket shot from the Suquamish camp on the bluff. That ended it and the enemies left.

Later still, the Skykomish came to present Suquamish and took women to make them slaves. When the white man came and said there would be no more slavery, they were released. This was the last time the enemy came, probably in the 1860s.

Leschi {ja}

The whites took the pastures for their stock. Leschi [ləšxiʔ, ləšxi(x)] started fighting over this. One Indian was a traitor to the white side and scouted for them. He was William Rogers. The soldiers were marching to the sound of fife and drum. Then Leschi knew where they were and told his men to shoot first "the one who hollers" (gives the commands). The rest would be easy because soldiers didn't know what to do with their leader gone.

The Indians cut a tree across the foot path along the White River. They hid in the willow trees on one side of the river. They caught the soldiers. One Indian stuck his hat over a log on a stick. When a soldier got up to shoot at the hat, the Indian killed him. Only two Indians were shooting, the others were loading for them. Some whites tried to get across on a foot log, but they were shot. One did get across, but they shot him on the other side. One Indian left his gun and the soldiers killed him when he went back for it. The whites were defeated and afterwards the place was called Slaughter. Now it is called Auburn.

The whites got Leschi's father. Leschi said, "Let the old man go. I'll die in his place." So Leschi came in and the whites took a rope and hanged him. He was strung up for a long time before he was taken down and pronounced dead. The rope was cut off his neck. As he lay on the ground, he started to come to life again. The Duwamish said, "If he comes to life again, he'll only kill us [get us killed]." So they killed him again there. They never got what they were fighting for and the whites still took possession anyhow.

Moses was a Yakama and a bad man. [Moses was a Columbia Salishan who died on the Colville reservation] He came over the mountains to help his uncle Leschi but he didn't stay long. He told his uncle that the ground was too soft and he might be shot. He went home. He had seen the bounty of the country and he came back with Yakama to attack the Nisqually and kill their cattle. If people tried to shoot Moses with a bullet, it couldn't hit him. He had a belt around his waist, and the bullets went into his belt instead of hitting him when he was shot at.

Finally, a Nisqually took a piece of iron, heated it in a fire, and hammered it like a knife that would fit into the barrel of his gun. He waited until Moses was coming at him on a horse and he shot Moses. The iron went right through his body, but it didn't kill him. He only fell off the horse. Moses had black powder pistols tied all over his body. When the Yakama saw him fall, they left all the cattle to make their get away. Moses kept fighting, using his pistols until he was out of ammunition. Then the Nisqually used spears to kill him dead. They cut him open to see what made him so mean. Inside of him they found a little man all covered with hair. That was what made him so mean.

Appendix

To compare with John Adam's account of Kitsap's fight, apparently directed against the Cowichan of Vancouver Island during the 1830s, here is a version Wilson George gave to Leon Metcalf, a Seattle musician who visited among the natives of Puget Sound in the early 1950s with a bulky tape recorder, preserving texts, messages, and conversations to be played back to other native speakers. He donated these to the Burke Museum at the University of Washington. Other versions of this or similar battles appear in Curtis (1913: 14) and Elmendorf (1993: 132, 136, 145).

By the best of circumstances, Violet Anderson Hilbert [taq̇ʷšəblu] took on the job of transcribing and translating these tapes, many of which involved her relatives. As a native speaker of Skagit and a university instructor, Mrs. Hilbert was especially gifted for this task. She is most comfortable with northern Lushootseed (Puget Salish), but the southern dialect differs only in minor features of vocabulary, agreement, and accent. These dialects are mutually intelligible, as shown by her translation of the southern Lushootseed saga of Fly (Hilbert 1985: 33-41).

Dr Vi Hilbert's work on the text of the Kitsap raid, as told at the Tulalip Reservation on 20 February 1952, has been rephrased by Jay Miller, with his explanations marked by square brackets [ ].

The place name ʔəhiẇ is prominent in this text. It has been translated as Portage because it marked the one between Puget Sound and the tip of Hood Canal. As such it was an important passage among the tribes allied with Kitsap.

A Kitsap Raid {wg}

My elders were visited by people from Portage. They were not just from one tribe. There were many different people who arrived and said to these old timers, "Let us go now to war on those people from the West [over there?]." [My elders responded,] "Let us all gather ourselves together so we can join on a raid, if that is what is on your mind, noble sir [siʔab].

Kitsap said, "Yes, I understand you. I hear what you folks are saying about raiding those well-known people. The ones who think that they should be important everywhere, although that is not so. We also have something that we want for ourselves. If any one of you thinks that they want to fight us about this, then we will fight them. [He wanted to be recognized as a leader on this expedition.] If this raid is on your minds, then I will go. I shall go along with you and I shall fight just as your other leaders fight while I am with you. I shall go I shall go and I shall fight."

[All was settled and the Suquamish joined.] The people went by canoe. They arrived at the place where Klallams lived and crossed over the water [Strait of Juan de Fuca] from there [to the southern tip of Vancouver Island.]

They visited the people at scukʷs [Sooke ?] and invited them to join. They were addressed, "It is best for you to accompany us, we go to the mean people across the water, way over there [up island]. This was at what they now call Vancouver Island at the present time and that was the name of the whole area. That was Vancouver Island.

[As an aside, Wilson said. "Its native name is different, but I can't recall its real name just now. My memory is getting short. It's particularly short now. I do not remember things very well. And I do not remember the native names for a lot of places and things. Yet they were raiding them [on the island]. They were the ones that many were going to [in order to fight.]

Then they found out that they did not have to go all the way to the land of the enemy to accomplish the raid. The mean ones from across the water were on the way to raid the Klallams.

Then the two forces met each other. The ones from across the water on Vancouver Island said, "Oh, we are not going to fight. We are too far away from our own land and you are far from yours. It is best not to fight. It is best that you just... If you folks give a man, one of your young ones, to us, that would be acceptable [to form an alliance through marriage]. If you provide a woman instead, it would be up to us to give you a young man."

All of those from Portage said, "No, we don't want anything like that. We are on our way to fight. We intend to fight you folks. Therefore, if you are willing, then we will fight now. It is best we just fight. We shall fight on the salt water. Offshore."

Kitsap said [to his allies], "Oh, the people from around here are skillful on the salt water. We won't be able to beat them if we fight them on the ocean."

[The allies responded,] "However, those of us from Portage have come here to fight and we can not just return home without a battle. That would belittle and disgrace our name [reputation]. That is why I think that we should intend to fight as long as you wish to fight."

So! The people from Vancouver Island had it settled now. They said, "All right. The mind of your leader is good. We are also ready to fight. And when he decides to fight, then we are ready."

So! They fought. The people gathered from Portage were bested because they were unsure of the water and their spears were short.

[In an aside, Wilson comments, "Spear is what the whites call this weapon. Theirs were short and those of the people from across the water were long.]

They were way short, those belonging to the people from Portage and they were capsized by the people from across the water. They were capsized and killed.

Kitsap, however, fought with a bow and arrow. [That was the style of the Suquamish. He fought bravely with arrows.] When he had used up all of his arrows, he just went to where there was a riptide and gathered up the arrows floating there until he had lots of them again. When he got back to the thick of the battle, he put them into his quiver. That was the way Kitsap got ahead of them and they could not beat him.

He would retreat, moving backwards. When they would advance, he would retreat. As he moved back and they moved closer, he would shoot the leader [sternman, steersman] who would tumble out of the canoe. The canoe would lose direction and veer sideways. When it was broadside of him, he shot across the rim at other members of the crew. His arrow would go right through the hull of the other canoe. [This way,] he managed to shoot the paddler sitting in the other seat, who died. Kitsap continued to kill [the enemy]. His people did not die [in the fight]. No!

One of them was shot, however. He was shot right in the eye by the sternman of an enemy canoe. He took the arrow and pulled it out. His eye came out with it. Talibot was his name. Talibot was the name of the man whose eye came out. He only paddled a little way before he collapsed in his canoe. He capsized. Someone nearby pulled him out and loaded him safely [into a canoe]. He had no eye now. He died now. Someone took his place in the canoe as captain [sternman]. Another warrior took the place of Talibot.

Kitsap fought on. He was chased. He would retreat so they thought he was going away. However, he just wanted to be chased [to have an advantage.] As those following came nearer, he would shoot their captain, who would flip out and die. As the canoe meandered, he would continue shooting until all [the crew] was finished off.

When he ran out of arrows, he would go after lots of them floating nearby in eddies and gather them up. By now, he was only using enemy arrows for his killing.

Suddenly, one of the allies made note aloud [of what Kitsap was doing]. "Kitsap is being chased by those from across the water. He does not retreat in order to get away from the raiders. He just wants to be chased so then he can shoot the one in the stern and kill him. When the canoe is broadside, he shoots again until everyone in the canoe is finished off.

Then another canoe chases him because they want to get Kitsap. That is what he wants! That is how he gets at those from across the water. Then he kills them until they are all gone. Until everyone in the enemy canoe quit shooting. After one canoe is finished off, another one arrives. But Kitsap kills all of them. They can not take Kitsap. Still he wants them to chase him. He isn't retreating in order to get away. NO! [He is luring them on.] He wants to be chased by those from across the water.

By the end of the battle, his strategy dawned on one of the enemy, who announced his observation. He said, "Kitsap is not running away from us. NO! He just wants us to chase after him, but I will not. I am finished, my friends. All of you folks stop now. No one chase Kitsap now. No one. He wants to be chased. He wants this [to happen]. That is the way he is killing your friends. You folks stop now. You folks stop right now. No one can kill him. The spirit power of Kitsap is mighty. It is special.

You folks see how he is shot [by our warriors] but he just deflects these arrows. They do not go into his body. They only go into his hair where they are available for him to use. He takes those which have been shot at him and he shoots them back, killing those who shot the arrows at him [intentionally]. Do not shoot at his head. You are giving him arrows. You folks stop now. My people, you must stop now. Stop this instant! "We have been beaten by Kitsap. Stop now. I am finished. You folks stop now, members of my tribe. I urge all of you, my people, to stop now. Then Kitsap will also stop and go home."

[And so it must have happened since Wilson George next said, "This is the end of my story."]

Index

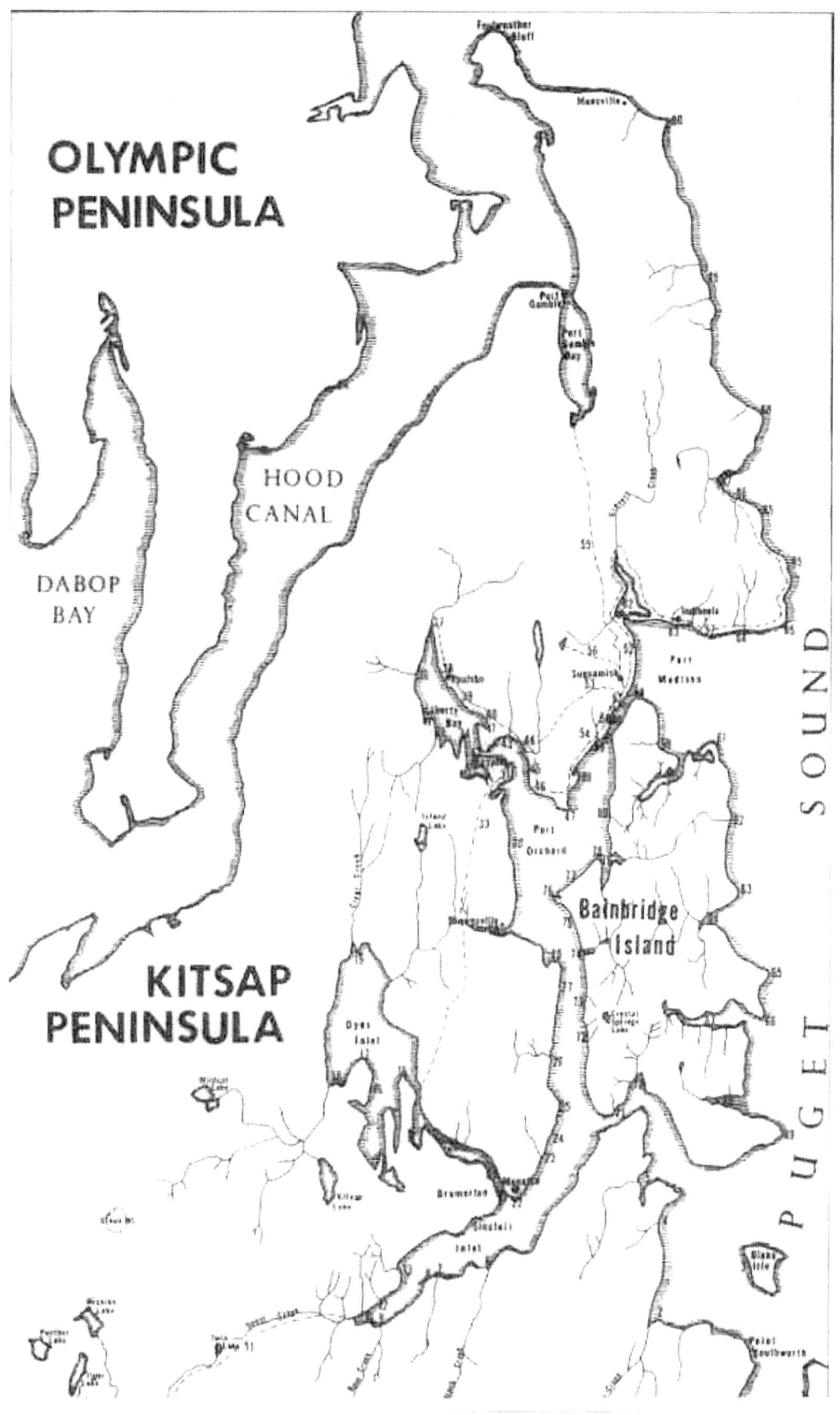

OLYMPIC
PENINSULA
HOOD
CANAL
DABOP
BAY
KITSAP
PENINSULA
PUGET SOUND
Bainbridge
Island

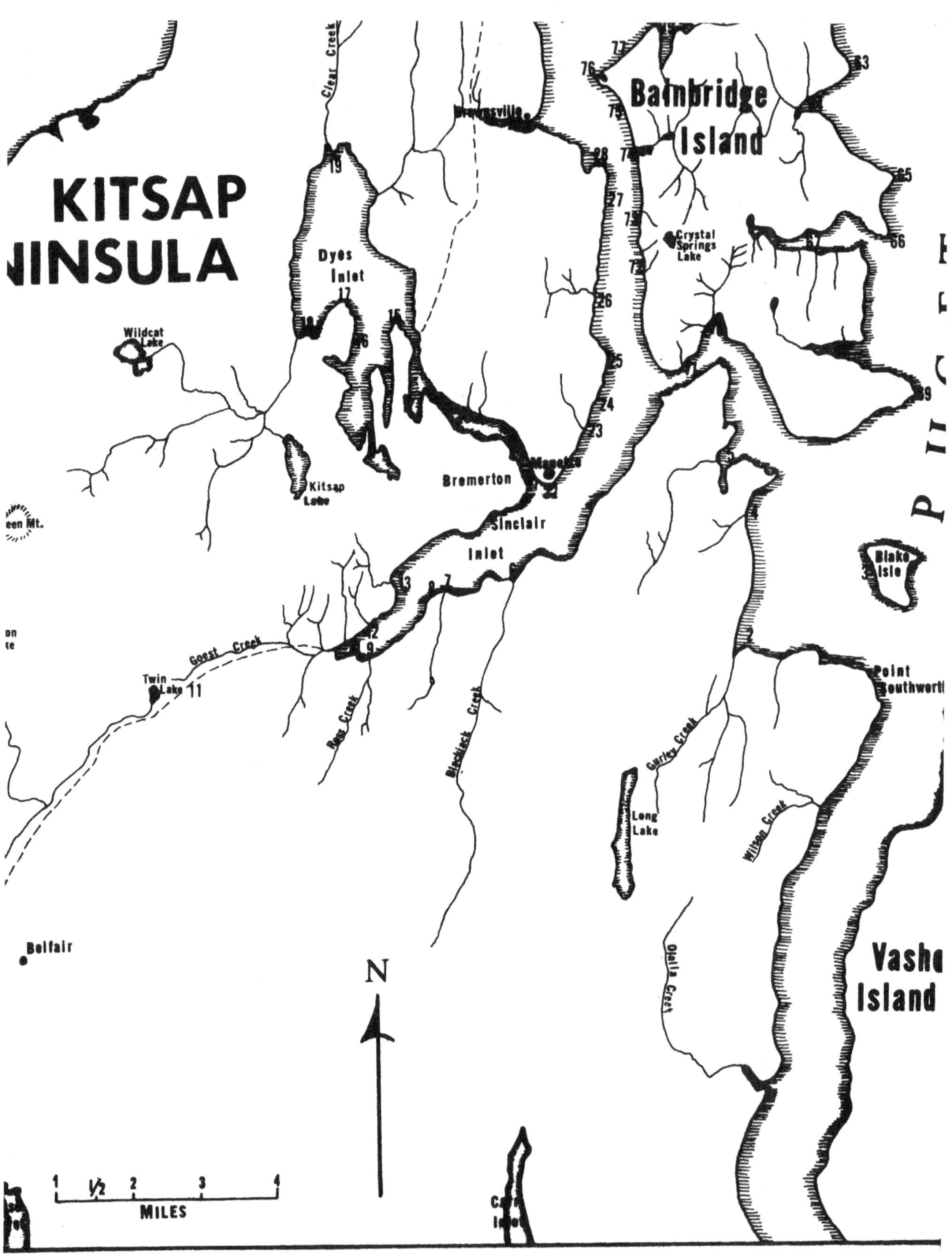

Clear Creek
Brownsville
Bainbridge Island
76
77
73
72
28
74
27
71
KITSAP
NINSULA
19
Dyes Inlet
17
15
16
Crystal Springs Lake
26
65
66
Wildcat Lake
25
24
23
een Mt.
Kitsap Lake
Bremerton
Manette
Sinclair Inlet
89
Blake Isle
on te
13
9 7
Goest Creek
2
9
Twin Lake 11
Ross Creek
Bischback Creek
Point Southworth
Gairley Creek
Long Lake
Wilson Creek
Belfair
Olalla Creek
Vashon Island
N
1   1/2   2   3   4
MILES
Ca Inlet

Suquamish Place Names

The main area occupied by the Suquamish Indians was on the eastern side of the Kitsap peninsula in Puget Sound. Following is a list of place names and trails with comments on the use of these areas. Text numbers correspond to those on the map and follow in order from south to north except at the northern end of Bainbridge Island where they circle the island and then precede north again along the peninsula.

1. wétbš One ~~informant~~ (JA) gave this as a Suquamish camping place. This is the furthest south that any point of land was named as a place frequented regularly by the Suquamish. The ~~informant~~ had never visited the area and was confused as to the name of the creek upon which it was located. Sometimes he gave it as Olalla creek; other times as Wilson creek. Wilkes visited the area in 1841 and places a village at the mouth of Olalla creek which he called "Teka village" (Wilkes 1858: 78). None of my ~~informants~~ recognized the name. Ed Sigo said that the present name for Olalla creek was derived from the Indian word for cattail, ólal. John Adams suggested that Wilkes' "*Teka*" may have been derived from the Indian phrase *te qá* meaning "lots or plenty there."

2. baq'ólbex^w This may have been a winter village although none of the ~~informants~~ were definite on this point. It may have been a seasonal camping place. Ed Sigo said that an old Indian told him that posts and parts of the frames of houses stood there when he was a boy (probably in the middle 1800's). Salmon were caught there as they ascended the creek.

3. tátčo This is the name for Blake island. It is the diminutive for the name of Vashon island to the south which was called taco. Blake island was used as a temporary camping place. It had good clam beds, and fish, ling cod and bullheads in particular, were speared in the surrounding waters. The west point and areas along the west shore were used as burial grounds.

    All of the ~~informants~~ agree that the Suquamish did not camp often on Vashon island. This was used mostly by the Puyallup. Since the Suquamish were on friendly terms with the Puyallup and often intermarried with them, they would sometimes visit Puyallup fishing and hunting grounds and other areas to the south, particularly persons who were related to the Puyallup or other tribes to the south by marriage. The place most often visited on Vashon island was Vashon point at the northwest end of the island. Deer hunting was good there during the summer.

4. q'áq'ad This was a summer camping area. It was known especially as a place where clams were dried.

5. q'éq'tx^{w}b This was a camping place that might be visited at any time of the year. It was known especially as a place to hunt ducks and deer. Flounders were speared in shallow water at night from a canoe that had a fire burning in it. Fish could be taken here at any time of the year, Salmon [131] berries were gathered along the creek.

6. c'yáčabad This was a camping place.

7. šábdop This name means "drying place." This was a camping place and was known especially as a place where salmon were dried. Salmon went up the creek in large numbers during salmon runs.

8. čašádx^w This point was used as a camping place during smelt runs.

9. dok'óy They camped here during dog salmon runs. Dog salmon in particular used this creek as a spawning grounds.

10. stačábac The camping grounds and stream at the head of Sinclair inlet as well as the whole inlet were known by this name. Dog salmon and silver salmon went up the stream. They were caught and dried here. The end of the inlet was shallow and devil fish were caught here. Clams were dug and dried. The area was noted for its abundance of huckleberries.

11. A trail led from the head of Sinclair inlet to Lynch cove at the end of Hood canal. This trail was used especially for fishing in the Union river. Early in the spring they would go to the Union river to catch steelhead. Sometimes they would dry the fish there. Other times they would carry the fresh fish back to their camp on Sinclair inlet and dry it there. The steelhead were caught with spears. Only the barbed points were carried. The spear shafts were made at the fishing place and were then abandoned. Deer hunting was particularly good around Twin lake.

12. sax^{w}sax^{w}áp means "jumping down" The Suquamish came to this place from all over to gamble and play games. They did this when food was plentiful or when there was a break in the seasonal food gathering activities. The place gets its name from a rock about five feet high on which jumping contests were held. The contestants jumped off the rock and tried to jump as far away from it as possible.

13. kbádeb kbáde are round, snail-like shell fish that used to be gathered here. This was a camping ground especially used for clam digging.

14. sq'yáwb q'*yáw* are long green grubs found in old logs. This camping place was located where the Bremerton City park now stands. Remnants of the shell mound were still visible in 1952. It was known as a good clamming, fishing, and duck hunting area. Deer were hunted inland.

15. x̱élelex̱ means "two groups fighting a battle". A myth concerning this point relates that there was a battle going on here when Transformer (*dók^{w}ebł*) came along. Transformer changed the warriors into rocks. The pile of rocks can still be seen here. This was a camping ground used especially for clamming.

16. g^{w}eg^{w}eáltx^w means "potlatch {invite} house". This house was built around 1880. It is said to have been the last potlatch house in the Suquamish area. Ellen George saw the uprights and rafters when she was a child. From her description this was a gable-roofed house

rather than the usual shed-roofed house. This may have been an attempt to imitate the gable-roofed houses to the north, or it may have been the result of European influence, or both.

17. gʷčálgʷel means the "canoe finding (look for) side". Canoes always drifted to this point if they got loose. It was not a camping place. [132]

18. spéwł This was a winter village site. Ed Sigo's father grew up here. There was a shed-roofed house here at that time. Ed Sigo is not sure whether the house was built before or after white settlers came to Puget Sound. Salmon were caught in the stream and deer hunting was good especially around Kitsap lake.

19. sáq'ad means "spear it" This name was given to the camping ground at the mouth of the creek, the creek itself, and all of Dyes inlet. There is no memory of there having been a winter village here. It was probably a seasonal camping ground. Silvers were the chief kind of salmon speared in the creek. Oysters and clams were plentiful on the beach. Inland, huckleberries and deer were abundant.

20. q'ʷasápc This was used as a clamming beach and camping area.

21. At the point where a bridge now connects Bremerton and Manette an Indian "fort" is said to have been located. None of my ~~informants~~ recall this. Mrs LA Bender who lived on the site in 1952 saw it when she first came here in 1888. It was a low wall made of dirt and rocks overlooking the entrance to the inlet, Mrs Bender was told by the Indians that it was used as a "fort." This area has yielded many artifacts to local diggers.

22. x̱áx̱a means "to cry out" or "to be taboo". Canoe burials were placed in the trees here.

23. skʷéksgʷeł means "blackening a dugout canoe with burning pitch". This was a camping place.

24. txʷdaʔabáltxʷ means "doctoring or shaman power house" txʷdaʔab means "shaman" or "shaman power". It was a place to seek doctoring power. Some powers came from the land and some came from the water. Those that came from the water resembled bears but were not. These were strong and dangerous powers (guardian spirits) and were hard to get. They gave a person the power to cure or kill others . They were more dangerous than the other guardian spirits or skláletot.

25. sčásab This was the name of the point. It was not a camping place.

26. q'ʷq'ʷlb means "where huckleberries are" They camped here while picking huckleberries, digging clams, or hunting deer.

27. syabálqo? means "high class water side" This place was named after a spring of water on the beach. They did not camp here but went inland for sallal and huckleberries.

28. qqʷáptb means "someone was bit on the buttocks" They camped here and fished for smelt in the fall. Inland, deer, grouse, and all kinds of birds were hunted. The point was named after the story of a woman who was supposed to have been bitten here by a shark.

29. c'ókɫxa They had smoke houses here and camped here while drying salmon. Dog salmon in particular were plentiful on this creek.

30. shé? means "something that is falling" The shoreline from Brownsville to Keyport was known by this name. It was not a camping place. It was named this because leaves fell into the water here. A certain plant about two feet tall grew along this shore. It was dug and small black things on the roots about the size of a marble were eaten raw. The plant was called xbxb. [133]

31. ɬ'bx̲os This name was applied to the whole peninsula where Key-port is now located. This was a camping ground,

32. ƛ̓ox̲ʷƛ̓ox̲ʷe means "oyster beds". Oysters and clams were gathered here.

33. A trail led from the camping grounds at Keyport to the camping grounds at Brownsville and then to the shore at the entrance of Dyes inlet.

34. qqʷés means "a narrow strip of land projecting into the water" They camped here while gathering clams and oysters.

35. béčlab This was a camping ground where salmon were dried. Only silver salmon went up this stream. The silver salmon came in October and November.

36. bádatoced Oysters were abundant at the mouth of this creek. They camped there while gathering oysters.

37. xʷóyečd This was one of the permanent winter villages. A shed-roofed house stood at the mouth of the creek. Several families lived in it. Various kinds of salmon were caught in the stream. Deer hunting was good up the stream. Mushrooms were found along the creek and were eaten raw.

38. čóčoɬac means "lots of maples". This was a camping area.

39. k'ayok'ayowádac means "kinnikinnik beach" This place was named after the kinnikinnik bush which grew here. The leaves of this bush were dried and smoked in alder stem pipes. This is said to have made them "drunk". After the coming of the whites the Indians mixed this leaf with tobacco (Haeberlin and Gunther 1930: 66).

40. xʷkʷálekʷed means "something wound around it" It was so named because of a tall rock which once stood there which was white around the top. This was a good clamming beach.

41. sax^wk^wásabsb A camping place for clamming, duck hunting, and catching flounders.

42. t'ałbág^wab means "it's croasways" The smelt fishing was good off this point.

43. ƛ̓ƛ̓táčac This was a camping ground.

44. spácpacab This is the sand spit where the ~~informant~~, John Adams, lived. This was a permanent camp where his family lived in the past. In some winter villages there might be several families. In this one there was only one. The people here were known as sqáaqabex^w meaning "many people".

45. słoxalde This was a camping area.

46. hóčbale There was an extensive marsh in this area which has now partially been washed away. John Adams had been told by the old Indians that a fort once stood here. It was made with tall fir poles set in the ground side by side forming walls. Holes were cut in the walls so that a person could look out. Mat houses were inside the enclosure. These were built as a protection against raids by northern Indians. This marsh was a good place to get cattails for mats, cranberries, and ducks. A plant was found there, the leaves of which were used as a "tea". The plant was called c'báčac. [134]

47. palák^weca This was the name of the point. Clamming was good on the east side.

48. sótč This was a winter village. There were several small shed-roofed houses there as well as mat houses. Ducks were plentiful there. Wilson George saw a herring trap there when he was a boy.

49. dax^wklébeal This was a camping place.

50. s?ácos means "face" It was the name of a high cliff here.

51. x^wčék'^w means "narrow pass" This name was applied to Agate passage. The same name was used for any narrow pass.

52. dax^wklébeal This was a permanent winter village. The structure that existed on this site has become known as "Old Man House." It was a shed-roofed house estimated by Gibbs to be about 520 feet long (Gibbs 1877: 215). Archeological evidence indicates that at least part of the house was built sometime between 1845 and 1855 (Snyder 1956: 23). The man after whom Seattle was named lived here. His name was syáł.

53. A trail started at "Old Man House" and ended at the head of Liberty bay.

54. A second trail started at "Old Man House", followed the bluff above the beach and joined the preceding trail.

55. A third trail went from "Old Man House" to the head of Port Gamble bay.

56. A fourth trail branched off the preceding one and led to a marsh where cranberries were gathered.

57. A fifth trail led north on the high ground above the beach as far as Apple Tree cove.

58. x̱alélos means "marked face" This is a rock on the beach at the northern tip of Bainbridge island on which there are petroglyphs. None of the ~~informants~~ knew its origin or significance.

59. x̱álq'ale This was a camping place.

60. dax̌ʷčókap This was a camping place. It was a good place to catch winter salmon. Deer hunting and blackberry picking were good in this area. In the second half of the 19th century many Indians lived here and worked at a lumber mill.

61. čawéč They camped on the sand spit. This was a good clam digging area and a good place for salmon trolling. Smith's Puyallup-Nisqually ~~informants~~ speak of this as a village (Smith 1940: 18). It is doubtful that this site was used as a permanent village site until after the white settlers had arrived in Puget Sound. The government tried to move some Duwamish from south of Seattle into this area in 1856 (Page 1857: 82-83). This was done on the mistaken assumption that, since the white government had appointed syáł as "chief" of both the Duwamish and Suquamish for treaty signing purposes, the two groups belonged to the same tribe. Most of the Duwamish do not seem to have remained in this area for long. Present ~~informants~~ say that there were a few shacks on the sand spit at this place but they knew it only as a temporary camping place. As pointed out by ~~informants~~, its position makes it particularly vulnerable to winter storms and, therefore, not a likely place for a winter village. [135]

62. c'tx̱a means "water falling over the bank" oc'tx̱b means "The water is spouting over the bank and falling". This was a camping place.

63. čagʷálweč means "the beach on the back side" It was not a camping area. There were good clam beds and a good salmon trolling area off the point.

64. daxʷkʷd saxʷb Literally this means "place which gets (has) jumping" There were camping places at the mouths of streams in this bay. Fish, deer, and huckleberries were plentiful.

65. daxʷkʷd saxʷb This is the same name as the one above. The whole area was referred to by this name. ~~Informants~~ knew of no reason why a name with this meaning was given to this area.

66. lax̱élks means "The point is wearing down" The root x̱él means that dirt is falling down from the bank to the beach. This was a camping area.

67. Two names have been given for this bay. Julia Jacobs gave the name elaledáltx^w which means "home of the eagles". John Adams believes the name yaboáltx^w was used for at least part of the bay. They camped on flat ground at the mouths of streams. The modern name of this bay is Eagle harbor. Smith's Puyallup-Nisqually ~~informants~~ spoke of this as the site of a village (Smith 1940: 18). My ~~informants~~ remember it only as a camping area. This may be another case of late occupation after the coming of white settlers.

68. c'ax^{w}lósb means "to have clay or hard mud" They camped on the low ground around the shore.

69. dax^{w}yak'ále This was the name of the point. There were temporary camping places on the flat land around the point.

70. sčelčélb means "bringing it home" This was a permanent winter village with plank houses, kcap, famous for his warrior power, is said to have lived there before the coming of the whites.

71. četeg^{w}áltx^w means "the house of čéte" An Indian named čéte is said to have made this his winter camping place before the coming of the whites. Only he and his family lived here.

72. dax^{w}x̱adeč means "place of covering over" This was a camping area.

73. pepadábac means "partly buried or covered" It is the diminutive form of pa'd, "to bury" plus -abac, "skin or outside". This was a camping place. It was given the name because sharks buried themselves in the mud along the shore. Number #72 above was given its name for the same reason.

74. x^{w}lélk'^{w}ap This was a camping place.

75. dax^{w}q^{w}oʒał There used to be a sandspit here where the Indians camped. It has been washed away.

76. káx̱tyo A fort of the same description as that at number 46 was said to have stood on this spit. Two ~~informants~~, John Adams and Ed Sigo, say that they saw the remains of some of the poles that formed the wall.. Poles ten to twelve feet high were placed in the ground next to each other (Suttles 1951b: 278; Haeberlin and Gunther 1930: 15). On the bank at the end of the spit was a burial ground. John Adams saw the graves when he was a boy. Cedar shakes leaning against each other were placed over the burials. Part of a shell midden is still exposed on this bank. [136]

77. báysx̱b This means "a girl just entering womanhood". It was a temporary camping place. A large white rock that used to stand here is said to have been a girl just changing to womanhood. She had been put outside so that she would not contaminate the fishermen and hunters. She was changed to rock when Transformer was changing the world.

78. sčečag^{w}álde means "a little beach ear" This was a good clamming beach and was used for temporary camping.

79. ƛ̓k^wédop This was a camping area.

80. páɬg^was means "to be separated or divided" This was a camping area for hunting, fishing, clamming and berry picking. Its name comes from the fact that it was a flat area with high banks on each side.

81. sacqéd was the name of the head of the pass. It was not a camping area.

82. dax^wc̓k^wéb The low land in this bay was a camping area. Salmon were caught with nets here. Deer hunting and berry picking were good up the stream. Potatoes were raised at the mouth of the stream before the whites were in the Puget Sound area (Suttles 1951a).

83. dax^wsésa This was a camping area.

84. dax^wkég^wc means "place of deer" This was a camping place.

85. kayópšed These three points all had the same name. They camped on these points.

86. dax^wp̓ók^we This means "where the p̓ók^w berries grow". This was a camping place. The p̓ók^w were gray berries that were eaten fresh and not dried.

87. qáqax̲^wc means "many crabapple trees". This was a camping place named after the wild crabapples that were gathered here. The name q̓ʼ^wekólob was given for this general area.

88. séstq This was a camping ground while they were trolling for spring and silver salmon. It was also a good place for catching herring. From here they went back to the headwaters of the creek that flows into the bay at #82 to catch salmon. Inland, deer hunting was good.

89. c̓apédyob They camped at the mouths of these two creeks while trolling for salmon or hunting deer inland.

90. hácks means "long point" and was the last area to the north where they camped regularly. They camped here while fishing for salmon or catching porpoise in the summer.

Suquamish Tales

Preface and Acknowledgments

Readers interested in the phonological and morphological interpretations on which materials in this volume are based are referred to Paper #8, published previously in this series, entitled; *Southern Puget Sound Salish: Phonology and Morphology*. Information contained in the previous volume is not repeated here.

Most of the acknowledgments made in the previous volume apply also to the present volume. In addition, I wish to thank the current president of the Sacramento Anthropological Society, Mark Grady, for preparing the map of Suquamish place names for publication and for other assistance in preparing this volume. I also thank Lynn Kauffman for typing the English translation of the texts, the bibliography, and introductory portions of the volume.

Warren A Snyder
Sacramento State College
August, 1968 [v]

Introduction

When I first began intensive field research on Southern Puget Sound Salish in the summer of 1953, I asked Suquamish ~~informants~~ with whom I had worked previously whether they knew of anyone who could tell the old myths and tales. All of them replied that they and other Suquamish they knew could tell only fragmented versions of the old folklore. I collected a few short texts from Lucy Mullholland of Suquamish in 1953.

When I resumed work in the summer of 1954 at Tulalip with Mrs. Mullholland's mother, Amelia Sneatlum, I collected only the few short fragmented tales which are included here, I decided to try to obtain linguistic texts by having Mrs. Sneatlum relate her autobiography. After the first few sessions this material proved to be so excellent that we added to it each session. It is presented here without editing or rearrangement in the order that Mrs. Sneatlum related it. The last two paragraphs were told at my last session with her. She requested that this statement be added. This should be understood as an ironical statement addressed to the "white world." Behind it, understandably, lie deep hostility and bitterness shared by many of these people.

~~Informants~~ lived long distances from each other, and it was seldom possible to bring two of them together. Small amounts of conversation were recorded the few times when Mrs. Sneatlum's daughter, Marie, and her son, Charles, were present while I was working with their mother.

At the beginning of the last period of field work during the summer of 1955, informants told me about an old Snuqualmie man. Jerry Kanim, who lived at Carnation, Washington. He was known to have told tales as a younger man. He was probably about eighty-two years old when I worked with him. He was feeble but mentally alert and interested in the work. He had not told myths or tales for many years, but he conscientiously searched his memory between sessions and was always ready at the beginning of each session with a tale that he had been going over in his mind.

Information on Suquamish place names was collected in 1952 as part of the research sponsored and supported by the Suquamish tribe in support of their claims case against the Federal government. The bulk of the information was provided by John Adams who was about eighty years old in 1952. He lived near Poulsbo. As a boy he hunted, fished, and camped throughout the area with older Suquamish men who told him the names of the places and how the places had been used in earlier times. Other [2] ~~informants~~ who contributed information included; Julia Jacobs of Indianola; Ellen George of Port Gamble; Wilson George of Tulalip; Ed Sigo of Shelton; Frank Harmon of Seattle; Celia Jackson of Bremerton; and Virgil Temple of Suquamish.

The dictionary contains only words that I have heard from my informants. More lexical material from Southern Puget Sound Salish may be found in ethnographic publications on Puget Sound Indians. Reference to some of these are included in the bibliography. The decision was made not to incorporate this lexical material into the present volume because of the many problems of phonological interpretation that would have to be decided upon if this material were to be put into the orthographic system adopted here.

Since I did not make an intensive study of the meanings of kinship terms. I have quoted from Marian Smith's *The Puyallup-Nisqually* 1940, where it is clear that her terms and my terms are identical or cognates. Those interested in a further analysis of kinship terms may also consult the 1935 article by Arthur C Ballard.

Since it is not possible at the morphological level to establish nouns and verbs as mutually exclusive paradigmatic classes, such classes are not marked in the dictionary. Whenever possible, roots have been isolated and presented as separate items in the lexicon with one or more examples of their occurence in morphological constructions. Usually roots have been glossed by use of the English infinitive. This is entirely a matter of habit and convenience and implies nothing about the structure of the Salishan language.

The Salish-English section of the dictionary follows the order of the standard English alphabet as closely as possible. The order is:

a, b, c, c′, č, č̓, d, e, g, gʷ, h, k, k′, kʷ, k′ʷ, l, ł, m, o, p, p′, q, q′, qʷ, q′ʷ, s, š, t, t′, w, x̲, xʷ, x′ʷ, y, ꝫ, ž, ƛ̓, ʔ • [2]

Tales

Texts

Table of Contents

Tales

I. Star Husband

1. The Snoqualmie people used to be living. Well, there was that food gathering place of theirs where they would be coming when things were ripe.

2. Then the women would go out to dig the food. Fern roots, bulbs, Indian carrots, and tubers would be gathered by the women. Then the men would go out to look for game. The men would go to the river. They would get some salmon. Then enough would be gotten by the women.

3. Well then, it was cooked on hot rocks by the women. Then the meat was broiled by the men. Then the salmon would be broiled.

4. Well then, all the people would come together. They would be standing in a circle around the food. Then they would look toward Our Father in the sky. They would give thanks for that food. Then they would sing. They were finished. Then they clapped hands and sat down.

5. One day a young woman spoke. She asked, "What do you think? We could go quickly to it and gather some food." Then the youngest one said: "Alright, we go out to gather some food. We'll go camping."

6. Then these women went out, These younger sifters will be camping. They were digging some food.

7. Then it was evening. They were camping. They were lying in bed, Then the sky was clearing. The stars were appearing to them as they lay in bed. They were looking up at the sky. The older one said: "Wish it was true that that red-eyed one was your husband and that that bright-eyed star might be my husband." The younger one tried to argue with her older sister. But she wouldn't argue. She was always talking about that star. [7]

8. Well then, they went to sleep. That star had been listening to their talking. While they were sleeping, the star came, took the woman, and went with her to the sky.

9. The woman woke up then. She was sleeping with a man. The same was true of the younger one who was also sleeping with a man.,

10. It was getting light. Then they learned that they were far away. The younger one said: "See, I tried to stop you! You wouldn't stop. Now look at your husband. That's what you wanted, that bright-eyed star. Well, his eyes are all pussy. The red-eyed one isn't so bad."

11. They were there in the sky married to the stars. When it was getting light, they went out to look for food, fern root food. They would bring their food home. They would cook it and serve it to their husbands.

12. One day, after they had been there a long time with those stars, the stars said to them: "You shouldn't be pushing too deep when you dig." The women would talk about it. "Why do they tell us not to dig too deep at that place?"

13. One day they said: "Alright now, we'll dig deep." Then they dug and dug and dug down deep.

14. Finally there was a hole. Way below they happened to see our world, Then they knew where they were. When they made the hole some wind came up. The stars became aware of what had happened and thought the hole had been made accidentally by the women.

15. The women were discussing it then. "How can we get home?" The youngest one said: "Alright, we'll gather some cedar limbs. We'll soften them until we have gotten enough."

16. They would go out then and gather food. They didn't bring much food back because they were gathering cedar limbs. One was softening them while one was breaking them,

17.   When they would come back they would be asked, "Why is it that you are not gathering much at that place?" They would say. "We're not finding [9] food because we're busy doing something," They were busy working to get back home.

18. Then they happened to find they had enough. Slowly they let it down toward earth. Well. did it nearly reach it? Yes, it did. They added some more. Then it was alright.

19. The youngest one had had a baby. Tomorrow they will go home, They tied it [the ladder] on a stick and buried it,

20. It was getting light in the morning. The women said to their husbands: "Tomorrow morning we will be gathering until we get enough food. Don't worry yourselves about our being late."

21. Well, it was getting light in the morning. They got ready. They went directly to the hole. The younger sister said: "You go first," She said. "Go fast. I'll be behind. I'll close the hole."

22. The youngest one went. Then the oldest one went. She closed the hole. Now they came down. They were coining down. They were getting back to earth. Now they realized that it was from here that they had been taken.

23. They went home to their relatives. They were telling them about the place where they had come down. They were telling the people, all of the people.

24. Then the people came. They saw the place where the women had come down. The people said: "We'll make a swing" [of the ladder]. "It will be a gathering place for lots of people. They will swing. The news will go to all tribes." Then it was learned by all people. They will be called to the swing. All the tribes came. The people swung then.

25. The woman's child was getting older then. Every day he would swing. He was being cared for by that old bull frog woman. The old one was blind.

26. The people came. The dog salmon tribe happened to hear that the child was being cared for at the place of the old woman. The dog salmon came. They will steal that child. Then the dog salmon arrived. They learned where the old bull frog was. Truly, the child was there. They [11] looked to see whether the child was ready.

27. Then the dog salmon went out looking for rotten wood. They wrapped it up small like the child. They said: "Tomorrow, as usual, everyone will be at the swing. Then we will grab the child. We will lay the rotten wood in his place."

28. Well then. the dog salmon went away with him. That child was stolen by the dog salmon. He was taken home by the dog salmon to their land.

29. The bull frog woman found out that the child was not there. It was no longer crying. The bull frog woman kept saying, "My grandson is just like a rotten stick."

30. The people heard. They paid attention to her talking. The people came. They looked into it. True! It was rotten wood bundled up. The child was gone. Then it was discovered that the child had been stolen.

31. Then the people gathered together. They tried to guess who could have stolen the child. They guessed where the child had been taken. One man guessed. He said: "The dog salmon were here. I have reason to believe that they stole the child. The dog salmon were here, and they went home, and, at the time of their going home, the child was absent." It happened that this guess was believed by all the people.

32. Then the people talked it over. Who will go to the land of the dog salmon to try to catch up with the child? All who happened to want to go were chosen. One was appointed to

go out. He wouldn't go far when he would turn back. He could not make himself go very far. Of all who were appointed to go, no one could make himself go.

33, Then Blue Jay was appointed. Blue Jay said: "I'll try." She was provided with meat and then Blue Jay left.

34. Well, she made it. She came to the land of the dog salmon. She happened to see a tree. There was a man sitting and working, making a flint arrow head. She found that this was the one she was looking for.

35. Blue Jay went and sat on a limb and was talking to him. He didn't pay any attention because he was working. [13]

36. She kept talking to him again and again. Then the man paid attention, The man took some flint chips and accidentally threw them in Blue Jay's face. Blue Jay said: "Why did something hit me in the face? I was being sent to look for you. Your relatives did not know who took you. I was told that *if.* I should happen to find you that I should take you home."

37. The man said: "How could you take me home?"

38. Blue Jay said: "I could pack you, I could cross the water with you to the land on the other side. Then you could walk home."

39. The man said: "Alright, alright, you take me across the water, I'll travel now."

40. Then Blue Jay rested herself. One day she said: "Tomorrow morning we will go home." The man was told by Blue Jay: "I will pack you."

41. Then the Blue Jay packed him and flew. They were crossing the water to land. Then she brought the man to the land.

42. The man said to Blue Jay: "Go home now. Tell my relatives I'll come home. I'll just be working."

43. Then Blue Jay went home. She came back and told them: "Your child will come. He'll be travelling. He'll be working. I'm not sure what his work will be." [23] [word analysis 14-21]

II. Transformer

1. Transformer had married a child of the dog salmon. The dog salmon child gave birth to Transformer's baby.

2. Before Transformer started for home [back to the Snuqualmie area] his child started to cry. He didn't know what to do for it. When he would leave, his child would cry. He would go back and take his child again. That's why he finally said that he would leave some of his hair for him.

3. He cut off some of his hair and gave it to his child. Transformer told his hair to watch the child, and told it that, if the child should cry, it should stop him. Then Transformer left. He would listen to his hair. Well, it was alright now. The child wasn't crying any more.

4. As he was travelling along. Transformer discovered that he was feeling different. He had some work to do.

5. He went back home to his land [among the dog salmon], [~~Informant~~ explains that he had received his power now and no longer needed Blue Jay to transport him across the water,] He found his wife and her relatives swimming. He told them to go down stream. The salmon went down stream. He shouted at them again. He told them to come up stream. The salmon came up stream. Transformer said: "In the future you will just be food for the people who are

coming soon. You'll be coming up the river." Now every year the salmon come up the river. That was the first work that he did.

6. Well, he went on with his work. He was changing everything now, He learned that he had been given this work to do.

7. All peoples heard about Transformer's changing everything. All the tribes said: "Alright, we'll kill him." They were lying in wait for him.

8. Transformer was travelling and he came to the land of the deer, He found Deer sitting down and working. Transformer was standing over the Deer behind him. Deer was singingi "This is for Transformer — Sharpening, sharpening, sharpening," Deer wanted to kill Transformer. Deer was sharpening a bone. [25]

9. Transformer was standing over Deer behind him. Transformer said to Deer: "That singing of yours just now was good. Sing it again," Deer sang it again. Transformer said: "Bring me that thing you're working on," Deer gave it to him. Transformer said: "Give me your hands." Deer gave his hands to Transformer. Transformer grabbed them. and stuck the bone into Deer's hands. Then Deer went jumping away. "You will be meat for the people who are coming soon."

10. Transformer travelled on. He was coming to the place where Mink lived. He asked Mink what he would like to be made into. Mink said: "What you make of me is up to you." "Alright, I'll make a snag out of you," "That's alright. Alright, you make a snag out of me."

11. Transformer went on then. He heard Mink shouting: "ho, ho, ho. You're going to make me a snag?" Transformer listened to him. Then Transformer went back. He came to Mink and grabbed him, "What shall I make you?" Mink said: "Make me what you want to." Transformer said: "Alright. I'll make you a stone." Mink said: "Alright." Transformer made Mink into a stone.

12. Transformer went on. Mink laughed at him, "That woman will make me a stone!" Transformer heard Mink laughing at him.

13. He went back. He was angry. He grabbed Mink. He cut him to pieces. Then he threw Mink away. That is the reason there are so many mink everywhere in this land now.

14. Transformer went on. He found Crane making a canoe. Whenever [Crane] would take hold of some sticks, the sticks would whip him. When he picked up a rock. it would pound him. In splitting the wood. Crane used his hands and head, driving the side of his head into the wood [using it as a wedge]. Crane was singing; "My hand, my hand is like the side of my head. My hand, my hand is like the side of my head."

15. Transformer came up and was watching Crane. Transformer felt pity for Crane. Transformer said: "I'm surprised you don't use a stick." Crane said: "Whenever I grab a stick it whips me. Whenever I grab a stone it pounds me. My skin is all bruised."

16. Transformer said: "I will help you." Transformer took the stick, broke it, and hit the pieces together. He said: "Take that stick and use it." Transformer then took the rocks. He knocked them together. He said: "The rocks and the sticks will be used by the people in the future." [27]

17. Then Transformer went on. He found someone trying to catch salmon on the river. He had caught a salmon. He would grab it and it would just slip [out of his hands]. He would hug it. He couldn't catch it.

18. Transformer was watching. He said: "Why don't you take a stick and club the salmon on the head?" The man said: "Whenever I grab a stick it just clubs me."

19. Transformer went and took sticks and pounded them together. He told the man to take the stick. The man took the stick. Transformer said: "That stick will be used by the people

who are coming soon. It will not club them." The man took a rock and it just pounded him. Transformer took them and pounded them together. Transformer said: "The stone will be used by the people who are coming. It will not pound the people."

20. Transformer was going on when he found some men standing by the river fishing for salmon. They had their heads together. They were closing off the river with their hair.

21. Transformer was watching. He went over and asked them what they were doing. He was told that they wanted salmon and that was the reason they were holding their hair together to close off the salmon at this place. Transformer said: "Why don't you take sticks and use the sticks?" The people said: "If we take a stick, it just whips us. If we take a rock, it just pounds us."

22. Transformer took the sticks and beat them together. He took the rocks and pounded them together. Transformer said: "You will take the sticks and rocks now and use them."

23. Transformer went on. He found Bear, He just slapped him. Immediately Bear started jumping and became bear. Transformer said: "You will be bear forever."

24. Transformer went on. He came to a lake. Beaver was paddling around doing things. Transformer said: "What are you doing. Beaver?" [29] Beaver said: "I'm just paddling around doing things on the lake."

25. Transformer called Beaver to come ashore. Beaver came ashore. Transformer went over to Beaver. Transformer asked: "What would you like to have me make you?" "I'm changing everything." Beaver said: "Make me what you wish." Transformer said: "Alright, you will be Beaver for the people coming soon. Your pelt will be clothes for the people who are coming." Beaver said: "Alright."

26. Transformer went on. He happened to see some smoke. He went toward it and saw something burning. Drawing near, he saw that person roasting something. He sneaked up on him. He saw that a man was roasting salmon. He stayed there. He wanted to wait until the man who was doing the roasting went to sleep.

27. Soon the man lay down and went to sleep. Then Transformer went over and turned the roast, When it was roasted. Transformer sat down and ate it. He ate it all. He took the salmon skin and rubbed it on the hands of the man. He rubbed it in his mouth. This done, he went into the brush, He was watching him. Soon the sleeping man will wake up.

28. He woke up. The first thing he did was to look at the fire. His roast wasn't there. The roasting sticks were lying there. He looked at his hands. He felt of his mouth. He said to himself: "Evidentally I ate my roast," But he was still hungry. He was thirsty. He went down to the river. While he was drinking, he happened to see his reflection in the river. His face looked different. He examined it again very closely. "Truly. I am different." Then Transformer came and said: "In the future, you will be Wild Cat." He jumped away. Then he was being Wild Cat,

29. Transformer went on. He came to some people far up the Tolt River. He came upon these people by chance. He asked: "What do you want me to make you?" The people said: "Make us what you wish." Transformer said: "I'm changing everything, I'll make you Elk, You'll be meat for the people who are coming soon. You'll be high in the mountains. Only good hunters will kill you."

30. Transformer went on. high into rocky mountains. He came upon some people high up in the rocks. He asked them: "How do you like these [31] rocky mountains where you are?" The people said: "We like the place where we are." Transformer said: "What would you like to have me make you?" The people said: "Make us what you wish." Transformer said: "I'm changing everything. I'll make you Mountain goats. You will be her on the high rocky

mountains. You'll be meat for the people who are coming soon. Your skin will be used for their clothes. Your fur will make good blankets for the future people."

31. Transformer went on. He came upon five men singing. Trans" former asked! "What are you doing?" They said: "We are children of fire. If we were to sing a song, it would burn the land." Transformer said: "Go ahead, sing your song." One man said: "I wouldn't sing it. If I should sing it, it would be dangerous. You could be burned." Transformer said: "It's alright for you to sing it. I want to learn it." The men said: "Alright."

32. Then they sang, "We are sons of the fire, We are sons of the fir." They would point anywhere and, when they pointed, fire would come from their hands. Transformer jumped into the water. He was told by the water "I'll be the first to burn. " Transformer jumped again, this time toward the woods. The tree told him: "I'll be the first to burn. " Someone yelled at Transformer: "It burns only where things are together. Come to me." Transformer went to the road. He watched the burning of the land.

33. Transformer said: "It is alright for the fire to burn the land. The berries will grow. This will be a berry gathering place for the people of the future. For this reason, the brush will be burned off this place again in the future. Only the big trees will be growing. This is the reason you will see the bark of the fir tree burned to charcoal. The people who are coming will discover that this land burned."

34. Transformer went on. He came to a river. He happened to see a child on the other side of the river. He had a big stomach. Transformer yelled at him; "Alright child, come and get me, " Everytime Transformer called, the child would answer by saying five times: "Child, come and get me. " Transformer was shouting: "Child, come and get me, " and the child was saying: "Child, come and get me."

35. After five times. Transformer became angry. He took off his clothes and waded out. He came ashore. The child went jumping away. [31] Transformer caught up with him. The child went into his house. Transformer went into his house. Transformer asked: "Where are your relatives?" The child answered five times: "Where are your relatives?" Whenever Transformer asked, the child would answer: "Where are your relatives?" Transformer became angry. He seized the child and cut him to pieces. He threw away the pieces in all directions. He threw the stomach toward the Klallam Indians. This is why the Klallam are big people with big fat stomachs.

36. Transformer went on. He happened onto some children on their way home. He asked them: "Where have you been?" The children told him: "We were seized by a witch. We got away. We are going home now." Transformer said: "You have no more relatives. I've changed everything. I'm asking you what you would like to have me make of you." The children said: "Make us whatever you wish to." Transformer said: "Maybe it would be best if you all stayed together." The children said: "Alright, we'll stay together." Transformer said: "I'll make you birds. Then you'll always be together."

37. Transformer seized the children and changed them. He let them go, and they flew off in all directions. He called them back. They came together. He called to them again. He told the children: "Alright, you will always be together." He turned them loose. They flew a little. Transformer was there watching them. The birds came and lit. Transformer said: "Alright now, the rain will come only when you fly a little, The people of the future will find out that the rain comes only when you fly a little." He said: "In the future you will indicate bad weather. When the weather is bad, you will fly a little."

38. Now he was through with his work. He went home to Snuqualmie and told his relatives: "Everything is done now. I have changed everything. There will be meat, and there will be berries and all kinds of food. You, my relatives, will be the first of the future people. You will look after the people of the future. Your name will continue on into the future. The people of the future will keep the name of Snuqualmie forever."

39. Now Transformer came back. There were still lots of people together swinging. He was watching. He was watching the Snohomish sitting high up on the mountain named Mt. Si. He was watching the swinging. Transformer thought; "There are very many people now. I could change things. I'll just clap my hands," He was able to stop the [33] swinging. He hold them that the swinging was finished. He pointed to the Snohomish, He told them: "You are Snohomish. You will be there on that place where you are sitting. You will be made into rock. It will only be when someone from Snohomish is near death that a rock will break off. Now it is done. Make yourselves ready. Everyone will change." Transformer said: "You are ready now."

40. Then Transformer clapped his hands. He told them: "You go now. You go now." Some went and flew and became birds. The same was true of everything – all the little animals in the land. The great man changed everything. When it was completed, the swing came down and turned to stone. It's still over there and is called "the swing." {ye?dó?ad}

41. Transformer left his relatives and took his cousin with him, They went to the sky to his star father. He was there talking with his cousin. He said: "Alright, you will be travelling in the daytime, I will be travelling at night." The moon travelled in the daytime. He travelled and burned everything. It was very hot. He came back and told bis brother, He told the sun! "I am very hot. Some of the people might die." He told the sun: "Alright, you try it yourself." Then the sun travelled. Everything was alright. The moon said: "Alright, I'll travel at night." That is the reason the sun travels during the day and the moon travels at night. [39] [word analysis 36-37]

III. Coyote Story

1. Coyote would travel around. He would see that river. Well, he would have the urge to say; "I wish there were some salmon in this river." Coyote was thinking; "How can I get a few salmon here?" He was motivated to say: "Alright, I'll try to bring some blue-back salmon from inland." Then Coyote went ashore. The blue-back salmon came in a canoe then. Coyote thought! "How are you going to get the salmon?"

2. He went to a sand bar. He was lying in wait for the salmon. He happened to see the salmon coming up stream. He yelled; "Jump to shore, salmon." He was standing above on the sand bar calling to the salmon. He told the salmon to jump to shore. The salmon jumped. He was jumped on by Coyote. Coyote grabbed him and jumped away with him.

3. He grabbed him and was jumping away with him. He was coming jumping along with the salmon. Night came. When it became light be arrived at the river called "blue-back salmon. " Immediately he put the salmon into the water. It was still alive! The salmon went down and stretched out on the bottom. Coyote was there looking at him. He was stretched out there. Coyote said: "There will be many salmon in this river. I will do it." He knows the salmon is stretched out there.

4.   Then Coyote went inland again. He went to the place where he had stalked the salmon. It was getting dark. Again he happened to see the salmon coming up the stream. He called! "Jump to the shore, salmon," Salmon jumped to shore. Coyote went and grabbed the salmon. He jumped away with it.

5.   When morning came the next day, he arrived at the river. He put the salmon into the water immediately. He happened to see there the first one of his he had brought back with him. It was there stretched out on the bottom. The one he had just brought back with him didn't go far before it stretched out.

6.   Coyote said: "I'll get a lot of salmon into this river." Five times salmon were brought by Coyote. At the fifth time he looked at them stretched out down there. Coyote said: "Why are they just stretched out there in only that place?" [41]

7.   He took a stick and went and stuck it into them. He found out that they weren't salmon! He felt around in the place with the stick. It was only moss! He was very disappointed. Coyote said: "In the future the name of this river will be just "blueback salmon river." [43]

IV. Swayok^w Story

1.   Five witches were living, xax̱áyklked and her grandson, Chipmunk, were living, x̱ax̱ayklked and the witches were related as cousins.

2.   Chipmunk would go out berry picking. He would sing and say: "I will eat these ripe berries, and, the ones that are not ripe, I will reach to them and push, yes, push, to grandmother." Grandmother told him: "Don't be singing about that pushing. You will be heard by the witches."

3.   Chipmunk went out to pick. He came upon some berries. He was picking. Then he sang! "I will eat these ripe berries, and. the ones that are not ripe. I will reach to them and push, yes, push, to grandmother."

4.   The witch was travelling along. She heard the singing. She went and came upon the Chipmunk singing and picking. The witch went after him. Chipmunk happened to see the witch. Chipmunk jumped away. The witch caught up to him. Chipmunk climbed to the top of a tree. The witch said: "Come down or you will get hurt." Chipmunk said: "I won't come down." The witch said: "Oh my grandson, you'll be hurt. Comedown." Chipmunk said: "You're not my grandmother."

5.   The witch stayed with him. Chipmunk took a limb and dropped it to her. The witch jumped after it. Chipmunk said: "See! You are different from my grandmother."

6.   He took a dry limb and broke it. Then he threw it far off. The witch caught up with it. Chipmunk came jumping down. He was running toward home. The witch caught up with him. They came to a fallen tree. Chipmunk crawled far underneath it. While he was crawling underneath the witch grabbed him. She just wanted to scratch him on the back. [43]

7.   Then Chipmunk ran to his grandmother. He told her! "Grandmother I'm being chased by the witch. Hide me!" His grandmother took him and covered him with cedar roots. Then the witch arrived. She came in. She asked: "Have you seen the child?" Grandmother said: "I haven't seen him."

8. The witch stayed there with grandmother. She happened to see grandmother's tattoo. "Oh, cousin, that tattoo of yours is good. How did you make it?"

9. Grandmother said: "I gathered some little rocks and just started a fire. I laid the rocks in it till they became red hot. Then I removed the fire so that only the rocks were left. I took off my clothes and I jumped on top of the little rocks. I turned myself over and over. When I was done, I removed myself from the rocks. Then I just scratched my skin. That is the reason you see this place tattooed. If you like it, you can tattoo yourself. I can help you."

10. The witch said: "Oh, cousin, alright, you help me. I want to tattoo myself as you have." Grandmother said: "Come. we'll gather little rocks together."

11. They gathered the little rocks. They started a fire. They laid the little rocks on the fire. The rocks were red hot. Then they removed the fire, leaving just the little rocks. She told the witch: "Quickly, undress and do to yourself as I did to myself." The witch undressed. She told her: "Quickly, just jump on those little rocks. Turn yourself over and over until you are done."

12. The witch said: "Oh, cousin, I am afraid." Grandmother said: "Quickly, or the little rocks will get cold." The witch was standing up and grandmother pushed her. The witch fell on top of the rocks. She rolled over just a few times.

13. The chipmunk jumped away. He found a pronged stick. He came back and gave it to his grandmother. Grandmother stuck it into witch's neck. When the witch was cooked, they covered her up. Grandmother said: "We'll get ready and go away." Then she went away with her grandson, Chipmunk. [47]

14. The witch's relatives looked for her. They found her cooked body. They said: "This must have been saved for us."

15. The witches sat down and ate some of the cooked meat. They became ill. They vomitted. They would say: "aaaa, this has the smell of our cousin." When they had finished, they said: "Alright, let's go home. That was our older sister that we ate!"

16. Coyote was travelling. He came upon the home of the witches. Their hearts were tied up outside on their house. Coyote looked at them. He thought: "What can I do with them?" He thought! "Alright, I'll ask my sisters."

17. His sisters were his bowels. His sisters stretched out of him now. He asked them; "What could I do with those things hanging up outside?" He was told by his sisters: "Well, those are the hearts of the witches. Take a stick and sharpen it on the end. Stick it in one and then in another."

18. Coyote stuck all five of them. He stuck all five. He stuck it in all of them. The witches died immediately. All five witches were killed by Coyote. Coyote said: "In the future children will play. There will be no witches to eat the children of the people who are coming near." [49] [word analysis 46-47]

V. Snow Bird

1. The black-faced Snow Bird was living with his relatives. Well, it was getting cold then. All the sticks were wet. Only the cedar snag was dry. Every day Snow Bird will gather wood. He put his back into gathering fire wood. He would be wiping his face with his hand ail covered with charcoal. It spread all over his face.

2. His relatives would talk about him, "Why is it that he never wants to wash his face?" One day they told him: "Alright now, wash your face." Snow Bird didn't say anything. They stopped telling him for one day, but very soon they told him again: "Alright now, wash your face. Your face is very black with charcoal." Five times he was told to wash his face. He said: "Alright, it's up to you. I'll wash my face now, but things won't be very good now." Then Snow Bird said: "I'll go down to the river now and wash my face."

3. Well, he went and sat down by the river. He looked up river toward the south. He cried out and said: "I wag told to wash my face," Then he washed his face. He looked up river toward South Wind. Then be sang: "I was told to wash my face. Yes, You will come now. South Wind."

4. South Wind paid attention. He heard that his uncle would be washing his face. "He has called me to come. Alright, I'll go."

5. Then. South Wind came. He came. The wind became warm. The snow in the mountains melted. The river came racing down. When it was over the water had flooded.

6. Snow Bird sang. He said: "Go up into the mountains my uncles, the elk. I wash my face."

7. His uncles, the elk, paid attention to him. They said: "We were told to go up to the mountains."

8. So the elk went into the high hills. The river ran swiftly. It ran swiftly. Everything was soaked.

9. The people said: "See now, you decided that he should wash his face without realizing the consequences of his doing it. It's our fault that [49] this great danger has come to the land."

10. Beaver wanted to take mouse as his wife. Mouse didn't like him. Mouse just said: "I don't want to make him my husband because his stomach growls."

11. When everything was flooded with water. Beaver rejoiced. Mouse was swimming around. Beaver would go by and would pass mouse. The mouse would yell: "I like you now. Beaver." Beaver would say: "Me? Me! My stomach is growling."

12. Now the mouse drifted. She floated inland. That is the reason the mouse is there now. If she had not floated to shore there would not have been any mice. Well, she floated in and that is the reason the mouse is there on the land now.

13. Now, if Snow Bird sings, his nephew, South Wind, comes from the south. Then Snow Bird flew south. He went to his nephew. Now when South Wind comes you can hear Snow Bird singing. You know that South Wind will come. [53]

VI. Laleewa

I. Once there was a tribe of people living. There were many people. Well, there was a man and his wife who had two grown sons and one little girl. The oldest son married a woman and they were living together. The man became sick and died. He left his wife and the old people.

2. Her in-laws liked the woman. The man's youngest son was the younger brother of the man who had died. Laleewa was the name of the young man. He would not be together with the other men. He was always by himself. People had reason to say that he was dumb. He just kept apart and watched those young men. He would not go with them but always kept apart.

3. One day Laleewa's father talked to him about his dead brother's widow, Laleewa's father and mother liked her.

4. [His father] said: "Alright now, ask your levirate relative if she would accept you? We don't want her to go to a different man."

5. Laleewa said: "It's only because I think she wouldn't like me because I'm sick. My skin is scarred, I'm afraid to talk to that woman."

6. His father said: "Alright, you just ask her if she would wait until you are over your sickness." Laleewa thought it over. He thought, "Alright, I'll ask her what she thinks about it. "

7. One day Laleewa went to her. The woman was sleeping. He was sitting near her. He took hold of her clothes and woke the woman.

8. She asked: "Who are you?" He said: "I am Laleewa." The woman didn't say anything. Laleewa said: "My father and my mother want you, I was told to ask you whether or not you want me. You can wait for me until I am over my illness." [55]

9. The woman did not say anything for a long time. Finally she said: "I cannot say anything now. It is better for you to go home now. Later I will tell you what I think."

10. Laleewa went home. One day the woman arrived. She was clutching a piece cut from her clothes where Laleewa had grabbed them. She was bringing it to Laleewa.

11. She told him: "This is the place where you grabbed me. I am bringing it to you, I do not want my skin to become rotten."

12. Laleewa took it and gave it to his mother. He told his mother: "Take it and put it away until I want it and then give it to me."

13. Laleewa thought it over. He thought, "What can I do for myself?" He thought, "Alright, I will travel now." He took his blanket and began to travel. He didn't tell anyone where he was traveling.

14. He went inland toward the mountains. He washed himself until his skin was good again. He came upon a lake back on a mountain. Then he began looking for it. He had reason to think that the lake looked as though the sort of thing he was looking for might exist there.

15. He thought it over. Then he thought, "Well, alright now, I'll dive in right here." He took some dried sticks and tied them together. He took a big rock and wrapped it with softened cedar limbs. Then he put it on a raft. Then he pushed [the raft] out. He came to the middle [of the lake]. Then he put the rock off into the water and held onto the rock.

16. He went down into the lake. He went down to the roof of a house. Someone said: "You (plural), open the house of the great spirit for him." It was said: "Bring him in."

17. He was brought in and a high class person talked to him. He was told! "Look at me and see what I am and you will be like me. You will have much food. You will only have to call the game animals, and they will come to your house."

18. He took his hair and rubbed it. His hair became very long. Then he was told to go home. He was taken from the guardian spirit's house at the bottom of the lake and was thrown out.

19. When Laleewa regained consciousness, he lifted his face to the hills. He had gotten what he was looking for. [55]

20. Then he went home. He arrived at the place where his little sister customarily played. She was sitting there. His little sister saw him. He called to her to come. His little sister was afraid. He called to her and told her not to be afraid, "It is I, I'm coming back. "

21. His little sister came to him. He told her: "Go home. Tell father and mother that I am arriving. Tell them to clean the house and get everything ready. Only when the house is ready will I come home."

22. The child went and told them, "The one who is my older brother is coming. He was up there. He said to tell you to clean the house and get everything ready. He also wants you to tell all the people to come to the house this evening."

23. The child went and told them this, but her father and mother just got angry with her. They said that her older brother died a long time ago. The child said: "My older brother is here now."

24. She ran back and told him. She said: "My father and mother just got angry with me again."

25. He called to his little sister. She went to him. He seized her head and rubbed it. The child's hair grew. Then he sent her off to go home to tell.

26. The child went home and told them again. Her father believed her this time. Her father happened to look at her hair. Then the house was cleaned. Everything in the house was made ready. The man went and told all the people. "My son is arriving and he wants you this evening."

27. Then the child went and told [her brother]: "It is done. The house is ready. They tell you to come home."

28. Then the man went home. He went in and went over and lay down, Evening came. The people, all the people, gathered together. Then they started singing. The people did the "go along with you." [The people did the ceremony of helping him to sing his power song and dance his power dance,] They danced and sang their powers every night.

29. [Laleewa] said: "I will dance and sing my power for five nights before I am finished." He sang and danced his power for three nights. Then he told his father; "Alright, you choose some very strong men. I will call the game animals. They will come to the outside of the house, and the game will be killed by these men." [59]

30. His father chose the young men. [Laleewa] sang. The people all watched to see if game would come. He sang and sang his power. Now elk were seen coming toward the outside of the house. Then the men killed the game. They cut it up. Then it was cooked and eaten by the people.

31. They went home and told the woman: "Your levirate relative has arrived. This food is the game meat of his power. "

32. The woman said: "Alright. I will go to see him."

33. On the third night she said: "Is it true that you have acquired a guardian spirit?"

34. Laleewa knew what the woman thought of him. [He thought] "She will come now to see about it."

35. As the fourth night was falling, the woman came to see. She did not come in but just peeked in. Laleewa knew she was peeking at him, so he turned around toward the other end of the house. The woman went to the end of the house, so Laleewa turned again toward the other end. She had failed. She couldn't see his face.

36. She went home. She said: "Tomorrow night I will come to see. I will go in."

37. On the last night she went. Laleewa spoke and told his mother: "That woman will come this evening. She will come in and you will get the place ready where she will sit. You will have that piece ready that she cut from her clothes. She gave it to me. She will come in."

38. Laleewa danced and sang his power till it was nearly daylight. Then Laleewa went and took the piece of clothing given to him by that woman. He went to the place where she was sitting and thanked her for having come and having watched. He gave it to her what she had given to him. [He said]: "Now I give it back to you. It is yours. Take it home with you."

39, Laleewa finished singing and dancing his power on the fifth day. The woman was crying. She went home and took with her what he had given her. She cried and cried. She wiped her face and it became scarred. She scratched it. Then she became sick. She became scarred over her whole body. She became sick and died. [61]

VII. Five Brothers

1. Five men who were brothers were living. The youngest one was named Sasobshid. When it would get light, the oldest one would go out traveling to look for food. One day at dawn he told his relatives: "I will go that way, and, if I kill anything, I will hang it up. If I am late. you will know that there is something that made me late."

2. He took his bow and arrows. Then he left. He traveled until he came upon some pheasants. He shot them. He took them and hung them on a pronged stick. He went on and came upon some grouse. He shot them, took them, and hung them up on a pronged stick. He went on and killed all kinds of birds. He was killing them and hanging them up on pronged sticks.

3. He walked on till night began to fall. He was looking for a place where he could camp. He came upon a big cedar tree. It was dry underneath the tree. He thought: "This is the place I will camp."

4. Night was coming. He made a sleeping place ready and lay down. He was still awake when he heard someone asking him from far away;

"Are you still awake, camper?" He said: "I am still awake." He heard the questioning from high up in the cedar tree.

5. It wasn't long when he was asked again. "Are you still awake, camper?" He answered and said: "I am still awake." He was asked five times. Finally, he did not answer. He was asleep. Soon he was asked again and it was found out that he was asleep.

6. Then the Cannibal Woman was coming down the tree. She went after the sleeping man, turned him over, and took out his heart. Well, she ate it. She just swallowed it. Then she took the man and threw him to one side.

7. Then the man was missing. His younger brothers were discussing it. They decided that evidentally he had come upon something that had made him be late.

8. One day the oldest one said: "I'll follow him to see what he found." He started to travel. He came upon the pheasant that was hung up. He went on and found the grouse that were hung on the pronged stick. He traveled on [63] killing all kinds of birds and hanging them up.

9. He traveled until it started to get dark. He began to think about where he would camp. He came to a cedar tree and happened to see there the camping place of his older brother. "Alright," [he thought], "I'll camp here." Night was coming, so he prepared his sleeping place and lay down.

10. Soon it was asking, "Are you still awake, camper?" He said: "I am still awake, " The questioning from high in the cedar tree stopped until it was asked again, "Are you awake yet,

camper?" He said: "I am awake yet." He was asked five times. Then he didn't answer. He was asleep. Soon he was asked again and he didn't answer.

11. Then the Cannibal Woman came down. She went after him. She took his heart and ate it. She just swallowed it. Then she took him and threw him to the place where she had thrown his older brother.

12. He was missing. His brothers were discussing it: "Why are they late? Evidentally there is something there that they found by chance." The oldest one said: "Tomorrow I will follow them."

1 3. When it started to get light, he started out. He came upon all the birds that had been killed by his older brothers. He walked until it became dark. He thought: "Where will I camp."

14. He came to the cedar tree that was dry around the bottom. He thought: "Oh, this will be a good place to camp." Now he saw that this was where his older brothers must have come to camp. He made a place ready to lie down. Then, as it became dark, he lay down.

15. Soon he was asked: "Are you still awake, camper?" He answered and said: "I am still awake. " The questioning stopped. Then he was asked again: "Are you still awake, camper?" He answered and said: "I am still awake." He was asked five times. Then he didn't answer. He was asleep. The questioning stopped. Then he was asked again: "Are you awake yet, camper?" He did not answer. He was asleep.

16. Then the Cannibal Woman came down. She went after him. She took his heart and ate it. She just swallowed the heart. The Cannibal Woman took him and threw him where his older brothers were.

17. The two men who were left were talking, "Evidentally there was something there that our older brothers came upon." [63]

18. The youngest brother had learned why his older brothers were missing. The youngest one was named Sasobshid. He had found out by chance what was killing his older brothers, but he wouldn't say anything about it.

19. In the morning his older brother said: "Tomorrow I will follow them."

20. When the next morning came, he started out. He came upon all the birds his older brothers had killed. He walked until it was becoming dark. He thought: "Where will I camp?" He came to the cedar tree. "Oh," he said: "this will be a good place to camp." He happened to notice that this must have been where his older brothers had camped.

21. He prepared a place to sleep. As it was getting dark, he lay down. Soon it was asking, "Are you still awake, camper?" He answered and said: "I am still awake." The voice stopped. Then it asked again: "Are you still awake, camper?" He said: "I am still awake." The question was asked five times. Now he didn't answer. He was asleep. The voice stopped and then it asked again, "Are you still awake, camper?" There was no answer.

22. Now the Cannibal Woman came down and went after him. She took his heart from him. It was taken by the Cannibal Woman. She threw him over with his brothers.

23. SasobshId was thinking it over. It happened that he had found out what was killing his older brothers. He was going to kill it. Sasobshid started to get ready. He chose a good arrow and slowly heated it in hot ashes.

24. When morning came he went out and followed after them. He happened to know where his missing brothers were.

25. He came to the cedar tree that was dry around the bottom. This was the place where his older brothers were lost, "Well, " [he thought] "I'll kill it when it gets light."

26. He prepared a place to sleep. He made a [dummy] man. He took off his clothes and put them [under the tree] and used them to make [a dummy]. As it was getting dark he went over and lay down next to the dummy. Soon he heard it. It asked, "Are you still awake, camper?" He said: "I am still awake?" The voice stopped. Then right away it asked again: "Are you still awake, camper?" He just said: "I am sti... , I am ... " [He made believe he was half asleep and only half answered.] [65]

27. When it found out he was asleep it stopped. Then it asked again: "Are you still awake, camper?" Sasobshid did not answer. He took his bow and one arrow that was heated and went around to the other side of the cedar tree.

28. He heard it coming. The Cannibal Woman was coming down. She went after the dummy. She was sitting on the dummy, Sasobshid came out and went nearer. The Cannibal Woman found out that the thing he had made was not a person. As soon as she stood up, he shot directly into her heart. She died immediately.

29. He went over to her and laid her on her back. Then he cut her open and took out the hearts of his brothers. Then he went after his brothers. He took them. came back, and laid them down. He took a heart and put it into his oldest brother. Then he took all the hearts and put them in his brothers.

30. When it was finished, he stepped over the youngest one. He stepped over him only once. When he stepped over him, his brother sat up immediately and regained consciousness. Then he stepped over the next older one. The first time he stepped over him, his brother Just lifted his bead and let it fall again. He stepped over him a second time. He sat up and regained consciousness.

31. He stepped over the next oldest one three times. He sat up and regained consciousness. Then he stepped over the oldest one. Nothing happened. Again he stepped over him. Nothing. He stepped over him five times, but he would not regain consciousness.

32. Sasobshid said: "Now, the oldest ones among the people of the future will die. The future people will be traveling and will camp at the dry places under the trees. In the future there will be no Cannibal Woman to eat the hearts of the people of the future. They will travel and they will camp. Then ... " [67]

VIII. Kingfisher

1. Crane is living. Kingfisher is his friend. They fish for all kinds of fish. Kingfisher is always lying in wait and spearing fish, Kingfisher is high, lying in wait high above the river.

2. Then night would come. Kingfisher would go home and Crane would go home. Then they would talk. Kingfisher would ask Crane: "What things can you hunt?" Crane replied: "There is my catch." Kingfisher went to look at the Crane's catch. Crane's catch consisted only of bullheads.

3. Then Crane said: "I wonder what you catch." Kingfisher said: "Come and look at the catch." Crane went and looked at Kingfisher's catch. It consisted of trout. Crane asked; "Where did you kill those?"

4. Kingfisher replied: "I always kill them over at the river, I watch the fish going upstream from on high. I spear them. If you want to know about it, you can come along with me. You can watch how I always Spear the fish."

5. Kingfisher then said to Cranes: "Your spear is long. You could spear the fish without even trying."

6. Crane went along with Kingfisher. They went there and got high up on a limb. They were watching the fish. As Kingfisher watched, he said: "See that trout?" He told Crane: "Go ahead now and spear it." Crane said: "You had better spear it." Kingfisher said: "Alright, I will."

7. Then Kingfisher jumped down and speared the fish.. He dove, got it, and came out with the fish. Then Kingfisher said: "Now you spear something." Crane said: "No, I can't dive as you do."

8. Now Crane went to a riffle in the river and started gathering food. He didn't get anything but bullheads. That is the only way he ever hunts. [69]

9. Kingfisher *is* good at spearing, but Crane cannot dive. He is afraid that he might stick his spear into a rock. That is the reason he will eat only bullheads while Kingfisher eats the good fish. [71]

IX. Pheasant Story

1. There were some people who were living. They were talking about who was a good hunter. Who was first in killing game, the Cougar, the Wolf, the Weasel, the Red-headed Woodpecker, or the Black Mountain Eagle? These men were saying they were good hunters.

2. The poor Pheasant was there. He would kill game when he wanted it. One day the men said to one another: "Alright, now, we'll go out and find out who the good hunter is."

3. They went out to compete with one another. By dark no one had anything to show to win the contest. The good hunters just returned without having killed anything.

4. The next day they went out again. None of them killed any game. This went on till the fifth day.

5. Then Pheasant said: "Tomorrow I will go along even if I can't kill any game. I'll just go along."

6. Day came and the good hunters went out. The Red-headed Woodpecker said: "You will hear my belt, I'm going out this way. Listen all the time."

7. Pheasant went out the other way. He was listening to the belt of the good hunter. [It sounded like] "*Katsa, katsa, katsa, katsa, katsa.*"

8. Pheasant went out the other way. He came upon game. It was a deer. He shot and killed it. Then he went home to his house. He asked for help. "Whoever is willing will help me. We will bring the game. It is out there dead where I killed it."

9. Some men went out with him and helped him. The big deer was packed out. It was brought downstream. It was brought in to Pheasant's house.

10. The news spread to the men that evening. "Pheasant has felled a big deer. He calls you together to come and visit him this evening. Pheasant has felled a big deer. He calls you to come and visit him this evening." [73]

11. The men came that evening. There was the big deer lying there. Pheasant said: "You will skin it and cut it up. You will spread it out among your relatives. Which of you will skin it and cut it up into small pieces? You will spread it around and eat it."

12. The deer was cut up, and the men gave out the meat. Pheasant said: "Don't give me a very big piece. It's alright if it's small. You take it and eat it." How Pheasant was thanked by the people!

13. Black Eagle came down from the sky. He asked Pheasant how he killed the deer. Pheasant said: "See this blanket! See that blanket! I pull a feather out of it and tie it onto the arrow. Then the arrow goes straight to the place I am shooting at. This blanket is my strength."

14. Black Eagle said: "I also have a blanket. I always stick one onto my arrow, but the arrow always curves."

15. Pheasant said: "See now! The feather from your blanket is very wide. Your arrow drifts and turns around. See mine! It is very good. This arrow always goes straight. That's the way I do it."

16. Black Eagle made a friend of Pheasant. "Alright, you will be my friend. We will always think alike."

17. Pheasant said: "I don't want to say, 'alright now, I'm a great hunter.' I just kill game when I want it."

18. Later all the good hunters wanted to kill Pheasant. They were angry that he should become a big man. He was just poor. Cougar and Wolf did not like Pheasant.

19. Pheasant just thanked these men. "It's alright for you to pity me. I am Just a poor man, I don't want to say I am a big man. Go ahead, go ahead, with what you are doing. It's just that whenever I am hungry, I just kill the game and eat it. That's all." [77]

20. Then Pheasant said: "I will not always be here in this land. The people of the future are coming. Soon the future people will be coming. Children will be coming. They will look for something to give them strength. I will be behind the young man. I will say to him: 'See this that I have made!' That man will become a good hunter by means of this blanket."

21. After everything was changed, all this was learned by young men living there. Pheasant said: "Look at me, child! See how I am made! I kill game for food everywhere."

22. Well, that is why you will not be hungry. You will always eat good meat. You will kill it. The young man will grow up. Truly, that is the reason the young man will grow up to be a good huntsman. [77]

X. The Origin of the Seasons

1. Bear has a younger brother, Rabbit.

2. One day Bear said: "Alright now, we'll gamble. Soon now the cold will come. We'll gamble. Then, if you beat me, it will be the way that you want it. If I beat you, it will be the way that I want it with respect to the way day and night will be. Now then, we'll gamble. And if you're going to beat me, sing your spirit power song." The Bear said: "If I beat you, it will be the way I want it."

3. Then they gambled. The Bear sat at the board and the Rabbit sat at the board. Then they gambled. Then Rabbit sang his power song from the north. He sang it and said: "Clear, clear, the sky. Dry, dry the sky." He called for freezing weather and cold. That is the song of the Babbit. Rabbit wanted it to get cold.

4. Then Bear sings for cloudy weather. Bear says: "Get warm, get warm." He calls for clouds.

5. Then they were gambling. The Bear was beaten by Rabbit. When the Babbit would be outguessed (made to fall) by the Bear, the Bear would jump at the Rabbit until the Bear was being beaten by the Rabbit. Rabbit won. It froze and became cold. It would crackle until it froze. The sky would clear.

6. Bear said: "You beat me. Now it will be the way you want it."

7. Then, for winning. Rabbit got the freezing weather. So now it freezes and gets cold. [79]

XI. The Hole in the Lake

1. The Snuqualmie people have two girl children. The oldest one possessed herself of a husband, a young man from Snuqualmie. Then the youngest one married a young man from Snohomish.

2. He was always here at Snuqualmie living with his in-laws. He was always together with the Snuqualmie man. One day he said: "Alright now, we'll go out to compete with each other for some game." The Snohomish said: "Alright." They asked their wives if they would like to go along. The women said: "We will go along."

3. Then they got themselves ready. They went up the river named the Tolt river. They killed some game, some elk, and broiled it. They had enough meat.

4. Then they started home. They came to the lake named "Salmon Soup." Here they rested. The Snuqualmie man said: "Behold this lake. It could be dangerous." The Snohomish asked: "Why is it dangerous?" Said the Snuqualmie man: "This lake has a hole in it." The Snohomish said: "I don't believe it. It is too small a lake for it to have a hole."

5. Their wives tried to stop their arguing. Then the Snohomish said: "I'm always diving in the salt water (Puget Sound). I can't find a hole in it." Said the Snuqualmie: "I dove, I was there in that hole. And that's the reason that I am telling you this."

6. The Snuqaalmie said: "If you do not believe it, we'll dive. You'll find out." The Snohomish said: "Alright, we dive. I want to know whether there truly is a hole."

7. Then they started to strip off their clothes. Their wives tried, but they would not stop. Then they went down to the lake. The Snuqualmie said: "I will be the first to dive." [81]

8. They went into the water. The Snuqualmie said: "I learned the Otter power. The Otter dives from one lake and comes out in another lake." The Snohomish said: "I learned the loon power. It dives everywhere in the salt water." Thus they dove, singing their power songs.

9. The Snuqualmie dove while the Snohomish waited. Then he also went, he also dove. The Snuqualmie went into the hole, but he did not go very far. He turned around and waited. Then he saw him (the Snohomish) coming. His wings were spread out. The Snuqualjmie was saying; "I'll grab him." The Snohomish came to where the Snuqualmie was waiting. The Snuqualmie grabbed him just at the end of his hair. He had him, but then the Snohomish went on.

10. The Snuqualmie waited for him to come back. Then he gave up. He came up out of the hole and came out of the water. He told the women: "He was going. I grabbed for him. but I didn't get him." They waited for him to come out. He did not come out. They gave up then.

11. They left and went home. They got back to their relatives and told them! "If he comes out, he will come back." But he never came back.

12. He had a father and a mother at Snohomish. They were always travelling by canoe. One day they were going along in a canoe. The tide was coming in in Puget Sound. Well, they travelled along very close to shore, and they came upon a person drifting there on the waves. They stopped and they looked into it.

13. They found out it was their child. His head was broken off. He did not have a head. He was going along with a tattoo of the loon on his chest. That is where they learned: "This is our child." He must have found something dangerous. They sent for this young man [the Snuqualmie] to come so that they could find out about this Snohomish man. They were told; "He dove into the lake, and he did not come out." [83]

XII. Mink Story

1. Mink was living over on that side of the river. Lots of people were living here [on this side]. Well, those children were always swimming.

2. One day Mink was sitting on the side of the river watching the swimming. While Mink was sitting there, many young women were swimming.

3. He was thinking about one particular girl. He wants her. "How can I get her?" [he thought]. He would grab his penis and stretch it. He was always stretching it so it would get longer.

4. One day his penis was long. He was sitting by the river and he tried his penis. He took it and shoved it out upriver and it drifted downstream, It came to the place where the women were swimming. He pushed it and it was just right.

5. Mink waited for them. Then the women came to swim. Mink was sitting there. Then he pushed it out upstream. His penis drifted downstream. It was coming to that woman. He pushed it now, and he got the woman.

6. Most of the other women were swimming. That one woman stood still there. Mink had her. The others would ask her; "Why is it that you just stand still there?" She couldn't tell them. Mink was working on the other side of the river.

7. They were through swimming now, but she couldn't go ashore. The women said: "We'd better go to see what's wrong with her now." The women went and grabbed the girl. They pulled her. She and Mink were copulating. She was being pulled to the other side of the river by her relatives. Mink was swimming in the water now. His penis came out.

8. A long time went by. The young woman became pregnant. She had a baby. Her mother and father said: "From whom has our baby gotten this child?" The people were called together now to see whose baby this child was. [85]

9. Men would come to look at the child. The child would just look away from them.

10. One day Mink went. He said: "Alright now. I'll examine this child." Mink came and stood in front of the child. Immediately the child said: "That is my father," The man [the girl's father] said: "Alright, you take Mink and make him your husband."

11. Then Mink was married. The girl's father was a high class man. He was given a canoe and two slaves by her father.

12. Later Mink and his wife were travelling along by canoe. One day they were travelling on salt water. Mink knew of a place where there were oysters. Mink said: "Stop over here."

13. They stopped travelling. Mink said that he would dive and get some oysters. Then he dove and came up with some oysters. He dove and came up with oysters many times. Then he dove again. Then he didn't come up. He was missing.

14. His wife was looking for him and happened to see her husband. He was eating and gnawing and his anus was extended and was also gnawing. She was ashamed. She told the slaves; "Go ahead, we'll leave him."

15. The slaves paddled the canoe. Mink came up and yelled: "Hey, I'm out now." The woman said: "Go ahead. We'll leave him."

16. They left Mink now. He was far behind. The woman threw her baby away. [Mink] was coming. He was catching up. He happened to see his baby being thrown overboard. He called to his baby: "Swim! Swim, my baby, toward your grandfathers, the snags."

17. Mink's baby swam toward the snags. That is why you can find Mink in the snags. [89]

XIII. The Old Man Becomes Young

1. Get ready! We're moving camp! The members of this tribe were looking at this very old man. He was always a bother to those who were living there. The old man was always sick, was very dirty, had sores on his body, had lice in his hair, and was getting blind.

2. A high class man said: "Well, what shall we do with this old man? He is always crazy and bothersome for the people. Right now I am ashamed of him. We will just leave him. It is alright if this old man dies."

3. Then they left him lying on the beach. Soon Crow came to this old man. Crow said: "Strengthen your mind, high class one, no matter what has been done to you. Sit up. I stole these burning coals and put them underneath a clam shell. Use them to build a big fire. Make a sweat house. Use it every day. Later the high class people will find out about it."

4. The next year the people who had left were coming back. They were still far off. Then they saw smoke. Who could be living here? We only left that old man. He has been dead for a long time.

5. They landed. Then they saw a tall, strong, good looking, young man. They asked him who he was. Then they were surprised to find it was the same person who had been useless. [89]

XIV. Cannibal Woman

1. The Cannibal Woman was walking along looking for some food. Her carrying basket was big. She was looking for children to eat. First she found the hunchbacked child. She grabbed him and put him in her carrying basket. Whenever she would put in another child, the little hunchback would lift himself up on top.

2. Now the Cannibal Woman's carrying basket is full. The hunchback is on top. The Cannibal Woman is returning. She will cook and eat these many children.

3. On arriving home, the Cannibal Woman builds a big fire. She heats some very large rocks which she will use for cooking them. She takes the children out and ties their hands and feet. She also splatters pitch on their eyes. Now the Cannibal Woman dances around and sings.

4. The little hunchback is intelligent and bright. He whispers to the children; "Listen! If the Cannibal Woman dances around in front of us again, grab her legs and pull on her legs hard. It is best if she falls in the fire."

5. That is just what they did. The Cannibal Woman screamed when she burned. The Cannibal Woman's entrails broke open. There were some little birds flying from the entrails of the Cannibal Woman.

6. Understand yourselves, children. Even if your body is ugly and you look ugly, if you have intelligence and are good. Then, even if a Cannibal Woman is big, you can win [91]

XV. The Coming of the Day

1. The coming of day. There were two walking along, the bear and the ant. The bear aJtid the ant began to argue as they were walking along, Bear said: "It will be a year before it is light again." But the ant, he said: "It will be dark and then it will be light." Then the ant won.

2. Now the ant will be eaten by the bear. The bear will sleep during the winter, and, when he wakes, he will walk around. He will walk around looking for bark. He will eat the ants on the bark.

3. In the place where day was, the daylight was inside a basket. Blue-jay went there and took the daylight. He took the daylight, out. He cut the daylight in half. We now have light as the result of Bluejay's work. That is why Blue jay's head is flat now. We now have light as the result of Bluejay's work.

XVI. Raven Gives Back the Tide

1. Raven had the tide. No one had the tide but Raven. He went out in his canoe to do something. Then Raven was coming home. His little son went down to the beach. His little son was seized by the people.

2. Then be wanted to get his little child back. He was told that only if he gave them the tide could he have the little child back. Then he gave them the tide, and the people gave back his little child. [95]

XVII. Transformer Changes Raven

1. The Transformer came to Raven. "Well, what do you want me to make you?" "I want you to make me something big so I could kill big things for food, fresh food." Transformer told him: "I will make you something."

2. Transformer seized some charcoal and put it all over the raven. He made him black. Then Transformer said: "You will only eat old or rotten food." [95]

XIX. Conversation
{Amelia (M), Marie (D), Charles Sneatlum (S) 1954}
Lucy Mullholland (D)

1. Amelia: You people talk now.

2. Marie: Edward has a white woman for a wife.

3. Am: That's the same white wife Edward had before. I wanted to find a way to see Edward about the death of his children. Edward's grandfather on his mother's side was a slave. Edward's father was descended from Chief Seattle. They used to say that we from *sblatx^w* were all slaves.

4. Charles: Maybe the mail is here now.

5. Am: The mail carrier couldn't be late.

6. M: The mail is always late on Monday. Did you get some mail?

7. Am: Only that paper,

8. M: Are you going to the store?

9. Am: I can't go to the store today.

10. M: When can we go to the store?

11. Am: Tomorrow we could go to the store.

12. Ch: I You got a letter from cayax^wtálot.

13. Am: Have you changed your shoes?

14. Ch: Yes, mother, I changed my shoes.

15. M: It's cloudy today.

16. Am: Is seɛstonaλ going with them?

17. M: Yes, she's going along,

18. Am. How many are going?

19. M: Everyone is going.

20. Am: When will they go?

21. M: We're going right now.

22. Am: What kind of drink do you have hidden in the other room?

23. M and Ch: (laughter) We don't have any drinks in the other room. [125]

24. Am: I don't know what to talk about now. You people on the other side of the room talk. x^wadé? might take pity on you and [take you to] the store.

25. M: What should we get?

26. Am: Get some bread.

27. M: Is that all you want?

28. Am: Yes, that's all, I guess. If I want something else, you can get it for me tomorrow.

29. Am: Is the cat inside?

30. M: No, outside.

31. Am: Bring the cat in.

32. M: I want the cat outside. The cat always stays outside.

33. Am: The box is falling. Don't let the box fall.

34. M: I want the box to fall.

35. Am:. It was a good gathering. They gambled by playing the bone game at Swinomish and ate dried salmon.

36. M:. Was it a good day?

37. Am: Yes, it was a good day. They had canoe races. I heard about It, but I didn't watch it. The British Columbia Indians and the Tulalip Indians gambled by playing the bone game. The BC Indians won, and the Tulalips lost. Only yáleced saw everything. We only ate dried salmon, and then we came back. We came home again. [129]

XX. Ethnographic Notes

1. Only high class children, descended from high class people, heard the teachings. From its grandmother and its grandfather the high class child would hear what was taught. The children were small when they were taught these lessons.

2. If you behave this way, you will grow up to be good. Early in the morning when the sun first rises, someone would whisper to the child: "Get up! Jump down to the beach and swim."

3. Your body and mind should always be clean and you will grow up to be high class. Do not lie in bed and cuddle up to keep warm. If you do that, some day it will come about that you will smell yourself. You could become sick.

4. Only those from the high class would grow old. If you will be lazy and stupid, you will not go far. You will be hurt in an accident. You will get some dangerous sickness. You will die. Only those from the lazy lower class will be called to by something dangerous.

5. The old people would cry to the children about these teachings, Do not lie. Lying is from the lower class. Even if you are made poor. are killed, or are whipped, never tell a lie. You will be fast because you are high class. Only slaves will be full of food. Don't call yourself high class. Others will point you out if you are high class. [130]

Amelia

I, Amelia Sneatlum, was born at a hop yard in Auburn on 28 September sixty seven years ago (in 1954, thus 1887). There was no hospital, and my mother starting picking hops again three days later. My father picked two or three boxes of hops a day for 75 cents a box. Food was cheap then. After picking hops, my parents went home to Port Blakely.

I married a man from Neah Bay, a Makah, but he died and I moved back to my father's house in Suquamish for two years. Then I married Sneatlum and moved to Tulalip. My mother had taught how to be good at home, and my relatives told me how to be good far off. If anyone came, I was to feed him or her. I should not fight anyone, though they be disliked. I should stay away from them instead of getting strong feelings against them. I was to be good to everyone.

My materal grandfather, *sɬbx̌ʷaltxʷ*, and grandmother, *wayatálot*, lived there until they died from poison. A daughter-in-law of *sɬbx̌ʷaltxʷ* died of suspected poison and they were killed in revenge and buried at Port Blakley. An Indian doctor was well paid to sing his power song. Now there are no more shamans, but they used to cure the sick. If a patient died, they [shamans] were killed. Any suspicious deaths possibly blamed on them also got them killed.

I watched my mother's father being carried out when he died. I did not see my grandmother die. I asked what they were carrying, and they said my grandfather had died. He was buried, but then youngsters were forbidden to see the dead because they might take us away with them. Today, everyone goes to a funeral, even the very young. In the past, the dead could not be taken out through a door. Instead, they went out through a window so no one would follow them. Today, the dead are removed through the door, though this is asking for trouble.

At Port Blakely, my brother Henry and I walked on the beach. He hunted and killed squirrels to take home. I don't recall eating them, but we took some home every day. Once, when I was young there, my brother and I were on the beach and he shot a squirrel but it did not die. We ran out of shot, but still it struggled. Finally we sang for it "Stop crying little sister," and it died. Then my brother himself died of typhoid fever, and I became the oldest. Only girls were left. I could no longer go walking. I helped my mother work, and I took care of the youngest.

My mother and I dug clams on the beach. We gathered berries. She would dry blackberries to be put in a sack. Four sacks were enough to last a winter. Huckleberries were picked, boiled, and put into a barrel. One was enough for a winter. Dog salmon, herring, and smelt were dried, along with clams and ducks. Back then there was a lot of food, but not now. That is why there are fewer people living. We never worried about food and clothing. Now we have to make do with dubious *pastəd* [whitemen's] food.

When I got to be the oldest child, I went out at night with my father to spear skate and flounder. A burning pitch torch was carried on the canoe. We ate many bottom fish, and gave many to others. Below, only the eye of the flounder could be seen, but it was speared and dropped into the canoe. I paddled, but I got sleepy and the canoe would shift. My father got angry and I woke up, but it was dark then and I was tired.

My father hunted deer, and I went along. He sold them in Seattle for ten cents a pound for venison. He used the money to buy flour, sugar, and molasses to take home to Suquamish. He hunted porpoises in Puget Sound, and we would play with the tiny ones. He hunted land otters to sell the fur. He also sold bear hides to get bread, sugar, and molasses.

Long ago, slaves speared flounders and gave them away. They gathered firewood for someone else (non-slave tainted) to cook these fish that everyone would eat.

Once all of us children went picking huckleberries with my mother. On the way home, we saw some salal berries so mother and I went ashore to pick them. Everyone else was in the canoe until my brother got out and the canoe drifted away. He started to cry, so we went back. My mother swam out to get the canoe and paddle it back to get us. We had lots of berries, but my father got angry because of this carelessness.

Once we were camping and selling clams in Seattle. My father went out at night and some Yakamas cut him on his side. He struggled home and collapsed into our canoe. In the morning, what looked like water inside turned out to be his blood. He had passed out. People were called. They grabbed him by the hair, shook him, and poured water over his head. But he kept passing out, and they kept shaking him awake. He was taken home, but he was feeble for a year until he got well. His name was *sbláatx*^w.

As a boy, my father was trained by his step-father. He had to bathe in Puget Sound each morning. Water-soaked cattails mixed with sand were rubbed over his body to make him strong. Every morning he bathed. That gave him the strength to survive his attack. After a year, he arose and was strong. Then he could paddle racing canoes, play baseball, run, and wrestle. His older brother would not discipline himself. He always fought their mother about bathing at dawn, and that uncle died a long time before my father.

Similarly, if my younger sister were awakened by our mother at night to go clamming, she would only cry. I went instead whenever my mother asked. That sister died a long time ago, and now only I am still alive. My mother always told me not to give up easily. I should live a long time in the world and be ready to do everything.

My father's mother *labex^wyod* lived at Port Washington and we went there. I went to school in Chico for about a year. Then we moved to Suquamish and I went to school seven miles away while I learned three books [grades].

When I was six, I went to Cushman school in Tacoma for three months. A male cousin was there to help me. I learned the ABCs, then my father took me home. I went back to Cushman when I was 14 years old. I had to wear shoes, but they made my feet hot, very hot. I learned about letters. I wrote my letters.

At Cushman I found that man, George Bob. We walked with him in a circle for exercise. Afterwards, other girls would tease me about him and I would cry. Letters came to me from home, but I did not know how to read. I carried around two from a man at home until they got lost.

Long ago, parents got a wife for their son. They gave money and gifts to her family. My father's parents gave $30 to those of my mother. No one told him about his own impending marriage. Later, he wanted another wife, but my mother objected because she was lower class.

My father came back from hunting, and this woman was there. My father said nothing. He had never seen her before. They lived together until my mother died and then he went on alone until he too died. My mother's brother used the money from my father's parents to arrange his own marriage. These arrangements were good long ago. Today, couples separate and a woman cannot be carefully chosen. She might even be low class and still marry well.

A man spoke to my father, who approved of our being married. I knew nothing. I never saw him previously. I was just told by my parents I was to be married. I cried for three days. My parents tried to instruct me, but I would cry again. They still talked and then I approved. We were married in town and stayed together until he died. That man was older, but I was only 18. He did not believe in religion, but my parents put on a feast of ducks and a cow. Many people came together and they sang for one day.

My husband went back to Neah Bay for a year, while I lived with my parents. Then I went to live with him, but I could not understand Makah speech. Only my male cousin there could translate for me. After twelve years, my husband died and I moved back to my father at Suquamish.

When my Neah Bay husband died, we had a boy and three girls. We went home to my father, and we lived by digging clams. After two years, I got another husband at Tulalip and I have lived there ever since.

At Neah Bay, I made baskets but they never sold. Today, white people will pay a lot of money for baskets. Makah used to kill whales from canoes. Sometimes, it took a week to haul it to shore. The whale was cut up and pieces sold for a dollar a foot. Enough was dried for one winter. Cooked with halibut, that was good food.

Andy Johnson was the last man to kill a whale. A month after the last whale was harpooned, he died. He fell and broke his leg. He would not go to a MD because he was afraid the leg would be cut off. He wanted to die with his own leg still on. Well, he did die, and only his son Sam Johnson survives.

My Tulalip husband was George Sneatlum, the grandson of Sneatlum from Sneatlum Point on Whidby Island. He had a lot of money. He would buy a car and hire someone to drive it, paying $10-20. He gave each of his relatives $25. Soon, the money was used up. He could not spend freely, then he died.

George Sneatlum had asked my father and my aunt to marry me. My aunt approved, but not my father. My mother was sick. She got chilled and sick while digging clams at night. She was in bed many months and died in 1913. My father died in 1950. I was left with my three children, Marie, Charles, and Lucy.

A whiteman once came to the home of Sneatlum and gave people black molasses and hardtack. Children played with the hard bread, and some people caulked their canoes with the molasses, but it would melt out in the sun. No one knew these were food.

Some Yakamas gave them a horse, and they tied it up inside their house. It got no food or water. It was just tied up there until it died near the fire.

My son George worked on the road for $48 a month. That was enough for food. One month George only got $20, then he was out of work. We only had that $20 for food so he went out by canoe to look for ducks, but he returned sick. In three months, he died. A year later, Freeman died. Then my family was only three, and Charles was 6 years old.

Once, Lucy and George were sick so we called a MD. He said Lucy was not sick. But we knew she was so people gathered with a drum and my father sang Crane power until Lucy got up and cried. Then they sang for George and both got well.

Another time Lucy was sick in Seattle. A MD was called and stuck her in the arm, but she did not improve so she was brought to this house at night and sung to by George, Wilson, and Albert until she got well. Her body shook. Then she went back to Seattle. People suspected that the Rainbow power of her father was making Lucy sick. Once he was lost in a fog in a canoe and the Rainbow spoke to him after he fell asleep. Then he found his way to safety.

Powers ran in families. Say and his stepfather were eating at the same table, but when Say passed him food, he became very angry because he could have gotten it by himself. Say called him stubborn for refusing help and predicted that they would die within a short time of each other if Say died first since there would be no one to care for the old man. Three months after Say disappeared, the old man also died.

Whenever a native doctor got angry at someone, he pointed and predicted a quick death. Even children who pointed at someone when they were angry could cause a death. The strict rule was that no one was ever to point at anyone. Another rule was that pregnant girl was told to be quick so her baby would not delay. Any child that fell should be caught before he or she reached the ground to prevent harm.

When many people lived in the same house, children could sleep with their parents or in other crowded places. They were never safe alone. Women cooked at the fire, baking bread and potatoes in hot sand and ducks and deer on roasting sticks. Then everyone ate.

The chief at Coupeville was *daxʷsdéƛab* and he had 12 wives who cooked clams, mussels, ducks, and deer. They went out for fresh water whenever he wanted to wash his hands, and then went out for something to wipe his hands with. They were all good women who did not argue. They were an ideal family.

My sister-in-law was poisoned and died. A policeman came for me and I went to her. Her husband told me to look for some clothes to put on her. Then I washed and dressed her. I finished just before I got sick. Her son-in-law brought me home, and I vomited all day and night because her corpse was poisoned and I touched it. I was very sick for two days and nearly died. The poisoner was said to be her own son-in-law. Her blind husband also died and that son-in-law inherited everything, including money. That was the whiteman's way of inheriting and it served the murderer well.

My aunt was married to an old shaman. She did not like the old man, and finally walked out on him. Her father chased her and whipped her with a gun. My aunt fell down, but when she could stand and walk, she left that old man forever. She went back to her father until she married John Hote and moved to Puyallup. He was blind. They had a cow and a horse. When they wanted to go to town, they milked the cow and he put a harness on the horse. In town, they sold apples, plums, and pears for 1 ¢ent a pound. They used the money to buy bread and sugar to take home.

They picked apples and John peeled them to dry. They did the same with plums. They also boiled plums and pears to put in jars to bury in the ground to last the winter. They made enough butter for the winter too. They had many sheep to shear for wool. My aunt then carded and knitted it into stockings to sell for money to buy cloth to make into many quilts.

John became "sick to sing" in the winter, and my aunt gave away these quilts, blankets, and money to those who helped him by singing and drumming. They gave away dried apples, plums, and butter. None of their children lived.

When John Hote died, my aunt came here to live until her own end. My aunt had saved $400 for her own coffin and funeral. She gave it to a man to use when that time came. But that man died. Nothing in writing showed it was my aunt's money so she lost it. She cried every day until she got sick and died without any money.

They had many chickens, but a skunk got after them at night. John dug around the outside of the fence and put a wide board against the side of the deep hole. That kept the skunk out. John Hote had fooled him.

Once John was washing his face by the door as my aunt walked out. He spilled that water over her. He was blind, but my aunt got angry at him. John assured her that he did not know she was there.

My aunt used her canoe to ferry people across the river. Once he heard her go across and back, but she was away a long time. When she got home and said she had just arrived, John whipped her with his cane, shouting "You landed a long time ago. Where were you?" My aunt left him over that. His relatives came to scold him, saying not to get mad or he would really be left alone and needy. From then on, he was good.

Annie Coates gave the last Puyallup potlatch. John Hote {Xot} called out the names of those who were given money. Suquamish and people from all over were there. A man from Neah Bay danced and gave away his work – bracelets, rings, earrings, and breast pins. Annie gave away many dollars to people whom John Hote would call by name. They were also given blankets, quilts, and water-tight baskets. People were well fed on beef, ducks, clams, salmon, and huckleberries. Everyone stayed together for two days and two nights. Annie was [then] poor. She had no money and few clothes, but still she wanted to give away to everyone to show her own worth.

The very high class would host a potlatch. He called everyone from all over, sang his power song, and gave away dollars, guns, canoes, and slaves. That *tosyálʔ'yalx^w*, son of *dax^wsdeƛ̓ab*, had *heyida?* = Wealth and Cloud powers: She was a woman with long hair coming from the east on a cloud. The father of Marie and Charles told me to tell them about that strong power so they could get and sing it when they were older. I know the song. Charles used to sing Wealth power in public, but now he only sings alone.

Chief Seattle had Thunderbird power, carved in the image of a duck rattle. It was the greatest power. When he got angry at anyone, he shouted at them and they would shake.

Chief Seattle warned at the Mukilteo treaty that we must watch and study these new transformer white people, and be good to them for our own safety.

[1968: 96-123]

Grammar Preface, Acknowledgments, Contents[2]

Warren Snyder was first introduced to this language in the winter of 1952 by John Adams of Poulsbo, Julie Jacobs of Indianola, and Ellen George of Little Boston. All were Suquamish living on the Kitsap peninsula. At that time the Suquamish tribe was sponsoring and supporting financially the author's research in relation to their claims case against the Federal government. In the summer of 1952 further research was sponsored by the Suquamish tribe for purposes of supporting their land claims against the Federal government. During both of these periods linguistic work was incidental to ethnographic research.

During the summer of 1953 intensive work on the language was begun. The field work was made possible by a grant from the Department of Anthropology at the University of Washington. The principal informant was Lucy Mullholland of Suquamish.

In the summer of 1954 linguistic work was continued with the mother of Mrs. Mullholland, Amelia Sneatlum, at Tulalip. Work was supported by a grant secured by Dr. Melville Jacobs from the University of Washington's Agnes Anderson fund. Up to that time only Suquamish informants had participated in the work.

In the summer of 1955 another grant from the Agnes Anderson fund made possible further research. The principal informants were a Snuqualmie, Jerry Kanim of Carnation, a Duwamish, Mary Charles of Muckleshoot, and a Suquamish, William Kitsap of Marysville. This was the last period of field research.

A phonological and morphological analysis of the language was submitted to the Anthropology department of the University of Washington in partial fulfillment of requirements for the Ph.D. in the spring of 1957. Supervision and assistance in this work came from Dr. Melville Jacobs, Dr. William W. Elmendorf, and Dr. Fang Kuei Li.

Two preliminary analyses of this language were made, one by Jay Ellis Ransom, 1945, and the other by Colin Ellidge Tweddell, 1950. The author found these works to be very valuable as bases from which to carry the analysis further and as bases for eliciting utterances in the early phases of the analysis.

I wish to thank all those mentioned above for the parts they have played in furthering this analysis.

Intermittently between 1958 and 1963 the author found time to translate previouslly collected texts provided primarily by Amelia Sneatlum and Jerry Kanim. Texts from the latter informant were recorded on tape. This allowed for some expansion and revision of the earlier analysis. [IV]

A letter to the author from Dr. Wayne Suttles in 1962 suggested a change in the interpretation of possessive pronominal affixes which allowed the author to remove constructions, now identified as the noun complex, from the class of verbs. This greatly simplified the analysis of the verb complex and led to a number of advances in morphological analysis (see under section 4.4.). I thank Dr. Suttles for his fruitful suggestions.

---

[2] Warren Snyder 1968 *Southern Puget Sound Salish 1: Phonology and Morphology, Sacramento Anthropological Society, Paper #8*. 83pp.

In the summer of 1967 the author read a paper given by Dr. Thomas M. Hess at the Second International Conference on Salish Languages. His suggested interpretation of the pronominal object suffixes in Snohomish applied equally well in the dialect analyzed here and resolved some formerly perplexing problems with which the author had struggled for several years (see under section 3.3.7.).

The author had hoped to return to the field to check old solutions, fill In gaps in the data, and follow new leads suggested during translation of texts. This has not been possible. The decision was made to publish the analysis at its present level of development with the hope that it will prove useful to others for whom informants are more accessible.

I thank the Sacramento State College Foundation for providing the Anthropology department at Sacramento State College with the linguistic typewriter by means of which I have typed this publication.

Finally, I thank the members of the Sacramento Anthropological Society, in particular the president, Donald G. Wood, for their efforts and support in publishing this analysis in their monograph series.

Warren A. Snyder
Sacramento State College
April, 1968 [v]

TABLE OF CONTENTS

Snyder, Warren
    1956 Archeological Sampling at "Old Man House" on Puget Sound. *Research Studies of the State College of Washington* #24 (1). Pullman, Washington.
  1968 *Southern Puget Sound Salish 1: Phonology and Morphology.* Sacramento Anthropological Society, Paper #8. 83pp.
  1968 *Southern Puget Sound Salish 2: Texts, Place Names, and Dictionary.* Sacramento Anthropological Society, Paper #9. 199pp.

{Snyder's Dictionary, with extracted appendices of
Botany, Geography, Mythics, Zoology, Loanwords
will be folded into
Ben Barrett's LUTWIK, an interactive Puget Salish file}

Salish-English ~ English-Salish ~ Dictionary

TABLE OF CONTENTS

Preface

This document was created from the dictionary portions of Snyder's publication by OCR processing and then editing with the purpose of recreating the typed document as close as possible to the original.

The following changes were made for clarity:
1. An equal sign was added between each headword and gloss, and between each sample sentence and gloss.
2. When two or more Lushootseed words were presented as alternatives separated by the word "or" in the original, the word "or" was replaced with a tilde.
    - swátyotd or sswátyotd → swátyotd ~ sswátyotd
3. When a definition was corrected or clarified, braces and the letters "ED" were added.
    - pyax̌é = plant used for food (looks like macaroni when cooked). {*rock rose, bitterroot*}
4. Accent marks above a consonant followed by a vowel were placed above the vowel.
    - stábawa sʔáɫd té?
    - syécb = news || yécb, to tell
5. Accent marks following a raised w were moved before the w.
    - gʷˊč → gˊʷč
6. On rare occasions, a spelling error or punctuation irregularity was corrected without note.
    - to bein front of someone or something → to be in front of someone or something
    - divide up, to; = cálq → divide up, to = cálq
7. Double pipes || were used to separate etymologies and comments from the main definition.
    - bˊċos = puss face || -os is a suffix meaning "face."
    - sƛeƛálqb = birds || Literally, "little animals."
8. For double quotation marks, straight quotes were used. For apostrophes, the curly version was used.

The Salish orthography used in the dictionaries comprises the following symbols plus an accent:

a, b, c, ċ, č, č̌, d, e, g, gʷ, h, k, k̇, kʷ, k̇ʷ, l, ɫ, m, o, p, ṗ, q, q̇, qʷ, q̇ʷ, s, š, t, ṫ, w, x̣, xʷ, x̣ʷ, y, ʒ, ǯ, ƛ̇, ʔ

This closely follows the general system used today, with the notable absence of a schwa (ə) letter and the following general correspondences:

Snyder	Hess & Hilbert
e	i
o	u
ʒ	dᶻ
ǯ	ǰ

It should be noted that the word "sápa" (grandfather= scapa) originally appeared on the "C" page but was moved to the "S" page.

~ A ~

á = to be somewhere
    áel = being here
    toáo = Was it there?
    tobaáaxʷdł halgʷa = Evidentally they were there again then.
áa = to put there
    gʷla oáatbaxʷ teeł x̣páy = Well, someone put the cedar sticks there.
áb = to give
    oábšed čed = I gave it to him.
ábaʔk = to bring || -aʔk may be an unidentified suffix while áb may be the root meaning "to give."
    tolaábaʔkd txʷal teeł stóbš = Someone was bringing it to the man.
abél = either...or; if
    abél déša te cwyóʔso čeł goébaš = If my children were here we could go (travel) somewhere.
    abel sáleʔ abel łéxʷ ṫalċ = either two or three salmon
ác = be there
    é ácac = Yes, it's there.
    gʷla ácac teeł daxʷoólax̣ads = Well, that is their food gathering place.
áca = I
    áca kʷe gʷšábad = I can dry it.
ácełtalbexʷ = people
ácgʷeł = middle
ádad = being
    łohóyel asésta akʷe cgʷá dx̣´č txʷal ádad teeł sl´x̣el yoxʷ teeł słáx̣el = It will be the way I want it with respect to the way day and night will be.
ágak = to groan
    oágak čed = I'm groaning.
ágʷ = under; underneath
    alágʷab ateeł x̣páyʔ = underneath that cedar tree
ál = to come to; to live at; to live
    toálelaxʷ čed alteeł = I lived there then.
    álʔal = home
    toálel = Someone was coming.
álaxʷ || ál is probably the directional prefix /al-/ being used here as a root. -axʷ is the suffix indicating momentaneous aspect.
    álaxʷ lák słáx̣el = On the last night.
aléʔs = even if
álk̓ʷ = the back of something
    alk̓ʷábac ate álʔal = the back of the house
    dálk̓ʷbed = behind me (my back to it)
álš = "siblings, cousins and persons of own generation and of opposite sex" (Smith 1940)

álʔal = house
áɫ = to be quick; to be fast
    dáyaxdɫ čeɫ laáɫ = We must be going fast.
aótx̣s = canoe || The word for this large canoe is probably a loan word from a northern language. See
    Haeberlin and Gunther, 1930, p. 34.
áɬx̣ad = north
ápls = apples (Eng. loan word)
askawéč = hunchbacked person
askékaweč = little hunchbacked person
ásxʷ = a seal
áš = to shove || It is probably á, to be there and -š, transitive, positional, intentive.
    tok´ʷdd gʷla toáš q̓éyoxʷ = He took it and shoved it upriver.
átbd = to die
    oátbd algʷa = They died.
    sátbd = death
áy = to know
    asáytxʷ čed asx̣ed teeɫ ƛ̓oshóyods = I know how he does it (his doing it).
ayayáš = to be dumb or stupid
áyxʷ = to want to; to have reason to
    gʷáyxʷ gʷáabs = Someone might have reason to want to go along.
áyʔ = to change things; to trade; to find
    tolaáyʔgʷasdaxʷ = Someone was changing things then.
    oáyʔtxʷ čed = I traded for it (have it traded) (or) I found it.
    oáyʔdob ate cé = She happened to be found by him.
áȝaq̓a = to turn around
    áȝaq̓acot = Turn around!
aȝaȝálos = fine in character; industrious
aƛ̓á = to give; to pass something to someone
    aƛ̓áčeb teeɫ k̓ʷás = Please pass the dried salmon.
aʔós = egg

~ B ~

báa = to widen
    obáatb teeɫ šágʷɫ = The road was widened.
bád = to be blind
    asbádel téʔeɫ = He is blind.
bád = father
bágʷ = to accuse; to blame
    obágʷad čed = I accuse (or blame) someone.
bákʷɫ = hurt accidentally
    asbákʷɫ čed = I'm hurt accidentally.
    obákʷldob čed atéʔ = I was hurt accidentally by him.
bálkʷ = to go back; to turn back
    ɫbabálkʷ = Someone would go back with someone again.

báloced = levirate relationship "all blood relatives of dead spouse; reciprocal" (Smith 1940)
    obálocedb = A man took his levirate relative as a wife.
báloq = to mix
    ƛ̓obáloqotb ateeł sgʷésdalb = It would be mixed with sand.
balyé = white man's or "legal" marriage
    tobalyéaxʷ čed = I got married.
báł = to doctor; a shaman's treatment of a sick patient.
    obáłatb ateeł txʷdáʔab = Someone is being doctored by the shaman.
báp = to bother
    ƛ̓obápad = Someone would bother someone.
báqoʔ = snow || This is probably bá-, repetitive aspect and qoʔ, water. Literally it would mean, "again water."
    obáqoʔb = It was snowing.
básčd = louse
báta = butter (Eng. loan word)
báyac = meat; flesh; skin; body
báysx̌b = a girl just entering womanhood
bážos = shag (a type of bird) {cormorant}
b´c = to pay
    ob´cd čed = I paid it.
b´c̓c̓ = snake
b´c̓os = puss face || -os is a suffix meaning "face."
b´č = to fall; to lie; to put down; to go down
    asb´čtxʷ = It's lying there.
    lab´čaxʷ teeł łokʷáł = The sun is setting.
    tasb´čaxʷ alpéed = Someone was lying in bed.
    ob´čš čed = I put it down.
bčágʷ = to lie down || bč, down; -agʷ, body or self
    tosbčágʷelsaxʷ = His lying down then.
bčálekʷ = to bet; to lay out; to put things down || bč, to put down; -álekʷ, collective object
    občálekʷ čed = I bet.
b´da = baby; small child
bdáʔ = to give birth; to lay an egg
    tobdáʔabaxʷ = Someone gave birth then.
b´dč = to tell a lie
    čexʷ txʷasb´dčaxʷ = You are a liar.
belál = kneel
    obelálab čed = I'm kneeling down.
bés = to choose
    obésed čeł = We chose it.
bét – ten cents (Eng. loan word, bit)
bét̓ = salmon soup
béƛ̓ = to chop up; to smash
    obéƛ̓ed čed = I'm chopping it up.
    obéƛ̓elšad čed = I smashed my leg.

bé? = to fall
    sbé? = Something that is falling
b´k̓ʷ = all; every
    tob´k̓ʷelaxʷ = It's all gone.
    b´k̓ʷ stáb = everything
    gʷla tob´k̓ʷelaxʷ teeɫ šodgʷáls = Someone ran out of shot.
bláḷegʷd = navel
blás = molasses (Eng. loan word)
b´lč = to answer
    ob´lčtb čexʷo ateeɫ acwéleqʷ = Was your question answered?
b´lxʷ = to pass by something
    ƛ̓olab´laxʷd ceeɫ sk̓ʷátad = Someone would be passing by that mouse.
b´ɫ = to drop; to let go of
    ob´ɫdxʷ = Someone dropped it accidentally.
    tob´ɫdaxʷ = Someone let it go.
b´ɫ = to be full of food
    asb´ɫaxʷ čed = I'm full of food.
bós = four
b´qsd = nose
b´q̓ = to swallow
    ob´q̓d čed = I swallowed it.
bq̓á?a = Neah Bay
b´qʷ = to be fat in the stomach
    lab´qʷelaxʷ = Someone is getting a fat stomach now.
b´š = to be lousy
    asb´šačad čed = I have lice on my head.
b´t̓k̓ʷ = to mix; to stir
    ob´t̓k̓ʷd čeɫ = We stirred it.
b´ƛ̓ = to feel of something
    ob´ƛ̓daxʷ = Someone felt of it.

~ C ~

cábadxʷ = two years
cádeɫ = she
cágʷeč = a tuber
cáksed = to stand || -sed or -ed may represent unidentified morphemes.
    ƛ̓ocáksedbaxʷ = Someone would be standing then
cák̓ = to spear; to stick something into something
    ocák̓ače čed = I have a sliver in my hand.
    ocák̓ad = Someone stabbed it.
cálq = to divide up
    ocálqd čed = I divided it up.
    ɫocálqd čeɫ te sq̓ʷláɫad = We're going to divide up the berries.
caɫdálb = to breathe
cáɫdɫ = breath

cáwał = to be hungry
    x̣áƛ̓txʷ čed gʷáteʔ čed łascáwał = I want it because I'm hungry.
cbáb = twice
cécal = feather
céck̓ʷ = surely; truly || The diminutive of c´k̓ʷ, straight or right.
cécq̓ʷ = old people
céleč = to be lazy
céq̓ = to poke (as a fire)
    océq̓ed čed = I poked it.
céʔ = she; her; this (feminine) || when this introduces a noun it usually occurs as /ce/.
céʔeł = that feminine person over there || When this introduces a phrase it usually occurs as /ceeł/.
c´k̓ʷ = straight; right
clác = five
cód = to say it; to tell it || có, an allomorph of cót; -d, transitive, direct, intentive.
    ocód čed = I said it.
code déʔe = here, over there
cóqʷa = my younger brother or sister "siblings, cousins and persons of own generation, of either sex,
    younger than speaker" (Smith 1940) || {d-}, my, plus sóqʷa becomes cóqʷa.
cót = to say; to think
    ocót teeł stóbš = That man (said) (thought)...
c´tx̣ = water falling over a bank
    oc´tx̣b = The water is spouting over the bank and falling.
cʔéloced = side of the road or door

~ c̓ ~

c̓ábed = an onion-like root
c̓ábt = a berry of the kinnikinnik bush
c̓ábtac = kinnikinnik bush
c̓áco = bow
c̓ákʷ = to wash
    oc̓ákʷc̓akʷ čed = I washed the clothes.
    oc̓ágʷačeb čed = I washed my hands.
c̓álbeȝ = reflection
c̓áło = to lie in wait for
    oasc̓áłob = Someone was lying in wait.
c̓ax̣ʷlós = clay
c̓báčac = a bush, the leaves of which were used to make a "tea."
c̓béq̓ = to scratch
    c̓béq̓ed = Scratch it!
c̓b´lked = mink

ċéċab = blanket
ċéq̓ʷ = to break
    asċéq̓ʷel té?eł = That is
c̓l = to beat in a contest
    tébecot oc̓ltb čeł = Try harder, we're being beaten.
    oc̓lálekʷ čed = I win.
ċód = to fail in health; to get weak
    asċódaxʷ čed = I'm failing (getting weak).
ċók = to suck
    oċókod čed = I sucked it.
ċóks = seven
ċoléq̓ʷ = to pinch; to squeeze a person with the hand
    oċoléq̓ʷed čed = I pinched someone.
    oċoléq̓ʷecot = Someone pinched himself.
ċólsxʷaya = bull frog
ċóqʷab = body
ċq̓´ʷt = butter clam
c̓´s = to drive into wood (a wedge)
    daxʷoc̓´sbs = His place of driving it into wood.
ċyátko = wild men said to wander in the woods and be dangerous (Smith 1940)
ċyék̓ = to wink
    oċyék̓alosbetb čed = Someone winked his eye at me.

~ č ~

čábaš = unmarried sisters of a man's living wife and the reciprocal; unmarried brothers of a woman's
    living husband and the reciprocal
čábeqʷ = "great grandparents; their siblings and cousins; reciprocal" (Smith 1940)
čád = to lean
    asčád = It's leaning.
čád = where?
    točádaxʷ čexʷ = Where were you?
čágʷaš = wife
čagʷáš = to be married
    teeł čagʷášbetagʷl dáčo teeł péeds halgʷa = Those who are married to each other have one bed.
čákʷ = to go to the beach; to come to
    tol čákʷ teeł laébaš = Someone is walking from the beach.
    točágʷaxʷ = Someone came to it (or beached).
čál = to catch up with; to chase; to reach
    očáldobaxʷ aceeł sk̓óy teeł q̓élbed = The canoe was caught up with by my mother.
    očálad čed = I chased him.
    točalálekʷo = Does it reach?
čáleš = hand (see čál above)

čáȝ = to hide
    očáȝel čed = I'm hiding.
čbólč = carrying basket (carried on the back and supported by a line across the forehead).
čéf = chief (Eng. loan word)
čék̓ʷ = to be stuck
    asčék̓ʷ = It's stuck.
čél = to bring home; to bring back
    ƛ̓osčélds halgʷa = their bringing it back
čéɫ = to build
    očéɫ čed ál?al = I'm building a house.
čéx̣ = to scream
    očéx̣ecot = Someone screamed.
čgóced = sand spit
čóba = to go ashore
    háy točóbaaxʷ teeɫ sbyáw = Then Coyote went ashore.
čókʷ = to peel
    očókod čed teeɫ ápls = I peeled the apples.
čóqbed = shavings (wood)
čóšad = star
čwál = to give up; to surrender
    točwálegʷdaxʷ = Then he gave up.
č'x̣ = to split; to divide; to crack
    oč'x̣gʷasd = Someone split it in half (divided it).
    čx̣gʷás = half-breed
    očx̣ák̓ʷčop čed = I'm splitting wood.
    očečx̣ák̓ʷčop = Someone is splitting kindling.
    ƛ̓ok̓étbaxʷ teeɫ q̓élbed ƛ̓asč'x̣ = It would be stuck on the split (cracked) canoe.
čyál = to hide something
    stáb kʷe sasčyálqo? lab alkʷe dyáde = What kind of drink do you have hidden in the other room?
č'ȝ = to sneak up on
    toč'ȝdaxʷ = Someone sneaked up on someone.

~ č̓ ~

č̓áč̓aš = child; a young person up to 'teens.
č̓ágʷatxʷ = one year
č̓áš = to spread all over
    pótaxʷ asč̓áš teeɫ acácos = It's spread all over your face.
č̓ásay = clam shell
č̓áxʷ = to club; to whip with a stick
    oč̓áxʷad čed = I whipped (clubbed) him
č̓á? = to dig
    oč̓á?ab akʷe spé?koc = He's digging potatoes.

131

čáʔa = to play; to make fun of
    očáʔa čed = I'm playing.
    očáʔabetb = Someone was made fun of.
čáʔo = smelt
čbáʔ = to pack; to carry
    tolasčbáʔad = Someone was packing (carrying) it.
čé = to have sores
    asčéabac = Someone has sores on the body.
čéb = to ask
    gʷla točéb kʷáxʷad = Well, someone asked for help.
čéq̓ʷ = to be dirty
    asčéq̓ʷel = It's dirty.
čéšay = spear
čét = to approach; to bring near
    čétaxʷdł čeł = We must almost be there.
    čéted teeł adčáleš = Give me your hands.
    tolačéčtel = Someone was drawing near (diminutive form).
čét̓ = to gnaw
    očét̓etb ateeł sk̓ʷátad = It was gnawed by the mouse.
čéx̣ = to fry
    očéx̣alekʷ čed = I'm frying things.
čéƛa = stone; rock
č̓′lp = to twist
    oč̓′lpd čed = I twisted it.
    asč̓′lp = It's twisted.
č̓′ł = to break
    asč̓′łgʷas = It's broken in the middle.
č̓ółac = maple tree
č̓′q̓ʷ = to be rotten; to be sore
    asč̓′q̓ʷel = It's rotten (sore).
č̓oyólč = a dish
č̓′x̣ = to crowd together
    ƛasč̓′x̣ed ateeł dáčo álʔal = They would be crowded together in one house.

~ D ~

dadáwšed = bone marrow
dáčo = one
dáčo sbqʷáče = one hundred
dádato = tomorrow
daxʷc̓axʷlósb = Port Blakely
dáy = later; shortly; just now
    dáyaxʷ čeł łopádad = Later we'll bury it.
dáyay = only; alone
    dáyayaxʷ teeł sax̣álos teeł asšáb = Only the cedar snag was dry.

132

dáʔ = to name
    gʷat kʷe asdáʔ = What is your name?
    sdáʔ = a name
dáʔxʷ = just now
    dáʔxʷ čed od´kʷš = I just put it in.
deábac = around
    toóx̣ʷaxʷ txʷal deábac ateeł x̣páyʔ = He went around the cedar tree.
débał = young
    te débał wyóʔso = These young children.
débł = we
dečákʷbexʷ = tribe (another tribe)
dečaxʷ = once
dédeʔ = that over there
dédeʔł = still; yet
    dédeʔł askó = still together.
déł = that's why; that is; there is
déłeł = the same; still; yet
    totágʷebaxʷ ateeł dqáse ceeł sláday tol alte déłeł tála = The woman was bought by my uncle from
    that same money.
déša = to be here
    todéša halgʷa = They have been here.
    déšaoʔxʷ čexʷo = Are you still here?
déw = inside
    asłédobaxʷ ácac asdéw = It happened to be tied up there inside.
déʔeł = that (referred to earlier)
    déʔeł teeł sb´das halgʷa = That was this child of theirs.
déʔł = whenever
d´gʷé = you (singular)
d´kʷ = to be in
    asd´kʷ = It's in.
dókʷ = to be angry with; to dislike
    asdókʷtobš = Someone is angry with me.
    ƛ̓asdókʷtxʷ čed teeł gʷcyáyos = I don't like working.
dókʷ = to be dangerous
    asdókʷ = It's dangerous.
dókʷebł = Transformer
dóqʷ = to be sick; to be weak
    asdóqʷ = Someone is sick or weak.
d´qʷ = to be rotten; to be spoiled
    lad´qʷaxʷ teeł łálc̓ = The salmon is spoiling.
    asd´qʷ = It's rotten.
dyáde = a room
dyóced = across; on the other side
    gʷla ƛ̓ogʷéadaxʷ teeł gʷát dyóced ateeł stólakʷ = She would be calling that person on the other side
    of the river.

~ E ~

é = yes
ébac = grandchild
ébaš = to travel; to walk
    ƛ̓oébaš teeł sbyáw = Coyote would be traveling (walking).
éd = to say
    oédegʷas čexʷ = You said something.
ées = to be in place; to stay
    toéestbaxʷ = It was in place.
éhal = to smell
    háʔł teeł soéhals = its smelling good
éhešd = parents or close relatives
ék̓ʷ = to clean; to wipe; to clear
    ék̓ʷed = Wipe it!
    togʷék̓ʷadaxʷ teeł š´q = The sky would clear.
    otxʷék̓ʷosb čed = I'm cleaning (wiping) my face.
él = to call; to sing
    toélaxʷ = Someone was called
    ƛ̓oéled algʷa = They would sing it.
élabac = outside; side
élagʷeł = side
eláled = eagle
elálegʷd = side of a person
élks = the end || -ks, nose or pointed end
    tok´ʷddaxʷ x̣ól élks akʷe sk̓ʷáӡo = He grabbed him just at the end of his hair.
éls = dollar
éł = to paddle a canoe
    ƛ̓oéłš čed = I would paddle it.
ełéč̓ = a piece cut out
éq̓ = to be pronged
    aséq̓ st´kʷab = a pronged stick
ésta = to be the reason; to be the truth; to be the way things are
    gʷla asésta kʷe txʷal oyécbtobeced = Well, that's the reason you are being told.
étot = to sleep
    asétot téʔeł = He's asleep.
éx̣ʷ = to lose; to throw away
    oéx̣ʷdxʷ čed = I lost it.
    oéx̣ʷed čed = I threw it away.
eƛ̓ób = enough || é ƛ̓ób = meaning "yes, enough" has also been recorded. eƛ̓ób may be derived from é
    ƛ̓ób.
éʔtot = to be sleepy
    aséʔtot téʔeł = He's sleepy.

~ G ~

gák = to clear away a crowd of people to make room for others
    ogákad te áceɫtalbexʷ = Someone cleared away the people.
gák̓ = to look for lice
    ogák̓ad čed = I'm looking for lice.
gˊk = sunshine
    asgˊkb = The sun is shining.
gˊk̓ = to open something
    ogˊk̓d čed te šágʷɫ = I opened the door.
góob = to bark
    ogóob teeɫ skobáyʔ = The dog is barking.

~ Gʷ ~

gʷá = to follow; to go along
    ɫogʷábed čeɫ halgʷa = We're going along with them.
gʷád = to sit
    ɫogʷádel čexʷo = Are you sitting down?
    ogʷáadelaxʷ halgʷa = They are sitting down now.
    asgʷégʷad = Someone is sitting quietly (diminutive form).
gʷád = to jump (fish)
    ogʷádel teeɫ ƛ̓xʷáyʔ = The dog fish are jumping.
gʷád = to stay with
    togʷádeletbaxʷ aswayók̓ʷ = The witch stayed with him.
gʷadákʷ = horn; wedge
gʷák = to teach
    deeɫ tosogʷáktbs teeɫ wyóʔso = That was what the children were being taught.
gʷákʷbexʷ = a tribe (general term)
gʷál = to instruct; to show how
    gogʷálčec čexʷ akʷe sčá̓ads teeɫ sʔáx̣oʔ = You could show me how to dig clams .
gʷásb = pelt or skin of an animal; fur
gʷát = who?
    gʷát kʷe ck̓ó = Who is with me?
    yécbtobš gʷát čexʷ = Tell me who you are.
gʷáteʔ = because
    oóx̣ʷaxʷ čed txʷal péed gʷáteʔ čed asx̣ˊɫ = I'm going to bed because I'm sick.
gʷáx̣ʷ = soon
    te gʷáx̣ʷ ɫoébaš te stóbš = In a little while the man will travel.
gˊʷc = to itch
    ogˊʷcb čed = I itch.
gˊʷč = to wade
    togˊʷčelaxʷ = Someone waded then.

gʼʷč̌ = to look for; to search
    ogʼʷč̌d čed = I looked for it.
    ogʼʷč̌b ateeɫ skáʒo = Someone is looking for squirrels.
gʼʷdbexʷ = blackberries
gʷé = to call for; to call together
    gʷla gʷédaxʷ čeɫ teeɫ áceɫtalbexʷ = Well, we called the people together.
    togʷéetbaxʷ adókʷebɫ = Someone was called for by Transformer.
    ɫogʷéed čeɫ ɫobáyac = We will bring (call together) the game.
gʷéč̌gʷeč̌ = to move residence
    ɫogʷéč̌gʷeč̌ čed txʷal xʷsx̌álab = I'm going to move to Klallam.
gʷédq = clam (gwiduck)
gʷégʷad = sit quietly || This is the diminutive form of gʷád.
gʷégʷax̱ʷ = very soon || This is the diminutive form of gʷáx̱ʷ.
    te gʷégʷax̱ʷ čeɫ kʷéleloɫ = Very soon we're going to pick berries.
gʷégʷe = to potlatch
    gʷegʷeáltxʷ = potlatch house
gʷéx̱ = to leak
    ogʷéx̱eb teeɫ syált = The water-tight basket is leaking.
gʷla = well; well then
gʷlál = to kill; to weaken
    ogʷláld čed = I killed it.
    asgʷlál čed ate sx̱ʼɫ = I'm weak from that illness.
gʷlápoʔ = you (plural)
    gʷlápoʔ teeɫ ocód = You (pl.) said it.
gʷɫ = from; of
    teeɫ gʷɫ sdókʷalbexʷ stóbš = That man from Snuqualmie.

~ H ~

há = Oh!
háac = horse clam (literally, "very long")
hác = to lengthen out; to provide
    ashác = It's long (or tall).
    gʷsháʒels = It's getting long.
    toháʒbetbaxʷ ateeɫ báyac = Someone was provided with meat.
hácaʒeč̌ = blackfish (a type of whale) || Literally, "a long top."
hadóʔ = humpbacked salmon
hákʷ = long ago; long time
    ashákʷ = It has been a long time.
    hágʷaxʷ = a long time now
haláʔab = very
    haláʔab čed asx̱écel = I'm very angry.
halé = to be alive
    tohaléoʔxʷ = It was still alive.
halgʷa = they

hál? = to stop something
    łohál?ads = His (future) stopping something.
háps = hops (Eng. loan word)
    xʷé? kʷe gʷsoháps aceeł cḱóy = My mother would not pick hops.
hárnesed = to harness (Eng. loan word)
    ƛ̓otoohárnesedetb ate žán x̣ót teeł stqéw = The horse would be harnessed by John Hote.
háw = to wish
    háwadł dé?eł acčéstxʷ = Wish it was true that that was your husband.
háw? = to go ahead
    háw? éled = Go ahead and sing it.
    háw? cáḱadaxʷ = Go ahead and spear it.
háy = to learn
    toháytxʷ čed = I learned about it.
háy = then
    háy toóselaxʷ = Then he dove.
há?d = to discuss; to talk over
há?ł = to be good
    ashá?ł čexʷ = You are good.
há?łdop = a smooth place || há?ł, good; -dop, place.
h′dew = to go into; to be in {*come in, welcome*}
    toh′dewaxʷ txʷal teeł ál?als. = He went into his house.
    tolah′dew = Someone went in.
    tohdéwtbaxʷ = Something was brought in then.
hé = to stand up; to stand on or in front of
    tashéeležaxʷ = Someone was standing on it then.
hékʷ = big; much; very
    xʷé? čed lahékʷ = I'm not big.
    hékʷ čeł ohá?łel = We had a very (big) good time.
helá = See!
héle = See!
héq = to push
    héqed = Push it!
héqalsd = boat pole (see the preceding entry)
héw = to go
    ohéwelaxʷ čed = I'm going ahead now.
    héwel txʷal tode dé?e = Go over there!
hób = to argue; to compete; to have a contest
    slahóbeltxʷs = Her (his) arguing about it.
    toóx̣ʷaxʷ teeł ołhób = They went out to compete with each other.
hód = to burn; to burn with fire
    ashód = It's burning.
    ohódoče = Someone burned his fingers in the fire.
hókʷ = to copulate
    ashókʷtob = Someone was being copulated with.

hóy = to do; to make

    tohóyod čed = I made it.

    ashóy = It's done.

hóygʷas = to marry || hóy, to do or make; -gʷas, collective object.

hóyob = to sell; to trade || hóyo, an allomorph of hóy; -b stative aspect.

    tohóyobtxʷaxʷ teeł łábed = Someone sold (traded) the fur.

hoyobáltxʷ = store

hóytd = material from which to make something

hóyʔ = goodbye

~ K ~

kaálos = tears || -alos, eye

kádaʔ = to steal

    xʷéʔ padáb kʷe ackádaʔ = Never steal.

kádayoxʷ = rat

kádxʷ = mouth

kákʷ = to rest

    hay tokákʷ skáyʔkayʔ = Then Bluejay rested.

kál = to circle

    bk̓ʷ teeł ácełtalbexʷ ƛ̓ocáksedbaxʷ askálaxʷ = All the people would stand in a circle then.

kalá = younger sibling (a derogative term)

kaláal = left side

kaláległʷd = person with an ugly body

kalálos = lazy; dumb

kaláʔab = person ugly in appearance

kalése = insane person

kaqél = lower class

kawéč = to be hunchbacked || -weč, back

káwx̣ = tin can

káyaʔ = grandmother "mother's mother; father's mother; all female siblings or cousins of parents' parents" (Smith 1940)

kbáde = a round, snail-like shellfish

kéq̓ = to confine

    okéq̓etb čed = I was put where I couldn't get away.

    skéq̓alekʷ = a policeman

kláde = snag

kládhob = bad weather

kláletot = to dream

    okláletot = Someone dreamed or had a vision.

    skláletot = spirit power

klbéd = useless

kók = to cook (Eng. loan word)

    tokókod čed = I cooked it.

kól = to hug
    okólod čed = I hugged someone.
kólab = grey hair
k´tktač = red-headed woodpecker
kyáp = to tickle
    okyápad čeł = We're tickling someone.

~ k̓ ~

k̓ák̓a = crow (bird)
k̓ák̓ed ~ c̓k̓ák̓ed = always
    k̓ák̓ed čed ƛ̓ołék̓ksd = I always hang it up.
    gʷla c̓k̓ák̓edaxʷ todéša = Well, he was always there then.
k̓ák̓l = reduplicated form of k̓ál, to fool; to deceive
k̓ál = to fool; to deceive
    ask̓álbed čexʷo céʔeł = Did you believe her (were you deceived)?
k̓áp = to bend
    ok̓ápad čed = I bent it.
k̓ásk = to jabber
    ok̓áskbetb čexʷ ate halgʷa = You're being jabbered to by them.
k̓aw = to bump
    ok̓áwač čed = I bumped my head.
k̓áyok̓ayo = kinnikinnik leaves
k̓´q̓ = to lie on the back
    ok̓´q̓daxʷ = Someone laid it on its back.
k̓éł = to hang up; to stick on
    tok̓éłš = Someone hung it up.
k̓ó = to accompany; to gather together; to be together
    gʷat kʷe ck̓ó = Who do I go with?
    tok̓óalekʷ teeł dbád yoxʷ teeł ck̓óy = My father and mother had a gathering.
    ask̓ó čeł = We're together.
k̓ó ~ sk̓óy = mother
k̓óxode? = little neck clam
k̓´ʒx̣ = guts; intestines

~ Kʷ ~

kʷáa = to send
    lakʷáatb čed = I was being sent.
kʷád = something
kʷágʷečd = elk
kʷáls = to boil; to cook by boiling
kʷát = to climb a tree; to go up
    okʷátač alteeł sčbédac = Someone climbed the fir tree.
    tokʷáteʒaxʷ alteeł asló? = He climbed up out of the hole.

139

kʷáta = quarter; twenty-five cents (Eng. loan word)
kʷáxʷ = to cure; to help
    xʷéʔ kʷe ckʷáxʷdob = my not getting better (being helped)
    kʷáxʷac akʷe skʷél = Help me with the berry picking.
kʷáʒab = moss
kʷbáčed = rainbow
kʼʷd = to catch; to get; to take
    okʼʷdtxʷ čeł = We have it caught.
    é kʼʷdd te k̓ʷás = Yes, take the dried salmon.
    okʷdábac = Someone hung onto something.
kʷdéd = to thank; to give thanks to || Literally, "grab to it."
    ƛokʷdédaxʷ halgʷa txʷal teeł sʔáłd = They would give thanks for the food.
kʷe = any; some
    kʷe ƛ̓ób sʔáłd = Enough food. || Literally, "some enough food."
kʷél = to pick
    bakʷélaxʷ teeł ck̓óy ateeł háps = My mother is picking hops again.
    skʷél = berry picking
kʷéʒ = to cover
    okʷéʒtb = It was covered.
kʷéʔkʷeel = skate (fish)
kʷéƛ̓ = red
    txʷkʷéƛ̓alos = red eye
kʼʷspł = trout
kʼʷt = to be stiff
    askʼʷtb teeł ʒášad = My leg is stiff.

~ k̓ʷ ~

k̓ʷáalxʷ = ducks (black ducks)
k̓ʷáltad = salmon skin
k̓ʷás = dried salmon
k̓ʼʷcdeʔ = rabbit
k̓ʷéc̓ = to be slanted; to tip
    ask̓ʷéc̓ = It's slanted
    ask̓ʷéc̓axʷ čeł = We're almost tipping over.
k̓ʷéč̓ = to cut up; to skin
    ok̓ʷéčed teeł łálc̓ = Someone cut up the salmon.
    łok̓ʷéč̓ed čelab = You will skin and cut it up.
k̓ʷéd = to count; how many?
    k̓ʷéded teeł laébaš = Count how many are walking.
    k̓ʷéd kʷe acχáƛ = How many do you want?
    k̓ʷék̓ʷd = a few (diminutive form)
    k̓ʷedáł = a few times
k̓ʷék̓ʷd = a few (see k̓ʷéd above)
k̓ʷél = to peek in
    ok̓ʷéled čed = I peeked in.
k̓ʷéłyoʔ = to live with in-laws
    task̓ʷéłyoʔ = Someone was living with his in-laws.

140

k̓ʷéƚ = to go down; to go down to the beach
    k̓ʷéƚaxʷ čeƚ txʷal swádač = We're going to the beach.
k̓ʷeyáxʷ = belly
k̓ʼʷl = to flatten
    ok̓ʼʷld čed teeƚ káwx̱ = I flattened that tin can.
k̓ʼʷƚ = to pour
    ok̓ʷƚd čed teeƚ qó? = I poured the water.
k̓ʼʷš = to count
    ok̓ʼʷšd čed = I'm counting it.

~ L ~

lahál = to gamble; to play the bone game
    tolahál = They gambled.
    slahál = bone game
lák = to be behind; to be last
    leƚlák čed = I'm further behind.
lalé? = other; different
    xʷé? kʷe sx̱áƛ̓txʷ čeƚ kʷe gʷsóx̱ʷs txʷal lalé? stóbš = We don't want her to go to another man.
lapaskʷé? = hardtack (Chinook jargon)
láx̱ = to remember
    memá?an? teeƚ casláx̱dxʷ teeƚ daxʷċaxʷlósb = I barely remember about Port Blakely.
láya = sky (in the language of Rabbit in a myth)
lá?a = to put away
    čexʷ ƚolá?aš txʷal yáw? čed ƚox̱áƛ̓eltxʷ = You will put it away only until I want it.
lá?b = to see; to examine
    aslá?bd čed = I see it.
    aslá?la?bd = Someone is looking at (examining) it.
lá?ƚdat = yesterday
lbyó? = to care for an infant
    tolalbyó?tobaxʷ = It was being cared for.
lʼċ = to step on; to run over
    olʼċdxʷ čed = I accidentally stepped on someone.
    lʼċd té?eƚ ateeƚ ǰášad = Step on it with your foot!
    olʼċdob té?eƚ ate kár = Someone was run over by a car.
    olʼċ te halgʷa ate sx̱ʼƚ = They were laid low by the epidemic.
lʼč̓ = to fill
    lʼč̓d teeƚ syált lab = Fill your baskets.
    aslʼč̓ = It's full.
lé = meaning undetermined
    olé čed gʷk̓ʼʷdd gʷx̱áƛ̓txʷ = I'd get it if I wanted it.
lél = to be far off; to go; to go away
    balélel = They are apart (far away from each other) again.
    x̱ól čexʷ olélcot = Just go away.
leƚál = through; by means of

141

léq̓ʷ = to slide; to slip.

    teeɫ goléq̓ʷ = That could slide (slip).

lesák = sack (French loan word)

léx̣ = to be messy

    asléx̣ = It's messy.

l´gob = teen-age boy

l´gʷlgob = young men

lkbéd = a soupy food made of flour and water

ló = to hear

    taslóod čelab = You will hear it.

    olótxʷ čed = I heard about it.

lóqʷ = the belly growls

    olóqʷocot = His belly growls.

lóʔ = a hole

    aslóʔ = It has a hole in it.

l´q = understand

    xʷe kʷe caxʷl´qbed teeɫ sx̣ódx̣ods halgʷa = I don't understand their language.

lqbéd = after; to be behind; to be back of it

    gʷla ɫoá čed lqbéd akʷe l´gob stóbš = I will be behind the young man.

l´q̓ = to go to get

    ol´q̓c = Come and get me.

l´q̓ʷ = to bite; to eat

    hay ɫol´q̓ʷtbaxʷ teeɫ ƛ́áƛ́aċap = Then the ant was eaten.

l´x̣ = to be light

    asl´x̣el = It's getting light.

    sl´x̣el = daytime

l´xʷ = to pierce; to stab

    ol´xʷod čed = I stabbed it.

    ol´xʷotb čed = I was stabbed.

~ ɫ ~

ɫáaxʷ = to learn; to find out; to know

    axʷ cótbed čed topóysnded ceeɫ sx̣áx̣as ɫáaxʷaxʷ xʷéʔawa = I used to think they poisoned their in-laws, but now I know they didn't.

ɫáč̓ = to extinguish a fire; to put out the fire

    oɫáč̓ad čeɫ teeɫ hód = We put out the fire.

ɫáčb = weasel

ɫágʷ = to leave

    tobaɫágʷɫaxʷ čed = Then I left mine again.

ɫágʷ = to take off

    toɫágʷeǯbaxʷ = Someone took off his clothes.

ɫákt = wide

ɫálap = tongue

ɫál = to arrive; to dock or land; to come ashore

    asɫálel čed alsoq̓ʷábš = I arrived (docked, came ashore) at Suquamish.

łálbexʷ = stranger || łal, to arrive, to come ashore; -bexʷ, people
łáł = to live at a place
    tasłáłel teeł sdókʷalbexʷ ácełtalbexʷ = The Snoqualmie people were living there.
łáx̣ = to be dark; to be night
    lałáx̣elaxʷ = It's getting dark.
    słáx̣el = night
łʼč = to arrive; to come back
    gʷla tołʼčesaxʷ teeł stóbs = Well, she (he) came back to that man.
    ołʼčeldxʷaxʷ čeł txʷal álʔal teeł skáʒo = We took the squirrels home for no reason.
łéč̌ = to cut
    ołéč̌ed čed = I cut it.
    ołéłečed = Someone cut it up small.
łečákʷčop = to cut wood
łéd = to hang up; to tie up
    asłéd = It's tied up.
    asłédabac = It's hung up outside.
    asłédkso alteeł = Is it hanging up there?
łedáp = to trawl for fish || łed, to hang or tie up; áp, bottom
    ołedáp čed = I'm trawling.
łék̓ = to hang up
    tołék̓kstb = It will be hung up.
łéxʷ = three
łéxʷače = thirty
łk̓ = other
    łk̓ábac = the other side
    łk̓áde = the other end of the house
łk̓álap = thigh || łk̓, other; ál, side; -ap, bottom
łób = to eat soup
    te syáb ołób alteeł łóp = The high class person drank soup in the early morning.
łokʷáł = sun
łók̓ʷ = to fly
    lałók̓ʷ teeł sk̓ʷálaš = The duck is flying.
łóp = morning (early)
łóq̓ʷ = to peel off
    asłóq̓ʷ = It's peeled.
    asłóq̓ʷ teeł sk̓ʷálaš = The duck's feathers have been taken off.
łq̓ále = digging stick
łʼqʷ = to be wet
    asłʼqʷ = It's wet.
łʼt = to sprinkle water
    ołʼtd čeł ateeł qóʔ = We sprinkled it with water.
łʼtb = to bounce
    aca teeł ołʼtbd = I'm bouncing it.

ɫ′x̣ = to spread out

    ɫ′x̣d = Spread it out!

    asɫ′x̣ = It's spread out.

~ M ~

memáʔanʔ ~ memáʔadʔ = small; little

~ O ~

ó = oh!

ól = to go out in a canoe; to paddle

    laóloɫ = someone is going out in a canoe.

    oóloloɫ teeɫ stkáx̣ʷ = Beaver was paddling out to do something.

ólal = cattail

ólax̣ = to gather; to gather berries and other foods and materials

    ƛ̓oólax̣ad čeɫ teeɫ sq̓ʷláɫad = We would gather berries.

óloɫ = marriage gift exchange

ol′x̣ʷ = to be strong

    asol′x̣ʷ čed = I'm strong.

    casol′x̣ʷ te ćéćab = That blanket is my strength (power).

oq̓éb = box

ós = to dive

    oósel = Someone is diving.

óš = to pity

    toóšbetb = Someone was being pitied.

ót = to stretch

    oótod = Someone stretched it.

óx̣ʷ = to go

    toóx̣ʷax̣ʷ čed tx̣ʷal skól = I went to school.

óʔ = to approve

    toóʔad = Someone was approving.

óʔɫaɫ = to bother; to trouble

    kʷe gʷacax̣ʷóʔɫaɫ x̣′č = your being bothered or troubled in the mind

~ P ~

pád = to bury

    topádadax̣ʷ čed teeɫ todbád = I buried my late father.

    spadálekʷ = a plant

padáb = period; time

padálekʷ = to plant || pad, to bury; -álekʷ, collective object

    ɫopadálekʷ čed = I'm going to plant things.

pádc = ten

padc yox̣ʷ kʷe sáleʔ = twelve

padc yox̣ʷ ta dáč̌o = eleven

padéč = to cover with dirt || pad, to bury; -eč, top

    ƛopadéžedaxʷ alteeł swátyotd = Someone would cover it with dirt.

padhádab = summer time

pák = to divide up amongst; to spread out amongst

    čelab łopákad = You will spread it out (divide it amongst).

    topákelaxʷ syécb txʷal teeł stóbobš = The news spread to the men.

páł = to separate or divide

    opáłgʷas = Things were separated.

páłač = potlatch || páł is probably the root listed above

pástd = white man (Eng. loan word, Boston)

patáb = when? || pa-, an allomorph of {pad-}, time; táb, to be or to mean

    patábdł kʷe shóyotbs até? = When does he seem to do it?

pat´s = winter time || pa-, an allomorph of {pad-}, time; t´s, to be cold

páƛ = to be enough

    páƛ gomemá?an?s = It's alright (enough) even if it is small.

péed = bed (Eng. loan word)

pékʷ = to sing a spirit song; to dance a spirit dance

    opékʷ čed = I sang my spirit song (or danced my spirit dance).

    pégʷed = Sing (dance) it!

    ogʷláld ateeł sopégʷeds = He killed by means of his singing (and/or dancing) his spirit power.

    pegʷedáltxʷ = smoke house where spirit songs were being sung

pépa = paper (Eng. loan word)

pérs = pears (Eng. loan word)

péšpeš = cat (Chinook jargon)

p´kʷ = to break off

    op´kʷotb x̣óola = Maybe it has been broken off.

    asp´kos = The head is broken off.

pláms = plums (Eng. loan word)

plélac = cherry tree (wild)

p´lx̣ʷ = to boil

    top´lx̣ʷd čed = I boiled it.

póh = to add to

    tobapóhodaxʷ = Someone added to it again then.

pókʷ = to be hilly

    aspókʷab = It's hilly.

póo = to drift; to drift away

    opóotb čed = I drifted away (in a canoe).

pós = aunt "female sibling of living parent; female cousin of parent and females of parents' generation" (Smith 1940)

pós = to hit by throwing something

    opósod čed = I hit it (by throwing something).

pót = very; very likely; much; often; soon

    pót asčéq̓ʷel = It's very dirty.

póysn = to poison (Eng. loan word)

    topóysndetb akʷe gʷát = Someone was poisoned by someone.

pó? = to blow

   opó?od čed = I blew it (made it move by blowing it).

   š'xʷb opó?alekʷ = The wind is blowing.

ptéd = to think about; to think it over; to ponder

   toptédgʷsbaxʷ = Someone was thinking now.

pyax̣é = plant used for food (looks like macaroni when cooked). {*rock rose, bitterroot*}

~ ṗ ~

ṗáć = to sew

   oṗáćad čed = I sewed it.

ṗák̇ac = rotten wood || ṗák̇, rotten; -ac, wood, tree, bush

ṗál = to come to; to regain consciousness; to revive

   oṗálelaxʷ čed = I'm regaining consciousness now.

   asṗálel = sober, not drunk

ṗápłč = to break open

   oṗápłčaxʷ teeł tosácegʷd ace ȝ´gʷa = The entrails of Cannibal Woman broke open.

ṗáyaq = to make a canoe

   oṗáyaq = Someone is making a canoe.

ṗáƛaƛ̓ = whatever || This is a reduplicated form of ṗáƛ̓, enough.

ṗá? = to try; to put to a test

   čed łoṗá?cot = I will try myself.

   toṗá?atbaxʷ = It was tried then.

ṗčáb = wildcat

ṗ´d = to float to shore

   oṗ´delaxʷ teeł q̇élbed = The canoe floated to shore.

ṗéć = to squeeze

   ṗéćalbexʷ = Milk the cow!

ṗéčt = to burn wood into charcoal; to be charcoal

   asṗéčtabac = The bark is made into charcoal.

ṗél = to flatten; to smash; the tide is in

   oṗéled čed = I flattened (smashed) it.

   oṗéled čed teeł saplál = I kneaded the bread.

   asṗél = It's smashed or the tide is in.

ṗépł = to be bright; to be smart

   asṗépł te askékaweč = The little hunchback is smart.

ṗéxʷ = to flood

   toṗéxʷebaxʷ = It flooded then.

ṗókʷ = a grey berry eaten raw

ṗós = to float

   asṗósob alteeł qó? = It's floating on the water.

ṗ´q̇ac = bark of a tree

ṗ´q̇ʷ = to drift; to float

   toṗ´q̇ʷaxʷ = It drifted then.

ṗsq̇ʷábac = Monday
ṗwáyʔ = flounder (fish)

~ Q ~

qá = many; lots
    qá ácełtalbexʷ = many people
qáa = large number; many
qacágʷac = ironwood
qál = to rain
    asqálab = It's raining.
qáp = to smell; to stink
    deeł á laqáp sqáq = This has the smell of cousin.
qáq = cousin
qáse = uncle "male sibling of living parent; male cousin of parent and males of parents' generation" (Smith 1940)
qáx̣ʷac = crabapple tree
q´b = to cuddle; to be warm
    q´bcot syáb oť´sel te swátyotd = Bundle up high class one, it's cold in the land.
    xʷéʔ kʷe łacasb´č alpéed gʷacasq´bcot = Don't lie in bed and cuddle up.
qéboʔx̣ʷ = raft
qeyá = to have ready, to loosen
    oqeyáad čed = I loosened it.
    asqeyáel = It's loose (ready).
ql´b = bad person
q´lob = eye
q´ł = to awake
    asq´łaxʷ čed = I'm awake.
qóʔ = water
qóʔqʷa = to drink || qóʔ, water
    qóʔqʷa čed = I'm drinking.
q´ṗ = to light on (bird)
    laq´ṗ = The bird is lighting.
    toq´qṗ = The bird lit lightly (diminutive).
qqʷés = peninsula (a narrow strip of land projecting into the water)

~ Q̇ ~

q̇ábas = to threaten
    oq̇ábasbetb čed = I was threatened.
q̇ál = to camp
    oq̇álb čeł alteeł šálbexʷ = We're camping outdoors.
q̇ál = to soak
    oq̇álad čed alteeł qóʔ = I soaked it in the water.
q̇álbad = camping area

 q̓áɫ = to come to
    tolaq̓áɫelaxʷ ateeɫ daxʷoɫétb = It was coming to that swimming place.
q̓ápoxʷ = nuts
q̓áq̓xʷoʔ = short
q̓awósds = cane; walking stick
q̓áx̣ = to uncover; to be visible
    oq̓áx̣eǯd čed = I uncovered it.
    asq̓áx̣eč = It's visible (uncovered).
q̓áxʷ = to freeze
    asq̓áxʷ = It's frozen.
    oq̓áxʷelaxʷ = It's getting frosty now.
q̓´d = to be late; to be slow
    k̓ák̓ed čed ƛ̓olasq̓´del = I'm always late.
    laq̓´d teeɫ q̓élbed = That canoe is slow.
q̓él = to carry in or on a canoe; to put in or on a canoe
    ƛ̓oq̓életbaxʷ = It would be carried in the canoe.
    q̓elágʷelaxʷ ceeɫ sk̓óy alteeɫ q̓élbed = My mother got into the canoe.
q̓élbed = canoe
q̓éyoxʷ = above; upriver
    toláʔbaxʷ txʷal q̓éyoxʷ txʷal stgʷáq̓ʷ = Someone looked upriver toward Southwind.
q̓láqted = a long wooden needle used in making cattail mats.
q̓láx̣ad = fence
q̓´ls = to cook by steaming on hot rocks; to steam
    toq̓´lstbaxʷ ateeɫ sɫáday = It was steamed on hot rocks by the woman.
q̓´qʷ = to bite
    oqqʷáptb = Someone was bitten on the buttocks.
q̓´sed = lean-to; umbrella
q̓wáde = suitcase
q̓x̣ólgʷatxʷ = South
q̓yáw = a long green worm found in old logs
q̓yóq̓ʷ = throat

~ Qʷ ~

qʷágʷ = to be sweet
qʷaláytxʷ = mat house
qʷáleɫ = pitch (of a tree)
qʷálk = others
qʷáqʷ = to cut open; to cut into
    qʷáqʷadaxʷ = Cut it open now!
qʷáqʷ = raven
qʷasyóʔ = porpoise
qʷát = to lay something down
    čed toqʷátš teeɫ čéč̓ƛ̓a = I laid down the little rocks.
    qá teeɫ sƛ̓álabac asqʷátqʷat = Lots of clothes are lying around.

q´ʷc = to slide
    oq´ʷcb čed = I'm sliding.
    oq´ʷcb te swátyotd = The earth is falling down.
q´ʷdes = whale
qʷé = to shout or yell to someone in the distance
    oqʷéad = Someone was shouting to someone in the distance.
qʷéb = to be prepared; to be ready
    qʷébecot oébaš čeł = Get ready, we're going to travel.
    asqʷébaxʷ čed = I'm ready.
qʷéc = to go downstream
    toqʷécaxʷ = Someone went downstream.
qʷéd = to be bearded
    asqʷéd čed = I have a beard.
qʷédos = beard || qʷéd, beard; -os, face
qʷóyst = cow
qʷoystáłce = beef
q´ʷqʷ = to burst
    oq´ʷqʷ = It burst.
q´ʷš = to be foggy
    asq´ʷšb = It's foggy.
    sq´ʷšab = fog

—Q̇ʷ—

q̇ʷál = to be cooked (broiled); to ripen; to get warm; to be painted or colored
    oq̇ʷálb čed teeł łálc̓ = I'm cooking the salmon.
    oq̇ʷálaxʷ te g´ʷdbexʷ = The blackberries are ripe.
    asq̇´ʷal = It's warm (or ripe or colored).
    oq̇´ʷalad čed = I painted it.
q̇ʷaqʷyélc = shinny game
q̇ʷás = to burn with steam
    oq̇ʷásače = Someone burned his fingers with steam.
q̇ʷáx̣ʷšad = toe nail
q̇ʷéb = to get off or get out of a canoe; to put or push off
    oq̇ʷébaxʷ čed alteeł q̇élbed = I got off the canoe.
    toq̇ʷébedaxʷ teeł čéƛ̓a = He pushed the rock off.
q̇ʷéq̇ʷalc = feather down
q̇ʷéxʷ = to be bruised
    asq̇ʷéxʷel = Someone is bruised.
q̇ʷéʔ = to soften
    čeł q̇ʷéʔed = We soften it.
q̇ʷláde = ear
q̇ʷáleč = food left after a feast to be divided amongst the guests
q̇ʷq̇´ʷl = huckleberries

~ s ~

sácab = spring salmon (Duwamish)

sáceg^wd = entrails

sádeł = he

ságak = to whisper
    oságakd čed = I whispered to him.

sák^w = to be rotten; to be old
    łodx^wsák^w = It will be rotten.

sále? = two

sále?ače = twenty

sálq̓ = to turn around
    osálq̓cot čed = I turned around.
    ƛ̓osálq̓ax^w teeł q̓élbed = The canoe would turn around.

sáł = to calm down; to stop being angry
    osáłel čed = I'm calming down.

sápa = grandfather

saplál = bread (Chinook jargon)

sáq̓ = to spear something; to throw a spear
    ƛ̓osáq̓ad čed teeł q´^wdes = I would spear the whale.

sáq̓^w = to fly
    tosáq̓^wax^w = It flew then.
    tosésaq̓^wax^w = It flew a little then (diminutive form).

sátbd = death

sáx̣ = to clear; to scrape
    osáx̣ad teeł sx̣alá?s = Someone scraped the board.
    sáx̣ sáx̣ te láya = Clear, clear the sky!

sax̣álos = cedar snag

sáx̣olč = fern root from which a medicinal tea was made.

sáx^w = to jump
    osáx^wabax^w = Someone is jumping.

sbádet = mountain

sb´k^w = A ball made of cedar or fir wood used in a shinny game (Haeberlin and Gunther 1930: 64; Smith 1940: 224)

sb´k^wa = crane

sblátx^w = place name

sb´q̓bq̓ = grouse

sbyáw = coyote

sckápsb = neck

sc̓ábt = elderberries

sc̓ále = heart

sc̓eqáysb = flower

sc̓wád = blue-back salmon

sčałbádb = step-father "husband of parent's female sibling" (Smith 1940)

sč̓álob = liver

sč´bed = bark of a tree

sčbédac = fir tree

sčdátxʷ = salmon; fish in general

sčétxʷd = bear

sčótx̣ = halibut

sčʼášed = limb or branch of a tree

sčbtláʔx̣ad = wing of a bird

sčʼéčʼ = mussels

sčʼéstxʷ = husband

sčʼóɫa = leaf

sčʼópċ = tail

sdáʔ = a name

sdókʷalbexʷ = Snuqualmie

sél = cloth (Eng. loan word, sail)

selálekʷ = a song || s-, nominalizer; el, to sing; álekʷ, collective object
     deeɫ selálekʷ ateeɫ k̓ʼʷcdeʔ = That is the song of the Rabbit.

seláwtxʷ = cedar shakes covering over a surface burial (Smith 1940, p. 202)

sélš = cloudy weather

séxʷ = to be wrong; incorrect

séʔtab = blanket

sgʷésdalb = sand; sand bar

sgʼʷlo = pheasant; chicken

sháȝb = tall person || s-, nominalizer; hác, long or tall; -b, stative aspect

shóp = bracelet

ská = older sibling "siblings, cousins and persons of own generation, of either sex, older than speaker"
     (Smith 1940)

skábac = top

skáda7 = theft; thief
     ɫohóyod skádaʔ = Someone will make a theft.

skálaltxʷ = roof

skáyo = corpse; dead person; ghost

skáyʔkayʔ = bluejay

skáȝo = squirrel

skégʷc = deer

skláletot = power; guardian spirit

skláȝotaɫ ~ kláȝotaɫ = nephew or niece || reciprocal of yaláp who is the sibling of a dead parent (Smith
     1940)

skótab = a cough (a form used in preference to stók̓ob when referring to another person's cough so that
     the cough will not get worse.)

skobáyʔ = dog

skól = school (Eng. loan word)

sk̓áȝo = hair

sk̓áƛ̓ = otter

sk̓áaƛ̓ = land otter

sk̓élaɫdalb = riffle in the river

sk̓ó = companion || s-, nominalizer; k̓ó, to be together

skʷátač = mountain

sk̓ʷtł = chipmunk
sk̓ʷáač = dogfish
sk̓ʷálaš = duck
sk̓ʷálo = animal skin
sk̓ʷásb = mountain goat skin
sk̓ʷátad = mouse
sk̓ʷdéʔecot = religion
sk̓ʷélp = root
slabéd = to be in front of someone or something
    slabéds teeł skobáyʔ = The dog is (dog's being) in front of someone.
slágʷac = cedar bark
slahábac = the front
slahál = bone game
slałáx̱el = evening || s-, nominalizer; la- continuative aspect; łáx̱, to be dark; -el, continuative aspect
sláʔbb = good looking person (see láʔb)
sléʔ = life; soul
sl′gob = child, 'teen-aged, unmarried
sl′x̱el ~ sl′x̱e = day || s-, nominalizer; l′x̱, to be light; -el, continuative aspect
sɫáday = woman
sɫátabed = herring rake
sɫáx̱el ~ sɫáx̱e ~ sɫáx̱ = night time
sɫéleš = saliva
sɫokʷálb = moon or month
sób = to smell something
    sóbod = Smell it!
sóbde = a good hunter
soládxʷ = dried fish
sólt = salt (Eng. loan word)
sóqʷa = younger sibling "siblings, cousins and persons of own generation, of either sex, younger than
    speaker" (Smith 1940)
soq̓ʷábš = Suquamish tribe
sošbábtxʷ = poor person
s′p = to be stiff
    teeł syált ass′p = That water-tight basket is stiff.
spadálekʷ = a plant
spadálekʷac = a seed
spécx̱ʷ = snow bird
speʔkóc = potatoe
sp′pc = bowels
sptadáx̱ = a cedar pole used in the spirit return ceremony (Suquamish) {*soul redeeming*}
sp̓ákʷ = a boil
sqálab = rain
sq′boʔ = breast; milk
sq̓áx̱ʷ = ice || q̓áx̱ʷ, to freeze
sq̓byó = skunk

s´qʷ = anus
sqʷécks = point of land
sqʷéqʷeč = oysters
sqʷéʔqʷale = grass
sq´ʷšab = fog
sq̓ʷál = heat
sq̓ʷéc̓ = widow
sq̓ʷláɫad = berries; fruit
stáb = what? thing? || s-, nominalizer; táb, to be or to mean
    stábawa sʔáɫd téʔ = What kind of food is this?
stákad = stocking (Eng. loan word)
stálaɫ = When neither of a child's parents are dead he or she is stálaɫ to his or her parents' siblings.
    (Smith 1940)
steqáyo = wolf
stétaɫ = wild men said to wander in the woods and be dangerous (Smith 1940: 129)
stetčól?bexʷ = bird
stewátɫ = a woman's canoe
stgʷáq̓ʷ = south wind
st´gʷd = salmon berry
stkáxʷ = beaver
st´ktkʷab = forest; trees || A reduplicated form of st´kʷab, tree.
st´kʷab = log; stick; tree
stóbš = man
stódq = slave
stók̓ob = a cough
stólakʷ = river
stólbš = cedar tree root
stólegʷd = blood || s-, nominalizer; tól, to cross over; -egʷd, body or self
stólel = a bridge
stqéw = horse
sɫédegʷd = cedar limbs that have been softened
sɫéleb = a song
sɫéq̓ʷel = smoke
sɫóʔol = herring
sɫ´s = winter
swádabš = Swinomish bribe {Swinomish *tribe*}
swádač = beach; tide
swátyotd ~ sswátyotd = land; earth; dirt
swawáʔ = cougar
swayók̓ʷ = witch; dangerous female spirit
sweʔál – work or the result of work
swókʷad = loon
s´x̣ = to dance
    os´x̣b = Someone is dancing.
sx̣ál = a mark; a letter

sx̣alá?s = board
sx̣áltad = cradleboard
sx̣áy?os = head (body part)
sx̣áʒb = onion-like plant
s´x̣b = a dance
sx̣´č = teachings; lessons
sx̣éċel = a shameful matter
sx̣édx̣edeb = secret society (dog eaters) || Literally, "a being what?"
sx̣éx̣č = intelligence (the diminutive of sx̣´č)
sx̣´ɬ = sickness
sx̣´ṗb = clam, cockle
sxʷásb = soapberry
sxʷċéċab = sweat lodge (Suquamish)
sxʷéxʷe = game animals || xʷéxʷe, to hunt
s´x̣ʷ = a place
sx̣ʷáde? = bullhead (fish)
sx̣ʷás = grease; fat; lard
sx̣ʷéƛ̓ay = mountain goat
sx̣ʷé? = Oregon grapes
syáb = high class person
syált = basket, water-tight
syáɬ = "Chief" Seattle
syáyos = work
syá?ya? = friends; relatives
syécb = news || yécb, to tell
sʒáladob = year
sʒalkét = long hair
sƛ̓álabac = clothes || s-, nominalizer; ƛ̓ál, to dress; -abac, outside or skin.
sƛ̓alhólc = cranberries
sƛ̓álqb = animal
sƛ̓aƛ̓wálde = earring
sƛ̓eƛ̓álqb = birds || Literally, "little animals."
s?ácos = face
s?álap = leg (from knee to buttocks)
s?áɬd = food || ?áɬ, to eat
s?áx̣o? = clam (generic term)
s?éledgʷs = chest (body part)
s?élečed = back (body part)
s?eléls = forehead
s?élks = point, head, or end of something

~ š ~

šáb = to dry
    ošábad čed teeɬ sq̓ʷláɬad = I dried the berries.
šágak = Indian carrot

šágʷɫ = door; road
šálbexʷ = outdoors; outside
šalbexʷáde? = outside of the house
šáw? = bone
šáxʷ = to swell
    ošáxʷaxʷ = It's swelling up.
šáy = to take out
    ošáyedaxʷ teeɫ sćále = Someone took the heart out of it.
šáy? = to surface; to come up after being submerged
    tošáy?axʷ = He surfaced (came up).
šbáb = to be poor
    tosošbábtxʷs = her being poor
šéc = to stick in
    tošécedaxʷ = Someone stuck something into something.
šéč = to rub
    ošéčed čed = I rubbed it.
    šéčšades = Rub my leg!
šéč̌ = to put away; to store
    šeč̌alwás = Put your paddles away. || -al, side; -wás, paddle
šesyákʷ = to stretch out || -akʷ, body or self
    tošesyágʷelaxʷ = It was stretched then.
šéš = to be scarred
    asšéšed te dbáyac = There are scars on my body.
šéščksače = ring
šéšolċ = bad weather
š′las = penis
šób = to be late; to be missing
    padáb sɫóḱʷs halgʷa kʷe gʷšóbad ateeɫ čáčaš = At the time of their going home the child could have
    been missing.
šodgʷáls = shot for a gun
sókʷa = sugar (Eng. loan word)
šól = to crawl; to move slowly down
    ošólagʷel ƛapábac = Someone crawled underneath.
    tošólšedaxʷ halgʷa = They slowly let it down.
šólakʷcop = fire drill
šóʒa = maggots
špágʷ = to come down to
    daxʷšpágʷes halgʷa = their place of coming down
š′q = to be high; to lift
    asš′q = It's high.
    oš′qšec halgʷa = They lifted it for me.
šqólgʷdxʷ = sky
štád = place where...
šw?áx̣ʷad = basket
š′xʷb = wind
šxʷódad = hot ashes

šʒál = to go out

    xʷéʔ kʷe gʷsošʒáltobs teeł skáyo lełál šágʷł = The dead person was not taken out through the door.

~ T ~

ta = this

táb = to be or mean in the sense of explanation or a course of action

    čed owéleqʷ gʷstábs teeł tolaóxʷtob = I asked what it could be that was being taken out.

    stáb = what? thing?

    łotátabbaxʷ čeł ateeł = We'll talk it over (discuss its meaning or what to do about it) then. || tátab, reduplicated form.

táč = to fall; to roll over

    otáč teeł = It's falling.

    otáʒad čed = I'm rolling it over.

táčad = birthmark

tádč = stomach

tádeʔ = here

táds = to dance

    otádsaxʷ ce ʒ'gʷa = The Cannibal Woman dances around.

tágʷ = to buy

    otágʷš čed = I bought it.

táktd = doctor (Eng. loan word)

tála = dollar; money (Eng. loan word)

talóp = dried spring salmon

tálx = to use

    teeł xʷéʔ kʷe gʷsotálxtobs = Those not used.

táł = truly

táqoʔ = to be thirsty || qoʔ, water

    totáqoʔaxʷ = Someone was thirsty.

táqos = to hand something over

    táqosc = Hand it to me.

táq̓s = to wait

    totáq̓sadedaxʷ = Someone waited for someone.

táq̓ł = to go to the mountains, high land, inland, or away from the water

    kʷéled tode déʔe táq̓ł = Pick those that are inland.

    tol táq̓ł = from inland

táš = to rub

    totášatbaxʷ = It was rubbed.

tátab = to talk over; to discuss the meaning || Reduplicated form of táb.

táwd = town (Eng. loan word)

táxʷ = to clap hands

    táxʷačeb halgʷa = They're clapping hands.

táʒ = to go to bed; to lie down

    otáʒelaxʷ čed = I'm going to bed now.

    táʒelaxʷ = Lie down!

tažábac = devil fish

tá?a = him; them (pointing)

t′č̓ = to point at; to stick into

    otčáde = Someone is pointing at something.

    áca teeł ot′čd = I pointed at it.

    totčábsbtbaxʷ = Someone was stuck in the neck.

téb = to be hard; to harden; very

    téb teeł čéƛa = This rock is hard.

    tébecot = Try harder (harden yourself).

tée = to give to

    otéečed = Someone gave it (handed it to someone).

tée?eł = those over there

téla = finally

télaxʷ = soon

    télaxʷ kʷe tosbčágʷelsaxʷ = Soon he lay down (his past laying down).

télb = right away; directly

    télb toátbd teeł swayóḱʷ = The Witches died immediately.

texḻá = to spread wings

    tolastexḻáadb = His wings were spread out.

té? = this, non-feminine || When this introduces a noun it usually occurs as /te/.

té?eł = that non-feminine thing or person over there || When this introduces a phrase it usually occurs

    as /teeł/.

tklós = owl

tlá = to attend to; to pay attention

    xʷé? kʷe tosastlábots gʷáte? toyáyos = He didn't pay attention because he was working.

tláč = to send for

    otláče čed = I sent for it.

tláw = to run

    otláwel čed = I'm running.

tléx̱ʷ = to be related by kinship

    teeł swayóḱʷ yoxʷ x̱ax̱áyklked tléx̱ʷ ?á?šad = The Witch and Chipmunk's grandmother were cousins.

tłél = to believe

    astłél čexʷo = Do you believe it?

tó = to spit

    tóasaxʷ = Spit now!

    otóod čed = I spit on someone (something).

tóbšadad = Yakima {*Yakama*} Indians

tóde = that

tode dé?e = that over there

tóḱ = to cough

    otóḱob čed = I'm coughing.

    stóḱob = a cough

tol = from

    teeł čáčaš tol alsdhóbš = That child from Snohomish.

tól = to cross over water
    ƛotóleltxʷaxʷ = Someone would go across (the river).
    stólel = a bridge
tolél = from afar
tóp = to pound
    ƛotópotb = It would be pounded.
tóx̣ʷ = just
    tóx̣ʷ ocótcot halgʷa = They're just talking.
t´p = to spear fish
    ot´pel = Someone is spearing fish.
t´q = to close
    t´qd teeł šágʷł = Close the door!
tqáče = eight
t´q̇ = to slap
    ot´q̇d čed = I slapped him.
t´q̇ʷ = to close off
    t´q̇ʷapšad = shoe or close off the bottom of the foot || t´q̇ʷ, to close off; -ap, bottom; -šad, foot
t´s = to hit; to punch
    ot´sd čed = I punched it.
tsólč = drum
txʷal = at; to; toward
    txʷal táwd = to town
    txʷal péed = to bed
txʷc´qʷoł = daytime
txʷdáʔab = shaman; shaman power
txʷlélap = Tulalip
t´x̣ʷ = to pull apart; to separate
    otx̣ʷogʷásed čed = I pulled it apart.

~ ƛ̇ ~

ƛ̇ábed = fur
ƛ̇ágʷt = to be on top of; noon
    oƛ̇ágʷt = It's on top.
    ƛ̇ágʷtd téʔeł = Put it on top.
ƛ̇álċ = salmon
ƛ̇álekʷ = elbow; upper arm; shoulder
ƛ̇áłgʷas = a cross
ƛ̇áqa = salal berries
ƛ̇áy = to go upstream
    laƛ̇áyel = Someone is going upstream.
ƛ̇béłd = rope
ƛ̇bólečd = barrel
ƛ̇´bš = to braid
    oƛ̇bšd čeł = We're braiding it.

ƛ́de = fern root
ƛ́dsweč = Chinese slipper (shell fish)
ɬéč = to swim
    oɬéčeb čeɬ = We swam.
ɬél = to sing
    ɬélebax^w = Sing it now!
    sɬéleb = a song
ɬéq̓^w = to smoke
    asɬéq̓^wel = It's smoky.
    oɬéq̓^wel = It's smoking.
    sɬéq̓^wel = smoke
ɬésd = arrow
ɬéso = young person
ɬéƛ = to bathe; to swim
    ɬoɬéƛeb čex^wo = Are you going swimming.
ƛ́k = to splatter on; to stick
    oƛ́kks čed = Something is stuck on my nose.
    oƛ́kšad čed = Something is splattered on my foot.
ƛ́któlg^wadx^w = east
ƛ́k̓^wáɬ = to pass out; to faint
    oƛ́k̓^wáɬax^w = He passed out.
ɬóbks = ling cod
ɬóc̓ = to shoot
    oɬóc̓od čed = I shot it.
ɬók^w = to guess
    asɬóg^wod čed = I guess that one.
    toɬók^wax^w = Someone guessed then.
    sɬók^w = a guess
ɬók̓^w = to go home; to take home
    oɬók̓^wax^w čed = I'm going home.
ƛ́q̓ = to mend
    ƛ́q̓šec = Mend it for me.
ƛ́s = to be cold
    ɬosƛ́sbsax^w = It will be cold then.
ƛx̌áb = to step; to take a step
    ƛx̌ábedax^w = Someone stepped over it.

~ W ~

wál = to be strong
    aswálwalax^w = Someone is very strong
wáq̓waq̓ = frog
wáƛ = to be fresh
    ɬowáƛ sʔáɬd = There will be fresh food.
welálade = side of the head

wéleqʷ = to ask
    towéleqʷedaxʷ halgʷa = They asked it then.
    swéleqʷ = a question
wlél = to be born; to be showing
    patábaxʷ kʷe gʷsowléls akʷe čáčaš = When will the child be born.
    towlélaxʷ teeł čóšad = The stars showed then.
wóxʷtad = sweat house (Duwamish)
wyóʔso = children

~ x̣ ~

x̣áb = to raid; to raid with the purpose of killing
    ox̣áb čeł = We're raiding.
x̣ác = to pull out feathers
    ox̣ácad čed = I pulled out the feathers.
x̣ác = to argue with someone
    ox̣ácab čed = I'm arguing with someone.
x̣áčo = lake
x̣ád = to cover; to wrap
    tox̣ádx̣adečtbaxʷ = It was covered over (or wrapped).
    tox̣áx̣daxʷ halgʷa = They wrapped it a little.
x̣ák̓ʷd = roasting sticks
x̣ál = to mark; to write
    tóx̣ʷ čed ox̣álš te čéƛ̓a = I just marked on that rock.
    ox̣ál čed = I'm writing.
x̣áq̓oʔ = backbone of salmon
x̣áx̣a = to cry out; to be sacred or taboo
    tox̣áx̣abaxʷ = Someone was crying then.
    padx̣áx̣a = Sunday
x̣áx̣a ~ sx̣áx̣a = affinal kin; in-laws (with the connotation of taboo, see entry above). "parents of living
    spouse and all blood relatives of living spouse in second, third, and fourth generations" (Smith
    1940)
x̣ax̣áyklked = name of Chipmunk's grandmother
x̣áy = to laugh
    ox̣áytxʷ čed = I made someone laugh.
    ox̣áyb čed = I'm laughing.
x̣áƛ = to be brushy
    hóyaxʷ óx̣ʷaxʷ txʷal x̣áƛ dókʷebł = When he was finished, Transformer went into the brush.
x̣áƛ̓ = to argue
    ox̣áƛ̓elaxʷ = They're arguing.
x̣áƛ̓ = to like; to want
    asx̣áƛ̓txʷ čed = I like (want) it.
x̣´b = heavy
    oxʷálbed čed x̣éqab x̣´b = I failed to lift it because it was too heavy.
x̣bx̣´b = a plant growing along the shore with small black bulbs on the roots which were eaten raw.

x̣´c = to fear
     asx̣´c čed = I'm afraid.
x̣´č = mind; thought
     asx̣éd kʷe adx̣´č = What do you think (how is your mind)?
x̣čóol = to relate one's genealogy
     ox̣čóolb = Someone is relating his genealogy.
x̣´d = to push
     x̣´dd = Push it!
x̣dé = to save or put away food
     hay x̣déedaxʷ kʷe pał´s = Then it was put away for the winter.
x̣éb = to grab
     łox̣ébed čeł = We'll grab it.
x̣éc = to be angry
     asx̣écel čed = I'm angry.
     sx̣écel = anger
x̣éċ = unripe; uncooked
     deeł x̣éċ = These that are not ripe.
x̣eċółd = backbone of dried salmon
x̣éd = how? what?
     asx̣édaxʷ čexʷ = How are you?
     asx̣édaxʷ kʷe aclóƛ̓ = What is your age?
x̣éh = to do something
     towéleqʷaxʷ ox̣éhd čelab = He asked, "what are you doing?"
x̣ék̓ʷ = to be mean
     x̣ék̓ʷ teeł stóbš = That man is mean.
x̣él = to slide down (dirt)
     ox̣él txʷal teeł swádač teeł swátyotd = The dirt is sliding down onto the beach.
     lax̣élks = The point is wearing down (place name).
x̣élex̣ = to fight a battle
     toóx̣ʷ čeł txʷal teeł ox̣élex̣ = We've been to the fighting (war).
     ox̣élelex̣ = Two groups are fighting a battle.
x̣éqab = very; too
     ox̣ʷálbed čed x̣éqab x̣´b = I failed [to lift it] because it was too heavy.
x̣éq̓ = to scratch
     ox̣éq̓alekʷ = Someone is scratching (on a board or something).
x̣éqʷ = to want
     asx̣éqʷbed = Someone wants it.
x̣étoċ = black
x̣éx̣ = to be aware
     te x̣éx̣dobot wyóʔso = Be aware, children.
x̣ćx̣c = to be ashamed
     tox̣éx̣eaxʷ = Someone was ashamed then.
x̣éx̣q̓aweł = to race; a race
x̣´k = to bundle up; to tie up; to wrap up
     asx̣´k = wrapped or bundled up
     ox̣ácad čed čed ox̣´kd alteeł t̓ésd = I pull out a feather and tie (wrap) it on the arrow.

x̣lédop = floor
x̣ʼɬ = to be hurt; to be sick
    asx̣ʼɬ čeɬ = We're sick.
x̣ɬáltxʷ = hospital
x̣ɬtéx̣ = to be like; to be just like
    x̣ɬtéx̣ yóq̓ʷayʔ = Just like a rotten stick.
x̣ódx̣od = to talk
    ox̣ódx̣odbed čed = I'm talking to someone.
x̣ók̓ʷadesd = breast pin
x̣ól = only; just
    x̣ólaxʷ čelab ɬosʔáɬd = In the future you will just be food.
x̣óola = maybe; perhaps
    x̣óola čed gotáʒelaxʷ = Maybe I should go to bed.
x̣óx̣ʷayʔ = duck (hell diver)
x̣óƛ̓ = to gnaw
    ox̣óƛ̓otb ateeɬ skobáy teeɬ šáwʔ = The bone was gnawed by the dog.
x̣ʼp = to break
    ox̣ʼpdxʷ čed = I accidentally broke it.
x̣páyʔ = cedar sticks
x̣páyac = cedar tree
x̣ʼƛ̓ = to bite
    ox̣ʼƛ̓d = Someone bit it.

~ xʷ ~

xʷalábaleʔ = jar
xʷálk̓ʷ = to be crazy; to be drunk; to interfere with others; to bother
    asxʷálk̓ʷ = Someone is drunk or bothering others.
xʷaltbálʔs = gun
xʷáy = to be hot; to become red hot
    tosxʷayésbs = It was red hot (its, past, being red hot).
xʼʷb = to throw
    oxʼʷbd čed = I threw it.
    oxʼʷbcot čed = I stumbled (threw myself).
xʷbǯál = black mountain eagle
xʼʷc = to come out; to take out or off
    toxʼʷcaxʷ = It came out then.
    oxʼʷcd = Someone took it out (off).
xʷčábk̓ʷ = cloud
xʷéd = to worry
    xʷéʔ kʷe ɬacoxʷédegʷdb = Don't worry yourself.
xʷékʷ = to crackle
    togʷxʷékʷadaxʷ alkʷe tosq̓áxʷsaxʷ = It would crackle until it froze.
xʷéɬ = to carry
    kʷe sx̣ál xʷéɬ = The mail carrier.
xʷéla = not

xʷét = to come down; to drop; to fall down
    toxʷételaxʷ teeł ye?dó?ad = The swing came down.
    toxʷételedaxʷ = Someone was dropping something to someone.
xʷéxʷe = to hunt; to gather
    oxʷéxʷeeloł čed = I'm going out hunting.
xʷé? = no; not
    xʷé?axʷ kʷe gʷsobésetbs = Her not being chosen then.
x´ʷkʷ = to wind around
    oxʷkʷálekʷed = Someone wrapped something around it.
xʷláb = as; like
    toxáxadaxʷ halgʷa xʷláb ateeł čáčaš = They wrapped it the way the child was wrapped.
    xʷé? kʷe gʷcósel xʷlab ad´gʷe = I could not be diving the way you do.
xʷṗós = to lift up the head (face).
    oxʷṗósb = Someone lifted his face.
xʷskáted = older sibling (term of address) "siblings, cousins and persons of own generation, of either sex,
    older than speaker." (Smith 1940)
xʷsƛ́álab = Klallam tribe
xʷtágʷe = down

~ x̣ʷ ~

x̣ʷahép = grunter fish
x̣ʷál = to fail
    ox̣ʷálbed čed x̣éqab x̣´b = I failed [to lift it because] it was too heavy.
    ox̣ʷál čed = I failed.
x̣ʷál = nine
x̣ʷáq̇ = to worry
    xʷé? kʷe stáb gʷla ƛ̇odxʷasx̣ʷáx̣ʷq̇egʷd = He wouldn't happen to worry a little about something
    (diminutive form).
x̣ʷá? = to be up
    tox̣ʷá? altóde = It was up there.
x̣´ʷc = to sharpen
    k´ʷdd kʷe st´kʷab čexʷ ox̣´ʷcksd = Take a stick and sharpen it on the end.
x̣ʷélč = to kneel down
    asx̣ʷélč čed = I'm kneeling down.
x̣ʷéqʷade? = thunder; thunder bird
x̣´ʷt = to rip something
    xʷé? gʷacx̣´ʷtd = Don't rip it.
x̣ʷéx̣ʷyap = to tell myths
x̣ʷé?w = to whistle
    oxʷé?wad = Someone was whistling.
x̣´ʷlč = sea; salt water; Puget Sound
x̣´ʷƛ̇ = to break
    ox̣´ʷƛ̇d = Someone broke it.
    tox̣´ʷƛ̇d teeł ǯášad = He broke his leg.

163

~ y ~

yábok̓ʷ = to fight

    xʷéʔ kʷe acoyábok̓ʷtxʷ teeł deeł agʷat = You should not fight with anyone.

yaláp = uncle "sibling of dead parent" (Smith 1940)

yasáwe = alderwood

yáwʔ = only; to have to be

    yáwʔ lełal teeł šwaláʔlbosd teeł gʷsšʒáltobs teeł skáyo = The corpse could only be taken out through the window.

yáx̱ʷd = flint arrowhead

yáyos = to work || -os is probably the suffix for "face."

    xʷéʔ gʷcx̱áƛtxʷ gʷcyáyos = I don't want to work.

yáƛ̓ = to scoop up

    oyáƛ̓ad čeł = We scooped it up.

yáʔbadad = a strong guardian spirit

yécb = to tell

    yécbtobš asx̱éd kʷe gʷacax̱ʷšábad te ƛ̓álc̓ = Tell me how you dry salmon.

yeʔdó = to swing

    oyeʔdóʔ čed = I'm swinging.

yeʔdóʔad = a swing

yléq̓ʷd = cedar root

yóbač = spring salmon (Suquamish)

yóq̓ʷayʔ = rotten stick

yoxʷ = and; together with

    dbád yoxʷ c̓k̓óy = My father and my mother.

~ ʒ ~

ʒák̓ = to fall; to make fall

    oʒák̓ txʷal teeł ashód = Someone fell into the fire.

    oʒák̓ teeł x̱páyac = The cedar tree is falling.

ʒákʷ = to move quickly; to shake; to swing

    gʷla ʒák̓ʷdoptobaxʷ alteeł sk̓áʒo = He was shaken by the hair at that place.

    oʒákʷacot = It's moving (swinging).

ʒálq = to turn

    oʒálqos čed = I turned my head.

    oʒálqd čed = I turned it over.

ʒáq̓ = to cohabit; to sleep together as husband and wife

    asʒáq̓txʷ ateeł stóbš = She was slept with by that man.

ʒáx̱ = to move something

    oʒáx̱tb teeł q̓wáde = Someone moved the suitcase.

    toʒáx̱ax̱ čeł txʷal soq̓ʷábš = We moved to Suquamish.

ʒáx̱ʷ = to melt

    oʒáx̱ʷaxʷ teeł sq̓áx̱ʷ = The ice melted.

ȝáƛ = to make a mistake; to be wrong
  oȝáƛab čed = I made a mistake.
  d´gʷe teeł asȝáƛab = You are wrong.
ȝ´des = tooth
ȝél = to be ashamed
  dáyaxʷ čed oȝéled = I'm just ashamed of him.
ȝéxʷ = first
  d´gʷe kʷe lełȝéxʷ = You are first.
ȝexʷbéd = before || Literally, "being first to it."
  xʷéʔ kʷe tosasláʔlaʔbtbs ate dbád ȝexʷbéd ateeł = She had never been seen by my father before that.
ȝeȝalálеč = Seattle {the city}
ȝéȝehe = to be pregnant
  toȝéȝeheaxʷ = Someone was pregnant then.
ȝ´gʷa = Cannibal Woman
ȝhál = right side
ȝhálegʷd = right side of body
ȝhálgʷł = right side of a canoe
ȝláče = six
ȝlaẋad = to visit
  oȝláẋadbed čed = I went to visit them.
ȝlólč = to walk around in a circle
  ƛoȝlólčaxʷ čeł = We would walk around in a circle.
ȝógʷ = to kick
  ȝógod = Kick him!
  oȝógʷc = Someone kicked me.
ȝólčo = waves
ȝóq = to drift; to float
  toláʔbdaxʷ halgʷa teeł oȝóqotb ateeł ȝólčo teeł ácełtalbexʷ = They happened to see that person floating on the waves.
ȝóẋʷat = to vomit
  oȝóẋʷat = Someone is vomitting.
ȝ´q = to bend down; to stretch out; to crawl
  oȝ´qel čeł = We're bending down.
  áca asȝ´qel = He was there stretched out.
  oȝ´qȝqel teeł wyóʔso = The children are crawling.
ȝ´q̓ = to sharpen
  oȝ´q̓tb askégʷc teeł šáwʔ = Deer was sharpening a bone.

~ ǯ ~

ǯáč = to flood; the water runs swiftly; the river overflows its banks
  toǯáǯaxʷ = It (the river) ran swiftly.
  asǯáč = It was flooding over.
ǯášad = leg or foot (from the knee down including the foot)

žéq̓ = to put into water; to soak
    télb tolažéq̓ed teeł šč̓datxʷ = Immediately he put the salmon in the water.
žó = to be joyful (Eng. loan word, joy)
    asžóel té? = He is happy.

~ ƛ̓ ~

ƛ̓á = to gather
    b´k̓ʷ sl´x̣e łoƛ̓áč̓op = Every day someone will gather wood.
ƛ̓ácapd = belt
ƛ̓ácas = island
ƛ̓áč = stomach
ƛ̓agʷéced = spear for catching bottom fish
ƛ̓ál = also
ƛ̓ál = to dress
    čed ƛ̓álšed ceeł skáyo = I dressed that corpse.
    sƛ̓álabac = clothes
ƛ̓álegʷd = plans; ideas
ƛ̓áx̣ʷ = to grow
    asƛ̓áx̣ʷ = It's growing.
ƛ̓áy? = river canoe
ƛ̓áƛ̓ac̓ap = ant
ƛ̓á? = to lie in wait for; to stalk
    tasƛ̓á?atbaxʷ = Someone was being stalked.
    toƛ̓á?adaxʷ = Someone was stalking.
ƛ̓´bč̓ = to listen to someone who is talking; to pay attention
    toƛ̓´bč̓tbaxʷ = It was listened to then.
ƛ̓´cbec = flint chips
ƛ̓éč = to tattoo
    dáyaxʷ há?ł teeł acƛ̓éč = Your tattoo is very nice.
ƛ̓éq̓ = to stick something onto something
    oƛ̓éq̓ed čed = I stuck it on.
    sƛ̓éq̓s = its being stuck on
ƛ̓´l = to desist; to stop; to let go
    togʷƛ̓´ldaxʷ halgʷa = They would stop it then.
    xʷé? kʷe acoƛ̓ábot = You didn't stop yourself.
ƛ̓ó = to be thin
    asƛ̓óel čed = I'm getting thin.
ƛ̓ób = alright
    toƛ̓óbelaxʷ = It was alright then.
ƛ̓óc̓ = to tie a knot
    oƛ̓óc̓od čed = I tied something in a knot.
ƛ̓ós = to face this way; to turn facing someone
    asx̣édaxʷ teeł adaxʷasƛ̓ósbaxʷ = Why is it that you are (standing) facing me in that place?

166

λ̓óxʷ = to be cold
    asλ̓óxʷel = It's cold.
λ̓óxʷλ̓oxʷe = oyster beds
λ̓´p = down
    otáčdxʷ λ̓´p = Someone accidentally fell down.
λ̓pábac = to be underneath
    λ̓pábacbed ate halgʷa = underneath them
λ̓pálko = bottom
λ̓´q̓ʷ = to tighten
    oλ̓´q̓ʷd čed = I tightened it.
    asλ̓´q̓ʷel = It's tight.
λ̓xʷáyʔ = dog salmon

~ ʔ ~

ʔáɬ = to eat
    oʔáɬdaxʷ čed = I eat it now.
ʔáx̣oʔ = to dig clams
    λ̓oʔáx̣oʔ čeɬ ateeɬ sʔáx̣oʔ = We would dig clams.
ʔáƛ̓ = to come
    slaʔáƛ̓ te slʼx̣el = the coming of the day
    ʔáƛ̓axʷ = Come here now!
ʔáʔšad = "siblings, cousins and persons of own generation and of same sex. Also used as a friendship
    term by men" (Smith 1940).

English-Salish

~ A ~

above; upriver = q̇éyoxʷ
accompany, to; to gather together, to be together = ḱó
accuse, to; to blame = bágʷ
across; on the other side = dyóced
add to, to = póh
affinal kin = x̣áx̣a ~ sx̣áx̣a
after, to be; to be behind = lqbéd
alderwood = yasáwe
alive, to be = halé
all, every = b´ḱʷ
alright = ƛ̇ób
also = ƛ̇ál
always = ḱáḱed ~ c̣ḱáḱed
and; together with = yoxʷ
anger = sx̣écel || x̣éc, to be angry
angry, to be = x̣éc
angry with, to be; to dislike = dókʷ
animal = sƛ̇álqb
animal skin = sḱʷálo
answer, to = b´lč
ant = ƛ̇áƛ̇ac̣ap
anus = s´qʷ
any; some = kʷe
apples = ápls
approach, to; to draw near (diminutive) = čéčt
approach, to; to bring near = čét
approve, to = ó?
argue, to = x̣áƛ̇
argue with someone, to = x̣ác
argue, to; to compete; to have a contest = hób
arm (upper); elbow; shoulder = tálekʷ
around = deábac
arrive, to; to come back = ł´č
arrive, to; to dock or land; to come ashore = łál
arrow = ťésd
arrowhead of flint = yáx̣ʷd
as; like = xʷláb
ashamed, to be = ʒél
ashamed, to be = x̣éx̣e

ashes; charcoal; coals; embers = ṗéčt
ashes, hot = šxʷódad
ask, to = wéleqʷ
ask, to = čéb
at; to; toward = txʷal
attend to, to; to pay attention = tlá
aunt = pós
awake = q´ł
aware, to be = x̣éx̣

~ B ~

baby; small child = b´da
back (body part) = s?éleced
back of something, the = álḱʷ
backbone of dried salmon, the = x̣ec̣ółd
backbone of salmon, the = x̣áq̇o?
bad person, a = ql´b
bad weather = šéšolc̣
bad weather, to be = kládhob
ball made of cedar or fir used in a shinny game = sb´kʷ
bark of a tree, the = sč´bed
bark of a tree, the = ṗ´q̇ac
bark, to (a dog) = góob
barrel = ťbólečd
basket = šw?áx̣ʷad
basket, carrying = čbólč
basket, water-tight = syált
bathe, to; to swim = łéł
be, to = ádad
be, to; to mean in the sense of explanation or a course of action = táb
be there, to = ác
be there, to = á
be together, to; to gather together; to accompany = ḱó
beach = čákʷ
beach; tide = swádač
bear = sčétxʷd
beard = qʷédos
bearded, to be = qʷéd
beat in a contest, to = c̣´l
beaver = stkáx̣ʷ

because = gʷáteʔ
bed = péed
beef = qʷoystáɫče
before = ʒexʷbéd
behind; after = lqbéd
behind, to be; to be last = lák
believe, to = tɫél
belly = k̓ʷeyáxʷ
belly growls, the = lóqʷ
belt = ƛ̓ácapd
bend, to = k̓áp
bend down, to; to stretch out = ʒ´q
berry of the kinnikinnik bush = c̓ábt
berry (a gray berry eaten raw) = p̓ókʷ
berries; fruit = sq̓ʷláɫad
bet, to; to lay out or put something down = bčálekʷ
big; much; very = hékʷ
bird, a = stetčólʔbexʷ
birds (literally, little animals) = sƛ̓eƛ̓álqb
birth, to give; to lay an egg = bdáʔ
birthmark = táčad
bite, to = q´qʷ
bite, to = x´ƛ
bite, to; to eat = l´q̓ʷ
black = xetóc̓
blackfish (a type of whale) = hácaʒeč
blackberries = g´ʷdbexʷ
blame, to; to accuse = bágʷ
blanket = séʔtab
blanket = c̓éc̓ab
blind, to be = bád
blood = stólegʷd
blow, to = póʔ
bluejay = skáyʔkayʔ
board = sxaláʔs
boat pole = héqalsd
body = c̓óqʷab
boil, a = sp̓ákʷ
boil, to = p´lxʷ
boil, to; to cook by boiling = kʷáls
bone = šáwʔ
bone marrow = dadáwšed
bone game = slahál

born, to be; to be showing = wlél
bother, to = báp
bother, to; to trouble = óʔɫaɫ
bottom = ƛ̓pálko
bounce, to = ɬ´tb
bow = c̓áco
bowels = sp´pc
box = oq̓éb
boy, teen-age = l´gob
bracelet = shóp
braid, to = ɬ´bš
branch or limb of a tree = sčášed
bread = saplál
break off, to = p´kʷ
break, to = c̓éq̓ʷ
break, to = x´p
break, to = x´ʷƛ
break, to = č´ɬ
break open, to = p̓ápɬč
breast; milk = sq´boʔ
breast pin = xók̓ʷadesd
breath = cáɫdɫ
breathe, to = caɫdálb
bridge = stólel
bright, to be; to be smart = p̓épɬ
bring = ábaʔk
bring home, to; to bring back = čél
bring in, to = hdéwʔ
bring near, to; to approach = čét
bring together, to; to call together = gʷé
brother or sister, my younger = cóqʷa
brother or male cousin of a man = ʔáʔšad
bruised, to be = q̓ʷéxʷ
brushy, to be = xáƛ̓
build, to = čéɫ
bullhead (fish) = sxʷádeʔ
bump, to = k̓áw
bundle up, to; to tie up; to wrap up = x´k
burn wood to charcoal, to; to be charcoal = p̓éčt
burn, to; to burn with fire = hód
burn with steam, to = q̓ʷás

bust, to = q´ʷqʷ
bury, to = pád
bush, the leaves of which were used to make a
    "tea" = ċbáčac
butter (Eng. loan word) = báta
buy, to = tágʷ
by means of = leƚál

~ C ~

call, to; to sing = él
call for, to; to call together = gʷé
calm down, to; to stop being angry = sáƚ
camp, to = q̇ál
camping area = q̇álbad
cane; walking-stick = q̇awósds
Cannibal Woman = ʒ´gʷa
canoe, river = ƛáy?
canoe (generic term) = q̇élbed
canoe (apparently a loan word from the north)
    = aótx̣s
canoe, woman's = stewátƚ
care for an infant, to = lbyó?
carry, to = čbá?
carry, to = xʷéƚ
carry in or on a canoe, to; to put in or on a
    canoe = q̇él
cat = péšpeš
catch, to; to take; to get = k´ʷd
catch up with, to; to chase; to reach a goal; to
    reach = čál
cattail = ólal
cedar bark = slágʷac
cedar limbs that have been softened = sṫédegʷd
cedar pole used in the spirit return ceremony
    (Suquamish) = sptadáx̣
cedar root = yléq̇ʷd
cedar shake covering over surface burials =
    seláwtxʷ
cedar snag = sax̣álos
cedar tree = x̣páyac
cedar; cedar sticks = x̣páy?
cedar tree root = stólbš

change things, to; to trade; to find = áy?
charcoal; coals; embers; ashes = ṗéčt
chase, to; to catch up with = čál
cherry tree (wild) = plélac
chest (body part) = s?éledgʷs
chicken; pheasant = sgʷló
chief (Eng. loan word) = čéf
"Chief" Seattle = syáƚ
child, small; baby = b´da
child, teen-aged, unmarried = sl´gob
child, young person up to teens = čačaš
children = wyó?so
Chinese slipper (shell fish) = ṫdsweč
chipmunk = sk´ʷtƚ
choose, to = bés
chop up, to; to smash = béƛ̣
circle, to = kál
clam, butter = ċq̇´ʷt
clam, cockle = sx̣´ṗb
clam, gwiduck = gʷédq
clam, horse = háac
clam, little neck = k̇óx̣ode?
clams (generic term) = s?áx̣o?
clam shell = čáway
clap hands = táxʷ
clay = ċax̣ʷlós
clean, to; to wipe; to clear = ék̇ʷ
clear, to; to scrape = sáx̣
clear, to; to wipe; to clean = ék̇ʷ
clear away a crowd of people to make room for
    others = gák
climb a tree, to; to go up = kʷát
close, to = t´q
close off, to = t´q̇ʷ
cloth (Eng. loan word, sail) = sél
clothes = sƛ̣álabac
cloud = xʷčábk̇ʷ
cloudy weather = sélš
club, to; to whip with a stick = čáxʷ
coals; embers; ashes; charcoal = ṗéčt
cohabit, to; to sleep together as husband and
    wife = ʒáq̇

cold, to be = ƚ´s
cold, to be = ƛ́óxʷ
come, to = ʔáƛ
come, to; to come back; to arrive = ƚ´č
come ashore, to; to dock or land; to arrive = ƚál
come down to, to = špágʷ
come down, to; to drop; to fall down = xʷét
come out, to; to take out or off = x´ʷc
come to, to = q̇áƚ
come to, to; to regain consciousness; to revive = p̓ál
come to, to; to live at; to live = ál
companion = sk̓ó
compete, to; to argue; to have a contest = hób
confine, to = kéq̇
cook, to (Eng. loan word) = kók
cook by steaming on hot rocks, to; to steam = q̇´ls
cooked, to be; to broil; to ripen; to get warm; to be colored = q̇ʷál
copulate, to = hókʷ
corpse; dead person; ghost = skáyo
cougar = swawá ʔ
cough, a = stók̓ob
cough, a = skótab
cough, to = tók̓
count, to = k̓ʷš
count, to; how many? = k̓ʷéd
cousin = qáq
cousin; sister; brother = ʔáʔšad
cover, to = kʷéʒ
cover, to; to wrap = xád
cover with dirt, to = padéč
cow = qʷóyst
coyote = sbyáw
crabapple tree = qʷáx̣ʷac
crackle, to = xʷékʷ
cradleboard = sx̣áltad
cranberries = sƛalhólc
crane = sb´kʷa
crawl, to = ʒ´ʊʒʊ
crawl, to; to move slowly = šól

crazy, to be; to be drunk; to interfere with others; to bother = xʷálk̓ʷ
cross, a = ƚáƚgʷas
cross over water, to = tól
crow (bird) = k̓ák̓a
crowd together, to = č̓´x̣
cry out, to; to be sacred or taboo = x̣áx̣a
cuddle, to; to be warm = q´b
cure, to; to help = kʷáxʷ
cut, to = ƚéč̓
cut open, to; to cut into = qʷáqʷ
cut up, to; to skin = k̓ʷéč̓
cut wood, to = ƚečák̓ʷčop

~ D ~

dance, a = s´x̣b
dance, to = táds
dance, to = s´x̣
dance a spirit dance, to; to sing a spirit song = pégʷ
dangerous, to be = dókʷ
dark, to be; to be night = ƚáx̣
daytime = sl´x̣el ~ sl´x̣e
daytime = txʷc´qʷóƚ
death = sátbd
deceive, to; to fool = k̓ák̓al
deceived, to be = k̓ál
deer = skégʷc
desist, to; to stop; to let go = ƛ´l
devil fish = tax̌ábac
die, to = átbd
different, to be; to feel or look different = lalé ʔ
dig, to = čá ʔ
dig clams, to = ʔáx̣o ʔ
digging stick = ƚqále
directly; right away = télb
dirt; land; earth = swátyotd
dirty, to be = č̓éq̇ʷ
discuss, to; to talk over = há ʔd
discuss, to; to talk about = tátab
dish = čoyólč
dislike, to; to be angry with = dókʷ
dive, to = ós

divide, to; to separate = páł
divide, to; to split = čxgʷás
divide up, to = cálq
divide up amongst, to; to spread out amongst = pák
do, to; to make = hóy
do something, to = x̣éh
dock or land, to; to come ashore; to arrive = łál
doctor (Eng. loan word) = táktd
doctor, to; shaman's treatment of a sick patient = báł
dog = skobáyʔ
dogfish = sk̓ʷáač
dollar = éls
dollar; money (Eng. loan word) = tála
door; road = šágʷł
down = xʷtágʷe
down = ƛ̓´p
dream, to = kláletot
dress, to; to put on clothes = ƛ̓ál
dried fish = soládxʷ
dried salmon = k̓ʷás
drift, to; to float = ȝóq
drift, to; to drift away = póo
drift away, to; to float = p̓´q̓ʷ
drink, to = qóʔqʷa
drive a wedge into wood, to = c̓´s
drop, to; to come down; to fall down = xʷét
drop, to; to let go of = b̓´ł
drum = tsólč
dry, to = šáb
duck = sk̓ʷálaš
duck, hell diver = x̣óx̣ʷayʔ
ducks, black = k̓ʷáalxʷ
dumb, to be = ayayáš

~ E ~

eagle = eláled
eagle, black mountain = xʷbǯál
ear = q̓ʷláde
earring = sƛ̓aƛ̓wálde
earth; dirt; land = swátyotd

east = t̓k̓tólgʷadxʷ
eat, to = ʔáł
eat, to; to bite = l̓´q̓ʷ
eat soup, to = łób
egg = aʔós
eight = tqáče
either...or; if = abél
elbow; upper arm; shoulder = tálekʷ
elderberries = sc̓ábt
eleven = padc yoxʷ ta dáčo
elk = kʷágʷečd
embers; ashes; charcoal; coals = p̓éč̓t
end; point; head = sʔélks
end of, the = élks
enough = eƛ̓ób
enough, to be = páƛ̓
entrails = sácegʷd
even if = aléʔs
evening = slałáx̣el
every; all = b̓´k̓ʷ
examine, to; to see = l̓´aʔb
extinguish a fire, to; to put out a fire = łáč̓
eye = q̓´lob

~ F ~

face = sʔácos
face this way, to; to turn facing someone = ƛ̓ós
fail, to = x̣ʷál
fail in health, to; to get weak = c̓ód
faint, to; to pass out = t̓k̓ʷáł
fall, to = béʔ
fall, to; to lie; to put down; to go down = b̓´č
fall, to; to roll over = táč
fall down, to; to drop; to fall down = xʷét
far off, to go; to go away = lél
fat; grease; lard = sx̣ʷás
fat in the stomach, to be = b̓´qʷ
father = bád
fear, to = x̣´c
feather = cécal

feather down = q̓ʷéq̓ʷalc
feel of something, to = b´ƛ̓
fell a tree, to; to make fall = ȝák̓
female relatives, including sisters and cousins from the male's point of view = álš
fence = q̓láx̣ad
fern root = t̓´de
fern root from which a medicinal tea was made = sáx̣olč
few = k̓ʷék̓ʷd
few times, a = k̓ʷedáɫ
fight, to = yábok̓ʷ
fill, to = l´č̓
finally = téla
find, to; to trade; to change things = áy?
fine in character; industrious = aȝaȝálos
fir tree = sčbédac
fire drill = šólakʷčop
first = ȝéxʷ
fish (generic term) = sčdátxʷ
five = clác
flatten, to = k̓´ʷl
flatten, to; to smash; the tide is in = p̓él
flesh; meat; human skin or body = báyac
flint chips = ƛ̓´cbec
float, to = p̓ós
float, to; to drift = ȝóq
float away, to; to drift = p̓´q̓ʷ
float to shore, to = p̓´d
flood, to = p̓éxʷ
flood, to; to run swiftly; to run over = ž̌áč
floor = x̣lédop
flounder (fish) = p̓wáy?
flowers = sc̓eqáysb
fly, to = sáq̓ʷ
fly, to = ɫók̓ʷ
fly a little, to = sésaq̓ʷ
fog = sq´ʷšab
foggy, to be = q´ʷš

follow, to; to go along = gʷá
food = s?áɫd
food left after a feast to be divided amongst the guests = q̓ʷáleč
fool, to; to deceive = k̓ák̓l
foot; leg from the knee down including the foot = žášad
forehead = s?eléls
forest; trees = st´ktkʷab
four = bós
freeze, to = q̓áxʷ
fresh, to be = wáƛ̓
friend; relatives = syá?ya?
frog = wáq̓waq̓
frog, bull = c̓ólsxʷaya
from = tol
from; of = gʷɫ
from afar = tolél
front, the = slahábac
front, to be; to have someone or something in front = slabéd
fruit; berries = sq̓ʷláɫad
fry, to = čéx̣
full of food, to be = b´ɫ
fur = ɫábed
fur; pelt or skin of animal = gʷásb

~ G ~

gamble, to; to play the bone game = lahál
game animals = sxʷéxʷe
gather, to = ƛ̓á
gather, to; to gather berries and other foods and materials = ólax̣
gather, to; to hunt = xʷéxʷe
gather together, to; to be together; to accompany = k̓ó
get, to; to grab; to catch = k´ʷd
get into a canoe, to = q̓elágʷ
get off or out of a canoe, to = q̓ʷéb
ghost; dead person; corpse = skáyo
girl just entering womanhood = báysx̣b
give, to = áb
give to, to = tée

give, to; to pass something to someone = aƛ̓á
give up, to; to surrender = čwál
glutted, to be; to be full of food = b′ł
gnaw, to = x̣óƛ̓
gnaw, to = čét
go, to = óx̣ʷ
go, to = héw
go ahead, to = háwʔ
go along, to; to follow = gʷá
go ashore, to = čóba
go away, to; to go far off = lél
go back, to; to turn back = bálkʷ
go down, to; to go down to the beach = k̓ʷét
go downstream, to = qʷéc
go home, to; to take home = t̓ókʷ
go into, to; to be in = h′dew
go out, to = šʒál
go out in a canoe, to; to paddle = ól
go to bed, to; to lie down = táʒ
go to get, to = l′q̓
go to the beach, to; to come to = čákʷ
go to the mountains, high land, inland toward
    land, or away from the water, to = táq̓t
go up, to; to climb a tree = kʷát
go upstream, to = łáy
good, to be = háʔł
good looking person, a = sláʔbb
goodbye = hóyʔ
grab, to = x̣éb
grab, to; to get; to catch; to take = k′ʷd
grandfather = sápa
grandmother = káyaʔ
grandchild = ébac
grass = sqʷéʔqʷale
grease; fat; lard = sx̣ʷás
great grandparent = čábeqʷ
grey hair = kólob
groan, to = ágak
grouse = sb′q̓bq̓
grow, to = ƛ̓áx̣ʷ
grunter fish = x̣ʷahép
guardian spirit; power = skláletot

guardian spirit, a strong one = yáʔbadad
guess, to = t̓ókʷ
gun = x̣ʷaltbálʔs
guts; intestines = k̓′ʒx̣

~ H ~

hair = sk̓áʒo
halibut = sčótx̣
hand = čáleš
hang on to something, to = kʷdábac
hang up, to = łék̓
hang up, to; to stick on = k̓ét̓
hang up, to; to tie up = łéd
hard, to be; to harden; very = téb
hardtack (Chinook jargon) = lapaskʷéʔ
harness, to (Eng. loan word) = hárnesed
have ready, to; to loosen = qeyá
have to be, to; it would be = yáwʔ
he = sádeł
head (body part) = sx̣áyʔos
head; end; point of = sʔélks
hear, to = ló
heart = sćále
heat = sq̓ʷál
heat, to = q̓ʷál
heavy = x̣′b
help, to; to cure = kʷáx̣ʷ
here, over there = code déʔe
here = tádeʔ
here, to be = déša
herring = stó̓ʔol
herring rake = słátabed
hide, to = čáʒ
hide something, to = čyál
high class person = syáb
high, to be; to lift = š′q
hilly, to be = pókʷ
hit, to; to punch = t′s
hit by throwing something, to = pós
hole, to have a = lóʔ
horn; wedge = gʷadákʷ
horse = stqéw
horse clam = háac

hospital = x̣ł áltxʷ
hot, to be; to become red hot = xʷáy
house = álʔal
how it is, to be = x̣éd
how many?; to count = k̓ʷéd
huckleberries = q̓ʷq̓´ʷl
hug, to = kól
humpy salmon = h´do
hunchbacked, to be = kawéč
hunchbacked person = askawéč
hunchbacked person, little = askékaweč
hungry, to be = cáwał
hunt, to; to gather = xʷéxʷe
hunter, a good = sóbde
hurt, to be; to be sick = x̣´ł
hurt accidentally, to be = bákʷł
husband = sčéstxʷ

~ I ~

I = áca
ice = sq̓áxʷ
ideas; plans = ƛ̓álegʷd
if; either...or = abél
in, to be = d´k̓ʷ
Indian carrot = šágak
inland = táq̓ł
in-laws; affinal kin = x̣áx̣a ~ sx̣áx̣a
in place, to be; to stay = ées
insane person = kalése
inside = déw
instruct, to; to show how = gʷál
intelligence = sx̣éx̣č
intestines; guts = k̓´ȝx̣
ironwood = qacágʷac
island = ƛ̓ácas
itch, to = g´ʷc

~ J ~

jabber, to = k̓ásk
jar = xʷalábaleʔ
joyful, to be (Eng. loan word, joy) = ǯóel
jump, to = sáxʷ

jump (fish), to = gʷád
just = tóx̣ʷ
just now = dáʔxʷ

~ K ~

kick, to = ȝógʷ
kill, to; to weaken = gʷlál
kinnikinnik bush = ċábtac
kinnikinnik leaves = k̓áyok̓ayo
Klallam = xʷsƛ̓álab
kneel, to = belál
kneel down, to = x̣ʷélč
know, to = áy

~ L ~

lake = x̣áčo
land; earth; dirt = swátyotd ~ sswátyotd
land otter = sk̓áaƛ̓
large number; many = qáha
last, to be; to be behind = lák
late, to be; to be missing = šób
late, to be; to be slow = q̓´d
later; shortly; just now = dáy
laugh, to = x̣áy
lay an egg, to; to give birth = bdáʔ
lay out, to; to put something down; to bet = bčálekʷ
lay something down, to = qʷát
lazy, to be = céleč
lazy; dumb = kalálos
leaf = sčóła
leak, to = gʷéx̣
lean, to = čád
lean-to; umbrella = q̓´sed
learn, to = háy
learn, to; to find out about; to know = łáaxʷ
leave, to = łágʷ
left side = kaláal
leg from the knee up to the buttocks = sʔálap
leg from the knee down, including the foot; foot = ǯášad

lengthen out, to; to provide with = hác
let go, to; to stop; to desist = ƛ̓´l
let go of, to; to drop = b´ł
letter; a mark = sx̣ál
levirate relationship = báloced
lie, to; to tell a falsehood = b´dč
lie, to; to fall or be down = b´č
lie down, to = bčágʷ
lie down, to; to go to bed = tá3
lie in wait for, to = ċáło
lie in wait for, to; to stalk = ƛ̓á?
lie on back, to = k̓´q̣
life; soul = slé?
lift, to; to be high; sky = š´q
lift the head, to = xʷp̓ós
light, to be = l´x̣
light on (bird), to = q´p̓
like; as = xʷláb
like, to; to want = x̣áƛ̓
like, to be; to be just like = x̣łtéx̣
limb or branch of a tree = sčášed
ling cod = ł̓óbks
listen to someone who is talking, to; to pay
    attention = ƛ̓´bč
live at, to; to come to; to live = ál
live at a place, to = łáł
live with in-laws, to = k̓ʷéłyo?
liver = sčálob
log; stick; tree = st´kʷab
long; tall = hác
long ago; a long time = hákʷ
long hair = s3alkét
look for, to = g´ʷč̌
look for lice, to = gák̓
loon = swókʷad
loosen, to; to have ready = qeyá
lose, to; to throw away = éx̣ʷ
louse = básčd
lousy, to be = b´š
lower class = kaqél
lying around, to be = qʷátqʷat

make, to; to do = hóy
make fall, to; to fell a tree = 3ák̓
make a canoe, to = p̓áyaq
make a mistake, to; to be wrong = 3áƛ̓
make fun of, to; to play = čá?a
man = stóbš
man in his 'teens = l´gob
many; lots = qá
maple tree = čółac
mark, a; a letter = sx̣ál
mark, to; to write = x̣ál
marriage gift exchange = óloł
married, to be = čagʷáš
marry, to = hóygʷas
marry, to (white man's or "legal" marriage) =
    balyé
mat house = qʷaláytxʷ
material with which to make something = hóytd
May (time period) = k̓ágʷalab
maybe; perhaps; uncertain = x̣óola
mean, to be = x̣ék̓ʷ
mean, to; to be the way in the sense of
    explanation or a course of action = táb
meaning undetermined = lé
meat; flesh; human skin or body = báyac
melt, to = 3áx̣ʷ
men, young = l´gʷlgob
mend, to = t̓´q̣
messy, to be = léx̣
middle = ácgʷeł
milk; breast = sq´bo?
mind; thought = x̣´č
mink = ċb´lkcd
missing, to be; to be late = šób
mix, to = báloq
mix, to; to stir = b´t̓k̓ʷ
molasses (Eng. loan word) = blás
Monday = p̓sq̓ʷábac
moon; month = słokʷálb
morning, early = łóp
moss = kʷá3ab

~ M ~

maggots = šó3a

mother = sḱóy ~ ḱó
mountain = sbádet
mountain = skʷátač
mountain goat = sx̣ʷéƛ̓ay
mountain goat skin = sḱʷásb
mouse = sḱʷátad
mouth = kádx̣ʷ
move quickly; to shake; to swing = ʒákʷ
move residence, to = gʷéčgʷeč
move residence, to = ʒáx̣ax̣
move slowly, to; to crawl = šól
move something, to = ʒáx̣
mussels = sčéč

~ N ~

name, a = sdá
name, to = dá?
name of Chipmunk's grandmother = x̣ax̣áyklked
navel = blálegʷd
Neah Bay = bq̓á?a
near, to be = čét
neck = sckápsb
needle of wood used in making cattail mats =
    q̓láqted
nephew = skláʒotał ~ kláʒotał
nephews and nieces = stálał
news = syécb
night, to be; to be dark = łáx̣
night time = słáx̣el ~ słáx̣e ~ słáx̣
nine = x̣ʷál
no; not = x̣ʷé?
noon = łágʷt
north = áłx̣ad
nose = b'qsd
not = x̣ʷéla
not; no = x̣ʷé?
now; just now = dá?x̣ʷ
nuts = q̓ápox̣ʷ

~ O ~

oh! = ó

oh! = há
old, to be; to be rotten = sákʷ
old people = cécq̓ʷ
older sibling (term of address) = x̣ʷskáted
on = álax̣ʷ
on top of, to be = łágʷt
once = dečax̣ʷ
one = dáčo
one hundred = dáčo sbqʷáče
onion-like plant = sx̣áʒb
onion-like root = ċábed
only; just = x̣ól
only; to have to be = yáw?
only; alone = dayáy
open something, to = g'ḱ
Oregon grapes = sx̣ʷé?
other = łḱ
other; different = lalé?
other end of the house = łḱáde?
others = qʷálk
otter = sḱáƛ
outdoors; outside = šálbex̣ʷ
outside; side = élabac
outside of the house = šalbex̣ʷáde?
owl = tklós
oysters = sqʷéqʷeč
oyster beds = ƛ̓óx̣ʷƛ̓ox̣ʷe

~ P ~

pack, to; to carry = čbá?
paddle, to; to go out in a canoe = ól
paddle a canoe, to = éł
painted, to be; to be ripe; to get warm; to be
    cooked = q̓ʷál
paper (Eng. loan word) = pépa
parents or close relatives = éhešd
pass by something, to = b'lx̣ʷ
pass out, to; to faint = łḱʷáł
pass something to someone, to; to give = aƛá
pass something to someone, to; to hand
    something over = táqos
pay, to = b'c

pay attention, to = tlá
pay attention, to; to listen to someone who is
    talking = ƛ´bč̓
pears (Eng. loan word) = pérs
peek in, to = k̓ʷél
peel, to = čók̓ʷ
peel off, to = łóq̓ʷ
pelt or skin of animal; fur = gʷásb
peninsula (a narrow strip of land projecting into
    the water) = qqʷés
penis = š´las
people = ácełtalbexʷ
period; time = padáb
person ugly in appearance = kaláʔab
person with an ugly body = kaláleg̓ʷd
pheasant; chicken = sg´ʷlo
pick, to = kʷél
pick hops, to (Eng. loan word) = háps
piece cut out = ełéč̓
pierce, to; to stab = l´xʷ
pinch, to; to squeeze a person with the hand =
    c̓oléq̓ʷ
pitch = qʷáleł
pity, to = óš
place, a = s´x̣ʷ
place for singing spirit songs = pégʷed
place name = sblátxʷ
place where... = štád
plans; ideas = ƛáleg̓ʷd
plant, a = spadálekʷ
plant growing along the shore. Small black bulbs
    on the roots were eaten. = x̣bx̣´b
plant, to = padálekʷ
plant used for food (looks like macaroni when
    cooked) = pyax̣é {*rock rose, bitterroot*}
play, to; to make fun of = čáʔa
plums (Eng. loan word) = pláms
point; head; end of = sʔélks
point at, to; to stick into = t´č̓
point of land = sqʷécks
poison, to (Eng. loan word) = póysn
poke, to (as a fire) = céq̓
poor, to be = šbáb
poor person = sošbábtxʷ

porpoise = qʷasyóʔ
Port Blakely = daxʷċaxʷlósb
potatoe = speʔkóc
potlatch = páłač
potlatch, to = gʷégʷe
potlatch house = gʷegʷeáltxʷ
pound, to = tóp
pour, to = k̓´ʷł
power; guardian spirit = skláletot
pregnant, to be = ʒéʒehe
prepared, to be; to be ready = qʷéb
pronged, to be = éq̓
provide with, to; to lengthen out = hác
Puget Sound; salt water; sea = x̣´ʷlč
pull apart, to; to separate = t´x̣ʷ
pull out feathers, to = x̣ác
punch, to; to hit = t´s
push, to = x̣´d
push, to = héq
puss face = b´ċos
put away, to = láʔa
put away, to; to store = šéč̓
put down, to = b´č
put in or on a canoe, to; to carry in or on a
    canoe = q̓él
put in water, to; to soak = ǯéq̓
put something down, to; to bet = bčálekʷ
put there, to = áa

~ Q ~

quarter (money, Eng. loan word) = kʷáta
quick, to be = áł

~ R ~

rabbit = k̓´ʷcdeʔ
race, to; a race = x̣éx̣q̓aweł
raft = qéboʔx̣ʷ
raid, to = x̣áb
rain = sqálb
rain, to = qál
rainbow = kʷbáčed
rat = kádayoxʷ

raven = qʷáqʷ

reach, to; to chase; to catch up with = čál

ready, to be; to be prepared = qʷéb

reason, to be the; to be the truth; to be the way
    things are = ésta

red, to be = kʷéƛ

red-headed woodpecker = k´tktač

reflection = ċálbeʒ

regain consciousness, to; to come to; to revive =
    ṗál

relate one's genealogy, to = xčóol

related by kinship, to be = tléx̌ʷ

relatives; friends = syáʔyaʔ

religion = sḱʷdéʔecot

remember, to = láx̌

rest, to = kákʷ

revive, to; to regain consciousness = ṗál

riffle in the river, a = sḱélałdalb

right away; directly = télb

right side = ʒhál

right side of a canoe = ʒhálgʷł

right side of body = ʒhálegʷd

ring = šéščksače

rip something, to = x̌´ʷt

ripen, to; to be cooked; to get warm; to be
    painted or colored = q̇ʷál

river = stólakʷ

road; door = šágʷł

roasting sticks = x̌áḱʷd

roll over, to; to fall = táč

roof = skálaltxʷ

room, a = dyáde

root = sḱʷélp

rope = łbéłd

rotten, to be = č´q̇ʷ

rotten, to be; to be old = sákʷ

rotten; sore = č´q̇ʷ

rotten; to be spoiled = d´qʷ

rotten stick = yóq̇ʷayʔ

rotten wood = ṗáḱac

rub, to = šéč

rub, to = tás

run, to = tláw

run out of, to; to be all gone; all; every; = b´ḱʷ

run over, to; to step on = l´ċ

run over, to; to flood; to run swiftly = žáč

~ S ~

sack (French loan word) = lesák

saliva = słéleš

salal berries = łáqa

salmon = łálċ

salmon; fish in general = sčdátxʷ

salmon berry = st´gʷd

salmon, blue-back = sċwád

salmon, dog = ƛx̌ʷáyʔ

salmon; dried spring salmon = talóp

salmon, humpbacked = hadóʔ

salmon skin = ḱʷáltad

salmon soup = bét̓

salmon, spring (Duwamish) = sácab

salmon, spring (Suquamish) = yóbač

salt (Eng. loan word) = sólt

salt water; Puget Sound; sea = x̌´ʷlč

same, the = déłeł

sand; sandbar = sgʷésdalb

sand spit = čgóced

save, to; to put food away = x̌dé

say, to = éd

say, to; to think = cót

scarred, to be = š´éš

school (Eng. loan word) = skól

scoop up, to = yáƛ

scrape, to; to clear = sáx̌

scratch, to = x̌éq̇

scratch, to = ċbéq̇

scream, to = čéx̌

sea; salt water; Puget Sound = x̌´ʷlč

seal = ásxʷ

Seattle {the city} = ʒeʒaláleč

secret society = sx̌édx̌edeb

see! = helá

see! = héle

see, to; to examine = láʔb

seed, a = spadálekʷac

sell, to; to trade = hóyob
send, to = kʷá
send for, to = tláč
separate, to; to divide = páł
separate, to; to pull = t´x̣ʷ
seven = ćóks
sew, to = ṗáć
shag (a type of bird) = bážos
shake, to; to swing; to move quickly = ʒákʷ
shaman; shaman power = txʷdáʔab
shameful matter, a = sx̣éćel
sharpen, to = x̣´ʷc
sharpen, to = ʒ´q̇
shavings (wood) = čóqbed
she = cádeł
shellfish (a round, snail-like shellfish) = kbáde
shinny game = q̇ʷaq̇ʷyélc
shoe = tq̇ʷápšad
shoot, to = łóć
short = q̇áq̇xʷoʔ
shot = šodgʷáls
shoulder; elbow; upper arm = łálekʷ
shout or yell to someone in the distance = qʷé
shove, to = áš
showing, to be; to uncover; to be visible = q̇áx̣
showing, to be; to be born = wlél
sibling = álš
sibling, older = skáʔ
sibling, younger = sóqʷa
sibling, younger = kalá
sick, to be; to be hurt = x̣´ł
sick or weak, to be = dóqʷ
sickness = sx̣´ł
side = élagʷeł
side; outside; side of body = élabac
side, the other = łk̇ábac
side of a person = elálegʷd
side of the head = welálade
side of the road or door = cʔéloced
sing, to = él
sing, to = łél

sing a spirit song, to; to dance a spirit dance = pékʷ
sink, to; to go down; to put down = b´č
sister-in-law = čábaš
sister or brother, my younger = cóqʷa
sister or female cousin of a woman = ʔáʔšad
sit, to = gʷád
sit quietly, to = gʷégʷad
six = ʒkáče
skate (fish) = kʷéʔkʷeel
skin, to; to cut up = k̇ʷéč
skin or body; meat; flesh = báyac
skunk = sq̇byó
sky; to be high; to lift = š´q
sky = šqólgʷdxʷ
sky (in the language of Rabbit in a myth) = láya
slanted, to be; to tip = k̇ʷéć
slap, to = t´q̇
slave = stódq
sleep, to = étot
sleepy, to be = éʔtot
slide, to = q´ʷc
slide, to = léq̇ʷ
slide down (dirt), to = x̣él
slow, to be; to be late = q̇´d
small; little = memáʔanʔ ~ memáʔadʔ
smart, to be; to be bright = ṗépł
smash, to; to chop up = béƛ̇
smash, to; to flatten; the tide is in = ṗél
smell, to; to stink = qáp
smell, to = éhal
smell something, to = sób
smelt = čáʔo
smoke = stéq̇ʷel
smoke, to = łéq̇ʷ
smoke house = pegʷedáltxʷ
smooth place = háʔłdop
snag = kláde
snake = b´ćć
sneak up on, to = č´ʒ
Snuqualmie = sdókʷalbexʷ
snow = báqoʔ

snow, to = báqoʔb
snow bird = spécxʷ
soak, to = q̇ál
soak, to; to put in water = ǯéq̇
soapberry = sxʷásb
soften, to = q̇ʷéʔ
some, any = kʷe
something; who? = gʷát
something = kʷád
song, a = st̓éleb
song, a = selálekʷ
soon = télaxʷ
soon = gʷáx̣ʷ
sore; rotten = č̓q̇ʷ
sores, to have = čé
soul; life = sléʔ
soupy food made of flour and water = lkbéd
south = q̇x̣ólgʷatxʷ
south wind = stgʷáq̇ʷ
spear = č̓éšay
spear for catching bottom fish = ƛ̓agʷéced
spear, to; to stick something into something =
    cák̓
spear fish, to = t̓́p
spear something, to; to throw a spear = sáq̇
spit, to = tó
splatter, to; to stick = t̓́k
split, to; to crack = č̓́x̣
spoiled or rotten, to be = d̓́qʷ
spread all over, to = čáš
spread out, to = ɬ̓́x̣
spread out amongst, to; to divide up amongst =
    pák
spread wings, to = tex̣lá
sprinkle water, to = ɬ̓́t
squeeze, to = ṗéc̓
squeeze a person with the hand, to; to pinch =
    c̓oléq̇ʷ
squirrel = skáʒo
stab, to; to pierce = l̓́xʷ
stalk, to; to lie in wait for = ƛ̓áʔ
stand, to = cáksed

stand up, to; to stand on or in front of = hé
star = čóšad
stay, to; to be in place = ées
stay with, to = gʷád
steal, to = kádaʔ
steam, to; to cook by steaming on hot rocks =
    q̇́ls
step-father = sčaɬbádb
step, to; to take a step = t̓x̣áb
step on, to; to run over = l̓́c̓
stick; tree; log = st̓́kʷab
stick, to; to splatter on = t̓́k
stick in, to = šéc
stick on, to; to hang up = k̓ét
stick something in the neck, to = tčábab
stick something into something, to; to spear =
    cák̓
stick something onto something, to = ƛ̓éq̇
stiff, to be = s̓́p
stiff, to be = k̓́ʷt
still; yet = dédeʔɬ
stir, to; to mix = b̓́tk̓ʷ
stockings (Eng. loan word) = stákad
stomach = tádč
stomach = ƛ̓áč
stone = čéƛa
stop, to; to desist; to let go = ƛ̓́l
stop something, to = hálʔ
store = hoyobáltxʷ
straight, to be; to be right = c̓́k̓ʷ
stranger = ɬálbexʷ
stretch, to = ót
stretch out, to = šés
stretch out, to; to bend down = ʒ̓́q
strong, to be = ol̓́x̣ʷ
strong, to be = wál̓
stuck, to be = čék̓ʷ
stupid person = ayayáš
suck, to = c̓ók
sugar (Eng. loan word) = šókʷa
suitcase – q̇wáde
summer = padhádab ~ shádab

sun = łokʷáł
sun is shining, the = gʹk
Suquamish tribe = soq̓ʷábš
surely; truly = céck̓ʷ
surface, to; to come up after being submerged =
    šáyʔ
surrender, to; to give up = čwál
swallow, to = b̓ʹq̓
sweat house (Duwamish) = wóxʷtad
sweat house (Suquamish) = sxʷc̓éc̓ab
sweet, to be = qʷágʷ
swell, to = šáxʷ
swim, to = łéč
swim, to; to bathe = łéł
swing, a = yeʔdóʔad
swing, to = yeʔdóʔ
swing, to; to shake; to move quickly = ȝákʷ
Swinomish tribe = swádabš

~ T ~

taboo; sacred; to cry out = x̌áx̌a
tail = sč̓óp̓c̓
take, to; to catch; to get = k̓ʹʷd
take off, to = łágʷ
take out, to; to go out = šȝál
take out, to = šáy
talk, to = x̌ódx̌od
talk about, to; to discuss = tátab
talk over, to; to discuss = háʔdad
tall; long = hác
tall person = sháȝb
tattoo, to = ƛ̓éč
teach, to = gʷák
teachings; lessons = sx̌ʹč
tears = kaálos
tell, to = cód
tell, to = yécb
tell myths, to = xʷéx̌ʷyap
ten = pádc
ten cents (Eng. loan word, bit) = bét
thank, to; to give thanks for = kʷdéd
that which was referred to earlier = déʔeł

that = tóde
that over there = déde?
that over there = tode déʔe
that's why; that is; there is = déł
theft; thief = skáda?
them; him (pointing) = táʔa
then = háy
there, to be = á
there, to be = ác
they = hálgʷa
thief; theft = skáda?
thigh = łk̓álap
thin, to be = ƛó
thing = stáb
think, to = x̌ʹč
think about, to; to think it over; to ponder =
    ptéd
thirsty, to be = táqo?
thirty = łéxʷače
this = ta
this, feminine = cé?
this feminine person there = céʔeł
this, non-feminine = té?
this non-feminine thing or person there = téʔeł
those over there = téeʔeł
thought; mind = x̌ʹč
threaten, to = q̓ábas
three = łéxʷ
throat = q̓yóq̓ʷ
through; by means of = lełál
throw, to = x̌ʹʷb
throw something away, to = éx̌ʷ
thunder; thunder bird = x̌ʷéqʷade?
tickle, to = kyáp
tide; beach = swádač
tide is in, the; to smash; to flatten = p̓él
tie a knot, to = ƛóc̓
tie up, to; to bundle up; to wrap up = x̌ʹk
tie up, to; to hang up = łéd
tighten, to = ƛ̓ʹq̓ʷ
time; period = padáb
tin can = káwx̌

tip, to; to be slanted = k̇ʷéċ
to; toward; at = txʷal
toe nail = q̇ʷáx̣ʷšad
together, to be = k̇ó
tomorrow = dádato
tongue = łálap
tooth = ʒ´des
top = skábac
town (Eng. loan word) = táwd
trade, to; to change things; to find = áyʔ
trade, to; to sell; to do; to make = hóy
Transformer = dókʷebł
travel, to; to walk = ébaš
trawl for fish, to = łedáp
treat, to; shaman's doctoring of a sick patient = báł
tree; stick; log = st´kʷab
tribe (another tribe) = deč̓ákʷbexʷ
tribe = gʷákʷbexʷ
trout = k´ʷspł
true, to be; to be the reason; to be the way things are; to be there = ésta
truly = táł
truly; surely = céck̇ʷ
try, to = ṗáʔ
tuber, a = cágʷeč
Tulalip = txʷlélap
turn, to = ʒálq
turn around, to = sálq̇
turn around, to; to face this way = ƛ̇ós
turn around, to = áʒaq̇a
turn back, to; to go back = bálkʷ
twelve = padc yoxʷ kʷe sáleʔ
twenty = sáleʔače
twice = cbáb
twist, to = č´lp
two = sáleʔ

~ U ~

uncle = yaláp
uncle = qáse

uncooked, to be; to be unripe = x̣éċ
uncover, to; to be visible = q̇áx̣
under = ágʷab
underneath, to be = ƛ̇pábac
understand, to = l´q
unmarried sisters of a man's living wife and the reciprocal. sister-in-law or brother-in-law = čábaš
unripe; uncooked = x̣éċ
up, to be = xʷáʔ
upriver; above = q̇éyoxʷ
use, to = tálx̣
useless, to be = klbéd

~ V ~

very; to be hard = téb
very = x̣éqab
very = haláʔab
very soon = gʷégʷax̣ʷ
very; very likely; much; often; soon = pót
visible, to be; to uncover = q̇áx̣
visit, to = ʒláx̣ad
vomit, to = ʒóx̣ʷat

~ W ~

wade, to = g´ʷč
wait, to = táq̇s
walk, to; to travel = ébaš
walk around in a circle, to = ʒlólč
want, to = áyxʷ
want, to = x̣éqʷ
want, to; to like = x̣áƛ̇
war; to fight = x̣élex̣
warm, to be; to cuddle = q´b
warm, to get; to be cooked; to be ripe; to be painted or colored = q̇ʷál
wash, to = ċákʷ
watch for, to = láʔlaʔb
water = qóʔ
water falling over a bank = c´tx̣
waves = ʒólčo
we = débł

183

weak; to fail in health = ćod
weak or sick, to be = dóqʷ
weaken, to; to kill = gʷlál
weasel = łáčb
wedge; horn = gʷadákʷ
well; well then = gʷla
wet, to be = łʼqʷ
whale = qʼʷdes
what? = stáb
whatever = ṗáƛaƛ
when = patáb
whenever = déʔł
where = čád
whip with a stick, to; to club = čáxʷ
whisper, to = ságak
whistle, to = xʷéʔw
white man (Eng. loan word, Boston) = pástd
who? something = gʷát
wide = łákt
widen, to = báa
widow = sɋʷéc
wife = čágʷaš
wild cat = ṗčáb
wild men said to wander in the woods and be
    dangerous = ćyátko
wild men said to wander in the woods and be
    dangerous = stétał
win, to = ćlálekʷ
wind, the = šʼxʷb
wind around, to = xʼʷkʷ
wing of a bird = sčbtláʔxad
wink, to = ćyékalos
winter = stʼs
winter time = patʼs
wipe, to; to clear; to clean = ékʷ
wish, to = háw
witch or dangerous female spirit = swayókʷ
wolf = steqáyo
woman = słáday
work = syáyos
work, to = yáyos
work or the results of work = sweʔál
worm (a long green worm found in old logs) =
    ɋyáw

worry, to = xʷéd
worry, to = x̣ʷáɋ
wrap, to; to cover = x̣ád
wrap up, to; to bundle up; to tie up = x̣ʼk
write, to; to mark = x̣ál
wrong, to be; incorrect = séxʷ
wrong, to be; to make a mistake = ʒáƛ

~ Y ~

Yakima {*Yakama*} Indians = tóbšadad
year = sʒáladob
year, one = čágʷatxʷ
years, two = cábadxʷ
yell or shout to someone in the distance = qʷé
yes = é
yesterday = láʔłdat
you (plural) = gʷlápoʔ
you (singular) = dʼgʷe
young = débał
young person = t̓éso

Bibliography

Allen, Henry

1950 Two Soul Recovery Songs. Recorded by Willard Rhodes in August and September. Reel 16. Bureau of Indian Affairs, Educational Division, American Folklife Center, Library of Congress, DC.

Amoss, Pamela

1975 Catalogue of the Marian Smith Collection of Fieldnotes, Manuscripts, and Photographs. Manuscript on file, Library of the Royal Anthropological Institute of Great Britain and Ireland, London.

1978 *Coast Salish Spirit Dancing* ~ The Survival of an Ancestral Religion. University of Washington Press, Seattle.

1981 Coast Salish Elders. *Other Ways of Growing Old*: 227-261. Pamela Amoss and Steven Harrell, eds. Stanford University Press.

1982 Resurrection, Healing, and "the Shake": The Story of John and Mary Slocum. Charisma and Sacred Biography. Michael Williams, ed. *Journal of the American Academy of Religion*, Thematic Studies XLVIII, Volume 48 (3-4): 87-109.

1987 The Fish God Gave Us: The First Salmon Ceremony Revived. *Arctic Anthropology* 24 (1): 56-66.

1990 The Indian Shaker Church. Handbook of North American Indians, *Northwest Coast*, Volume 7: 633-639. Wayne Suttles, ed. Smithsonian Institution Press, Washington DC.

Asher, Brad

1995 A Shaman-killing Case on Puget Sound, 1873-1874. American Law and Salish Culture. *Pacific Northwest Quarterly* 86 (1): 17-24. Winter 1994/95.

1999 *Beyond the Reservation*: *Indians, Settlers, and the Law in Washington Territory, 1853-1889*. Norman: University of Oklahoma Press.

Ballard, Arthur C

1927 Some Tales of the Southern Puget Sound Salish. *University of Washington Publications in Anthropology* 2 (3): 57-81.

1929 Mythology of Southern Puget Sound. *University of Washington Publications in Anthropology* 3 (2): 31-150.

1935 Southern Puget Sound Kinship Terms, *American Anthropologist* 37 (1).

1950 Calendric Terms of the Southern Puget Sound Salish. *Southwest Journal of Anthropology* 6: 79-99.

1951 Deposition on Oral Examination of Arthur Condict Ballard. November 26, 27, 28. Testimony before the Indian Claims Commission of the United States, Docket 98. Carolyn Taylor, court reporter. Manuscript on file, White River Historical Society, Auburn, Washington.

1957 The Salmon Weir on Green River in Western Washington, *Davidson Journal of Anthropology* 3 (1). Seattle: University of Washington Anthropology.

Barnett, Homer

1955 *The Coast Salish* of British Columbia. Studies in Anthropology 4. Eugene: University of Oregon Press.

1957 *Indian Shakers*, A Messianic Cult of the Pacific Northwest. Carbondale: Southern Illinois University Press.

Bates, Dawn, Thom Hess, and Vi Hilbert
 1994 *Lushootseed Dictionary*. Seattle: University of Washington Press.
Bishop, Thomas
 1916 Applications For Enrollment and Allotment, 1911-17. Records Relating to Enrollment of Washington Indians. Special Agent Charles E. Roblin. National Archives.
Bishop, Kathleen, and Kenneth Hansen
 1978 The Landless Tribes of Western Washington. *American Indian Journal* 4 (5): 20-31.
Blalock, Susan
 1979 List of Suquamish Settlements. Suquamish Tribal Library and Archives.
Boas, Franz, and Hermann Haeberlin
 1927 Sound Shifts in Salishan Dialects. *International Journal of American Linguistics* 4 (2-4): 117-136.
Buchanan, Charles
 1916 Rights of the Puget Sound Indians to Game and Fish. *Washington Historical Quarterly* 6 (2): 109-118.
Bruseth, Nels
 1950 Indian Stories and Legends of the Stillaguamish, Sauks and Allied Tribes. Arlington (WA) Times Press.
Buchanan, Charles
 1916 Rights of the Puget Sound Indians to Game and Fish. *Washington Historical Quarterly* 6 (2): 109-118.
Castile, George P, ed.
 1982 The 'Half-Catholic' Movement: Edwin and Myron Eells and the Rise of the Indian Shaker Church. *Pacific Northwest Quarterly* 73: 165-174.
 1985 *The Indians of Puget Sound*: The Notebooks of Myron Eells. University of Washington Press for Whitman College, Walla Walla, WA.
Collins, June
 1949 John Fornsby: The Personal Document of a Coast Salish Indian. Smith 1949: 287-341.
 1950a The Indian Shaker Church. *Southwestern Journal of Anthropology* 6 (4): 399-411.
 1950b Growth of Class Distinctions and Political Authority Among the Skagit Indians during the Contact Period. *American Anthropologist* 52 (3): 331-342.
 1952 The Mythological Basis for Attitudes toward Animals among Salish-Speaking Indians. *Journal of American Folklore* 65 (258): 353-359.
 1966 Naming, Continuity, and Social Inheritance among the Coast Salish of Western Washington. *Papers of the Michigan Academy of Science, Arts, and Letters* 51: 425-36.
 1974 *Valley of the Spirits* ~ The Upper Skagit Indians of Western Washington. Seattle: University of Washington Press.
 1979 Multilineal Descent: A Coast Salish Strategy: 243-254, *Currents in Anthropology*. Robert Hinshaw, ed. The Hague: Mouton.
Curtis, Edward
 1913 *The North American Indian*, being a series of 20 volumes picturing and describing the Indians of the United States, the Dominion of Canada, and Alaska. Written, Illustrated, and Published by Edward S. Curtis. Frederick Webb Hodge, ed. Volume 9: Coast Salish. Norwood, Mass.

Dorsey, George

1898 Accession 660: Salish of Puget Sound and Lake Washington. Chicago: Field Museum # 55848 - 55960.

1902 The Duwamish Spirit-Canoe and Its Use. Bulletin Free Museum of Science and Art, University of Pennsylvania 3 (4): 227-238.

Drucker, Philip

1937 Diffusion in Northwest Coast Culture in the Light of Some Distributions. PhD Dissertation, University of California at Berkeley.

Eels, Myron

1884 Census of the Clallam and Twana Indians of Washington Territory. *American Antiquarian* 6: 35-38.

1887 The Indians Of Puget Sound (nine parts). *American Antiquarian* 9.

1889 The Twana, Chemakum, and Klallam Indians of Washington Territory. Smithsonian Annual Report For 1887: 605-681.

1985 *The Indians of Puget Sound ~ The Notebooks of Myron Eells*. George Pierre Castille, ed. Seattle: University of Washington Press.

Elmendorf, William

1946 Twana Kinship Terminology. *Southwestern Journal of Anthropology* 2: 420-432.

1948 The Cultural Setting Of The Twana Secret Society. *American Anthropologist* 50: 625-633.

1960 *The Structure of Twana Culture* ~ with Comparative Notes on the Structure of Yurok by Alfred Kroeber. Washington State Research Studies, Monographic Supplement 2, Washington State University, Pullman.

1961a System Change in Salish Kinship Terminologies. *Southwestern Journal of Anthropology* 17 (4): 365-382.

1961b Skokomish and Other Coast Salish Tales. Washington State University Research Studies 29 (1): 1-37, (2): 84-117, (3): 119-150.

1971 Coast Salish Status Ranking and Intergroup Ties. *Southwestern Journal of Anthropology* 27: 353-380.

1982 Deposition of February 25 and 26. Davis, California. Civil # 9213 - Phase I.

1989 Skokomish Sorcery, Ethics, and Society: 147-182. *Systems of North American Witchcraft and Sorcery*. Deward Walker, ed. 1970, Anthropological Monographs of the University of Idaho 1, University of Idaho, Moscow.

1993 *Twana Narratives*. Native Historical Accounts of a Coast Salish Culture. Seattle: University of Washington Press.

Galin, Anne

1983 Spatial Organization in Lushootseed Culture, Texts, and Language. New York: Columbia University, Ph.D. Dissertation.

Gibbs, George

1877 Tribes of Western Washington and Northwestern Oregon. United States Geographical and Geological Survey of the Rocky Mountain Region, Part II: 157-241. Department of the Interior. *Contributions to North American Ethnology*, Vol. #I. Washington DC.

1970 Dictionary of the Niskwalli (Nisqually) Indian Language, Western Washington. Reprinted The Shorey Book Store, Seattle. Originally published 1877, Contributions to North American Ethnology #1: 285-361.

Guilmet, George, and David Whited
 1989   The People Who Give More: Health and Mental Health among the Contemporary Puyallup Indian Tribal Community. American Indian and Alaska Native Mental Health Research Journal. Volume 2 (Winter), Monograph #2: 1-141.
Guilmet, George, Robert Boyd, David Whited, and Nile Thompson
 1991 The Legacy of Introduced Diseases. *American Indian Culture and Research Journal* 15 (4): 1-32.
Gunther, Erna
 c1930-1940 Field Notebooks. Manuscript on file, Burke Museum, Seattle.
Haeberlin, Herman K
 1916-1917   Puget Salish, 41 Notebooks. Microfilm #2965 on file, National Anthropological Archives, Washington, DC.
 1918 SbEtEtda'q, A Shamanic Performance of the Coast Salish. *American Anthropologist* 20 (3): 249-257.
 1924 Mythology of Puget Sound. *Journal of American Folklore* 37 (143-144): 371-438.
Haeberlin, Herman and Erna Gunther
 1930 The Indians of Puget Sound, *University of Washington Publications in Anthropology* #4 (1): 1-84, Seattle.
Harmon, Alexandra
 1995   A Different Kind of Indians. Negotiating the Meanings of "Indian" and "Tribe" in the Puget Sound Region, 1820s-1970s. Ph.D. dissertation, Department of History, University of Washington, Seattle.
 1999   *Indians in the Making*: *Ethnic Relations and Indian Identities around Puget Sound*. University of California Press.
Harrington, John Peabody
 1910 Field and Class Notes, University of Washington, Seattle. Manuscript on file, Folders 36, 37. Microfilm reel 015, National Anthropological Archives, Washington DC.
 1910 Lummi/Duwamish. Microfilm of Fieldnotes. (Cited by frame in the text).
 1942 Chemakum /Clallam /Makah /Quileute fieldnotes.
Indian Claims Commission
 1952 Suquamish Tribe of Indians vs. The United States of America. Docket 132.
Hess, Thom
 1971 Prefix Constituent With /x^w/. *Studies in Northwest Indian Languages*. James Hoard and Thom Hess, eds. Sacramento Anthropological Society, Paper #11: 43-69.
 1976 *Dictionary of Puget Salish*. Seattle: Seattle: University of Washington Press.
 1977 Lushootseed Dialects. *Anthropological Linguistics* 19 (9): 403-419.
Hilbert, Vi taq^{w}šəblu
 1976 Recording in the Native Language. *Sound Heritage* IV (34): 39-42.
 1979 *Yehaw*. Seattle: Lushootseed Press.
 1980a Ways of the Lushootseed People: Ceremonies and Traditions of the Northern Puget Sound Indians. Seattle: United Indians of All Tribes Foundation, Daybreak Star Press.
 1980b Haboo. Seattle: Lushootseed Press.
 1985 *Haboo*: Native American Stories From Puget Sound. Seattle: U of Washington Press.
 1996 *Haboo* ~ Lushootseed Literature in English. Lushootseed Press.

Hilbert, Vi taqʷšəblu, Jay Miller, and Zalmai Zahir
  2001 *Puget Sound Geography*. Revised Thomas T Waterman Ethnogeography. Seattle: Lushootseed Press.
Horr, David Agee
  1974 Coast Salish And Western Washington Indians v. Indian Claims Commission. Findings. New York: Garland Publishing, Inc.
Indian Claims Commission
  1952 Suquamish Tribe of Indians vs. The United States of America. Docket 132.
  1974a Commission Findings. Docket No. 109, Duwamish Tribe of Indians. Coast Salish and Western Washington Indians V: 29-51. David Agee Horr, ed. NY: Garland Series.
  1974b Commission Findings. Docket No. 98, Muckleshoot Tribe of Indians. Coast Salish and Western Washington Indians V: 101-132. David Agee Horr, ed. NY: A Garland Series.
  1974c Commission Findings. Docket No. 132, Suquamish Tribe of Indians. In Coast Salish and Western Washington Indians V: 620-644. David Agee Horr, ed. NY: A Garland Series.
Kane, Paul
  1925 *Wanderings of an Artists* among the Indians of North America, From Canada to Vancouver's Island and Oregon through the Hudson's Bay Company's Territory, and Back again. Toronto: The Radisson Society of Canada. [1858].
Kruckeberg, Arthur
  1991 *The Natural History of Puget Sound*. Seattle: University of Washington Press.
Kuipers, Aert
  2002 Salish Etymological Dictionary. U of Montana, *Occasional Papers in Linguistics* #16.
Lane, Barbara
  1973 Political and Economic Aspects of Indian-White Culture Contact in Western Washington in the Mid-19th Century. May 10. United States v. Washington.
  c1974 Anthropological Report on the Identity, Treaty Status, and Fisheries of the Skokomish Tribe of Indians. 86pp.
  1974 Identity, Treaty Status and Fisheries of the Suquamish Tribe of the Port Madison Reservation. 52pp.
Lushootseed Press
  1995 Aunt Susie Sampson Peter; The Wisdom of a Skagit Elder. Transcribed by Vi Hilbert. Translated by Vi Hilbert and Jay Miller. Recorded by Leon Metcalf. Seattle.
  1995b Gram Ruth Sehome Shelton; The Wisdom of a Tulalip Elder. Transcribed by Vi Hilbert. Translated by Vi Hilbert and Jay Miller. Recorded by Leon Metcalf. Seattle.
  1995c Petius Isadore Tom; The Wisdom of a Lummi Elder. Seattle.
  1996 Lady Louse Lived There. Janet Yoder, ed. Complied by Vi Hilbert, Illustrated by Brad Burns. Seattle.
Maclachlan, Morag
  1998 The Fort Langley Journals, 1827-30. Vancouver: University of British Columbia Press.
Meany, Edmund
  1924 Chief Patkanim. *Washington Historical Quarterly* 15: 187-198.
  1957 Vancouver's Discovery of Puget Sound. Portraits and Biographies of the Men Honored in the Naming of the Geographical Features of Northwestern America. Portland: Binford and Mort Publishers. [1907]

Meeker, Ezra
 1980 *The Tragedy of Leschi*. Everett: The Printers. [1905]
Michaud, Ellen
 1977 Women of the Puget Sound Coast Salish Indians. An Inquiry into their traditional role in socialization, religion, and economics. University of Washington: BA Thesis.
Miller, Jay
 1976 The Northwest Coast of What? Paper presented at the Conference on Northwest Coast Studies, Burnaby, BC.
 1980 High-Minded High Gods in North America. *Anthropos* 75: 916-919.
 1981   The Matter of the (Thoughtful) Heart: Centrality, Focality, or Overlap. *Journal of Anthropological Research* 36 (3): 338-342.
 1985a   Salish Kinship: Why Decedence?   20th International Conference on Salish and Neighboring Languages: 213-222. August 15-17, University of British Columbia.
 1985b   Art and Souls: The Puget Sound Salish Journey to the Land of the Dead. Paper presented at the 5th Conference of the National Native American Art Studies Association, Ann Arbor.
 1988 *Shamanic Odyssey: The Lushootseed Salish Journey to the Land of the Dead*. Menlo Park: Ballena Press.
 1990 *Mourning Dove ~ A Salishan Autobiography*. University of Nebraska Press, Lincoln.
 1992a Native Healing in Puget Sound: Portrayal of Native American Health and Healing: 1-15. *Caduceus* ~ A Museum Journal for the Health Sciences. Winter.
 1992b A Kinship of Spirit: Society in the Americas in 1492: 305-337. *America in 1492*. Alvin Josephy, ed. NY: Alfred Knopf.
 1992c North Pacific Ethno-Astronomy: Tsimshian and Others: 193-206. *Earth and Sky*: Visions of the Cosmos in Native American Folklore. Claire Farrer and Ray Williamson, eds. University of New Mexico Press.
 1992d   Society in America in 1492.   America in 1492.   Selected Lectures from the Quincentenary Program. Harvey Markowitz, ed. The Newberry Library, D'Arcy McNickle Center for the History of the American Indian, Occasional Papers in Curriculum Series 15: 151-169. Chicago.
 1994 The Wisdom of Aunt Susie Sampson Peter, A Skagit Elder (Lushootseed~English).
 1995a The Wisdom of Ruth Shelton, A Tulalip Elder (Lushootseed~English).
 1995b The Wisdom of Isadore Tom, A Lummi Elder.
 1996 Seattle (si'ał): 574-576. Encyclopedia of North American Indians. Frederick E. Hoxie, ed. Houghton Mifflin Company, Boston.
 1997 Back to Basics: Chiefdoms in Puget Sound. *Ethnohistory* 44 (2): 375-387.
 1998   Middle Columbia River Salishans. Smithsonian Handbook of North American Indians. *Plateau*. Deward Walker, ed. Volume 12: 253-270.
 1999   *Lushootseed Culture and the Shamanic Odyssey*: An Anchored Radiance. Lincoln: University of Nebraska Press.
 2000   Inflamed History: Violence Against Homesteading Indians in Washington Territory. *North Dakota Quarterly* 67 (3/4): 162-173.

2004   Winds, Waterways, and Weirs.   Ethnographic Study of the Central Link Light Rail Corridor. Sound Transit, Contract Rta/Lr 69-00. Boas Project No 20005.D (Astrida Blukis Onat, PI). Seattle.

2014   Elders Dialog ~ Ed Davis and Vi Hilbert Discuss Native Puget Sound Language, Culture, and Heritage. (Lushootseed~English). 4Culture, King County Lodging Tax.

2015   Evergreen Ethnographies ~ Hoh, Chehalis, Suquamish, and Snoqualmi of Western Washington. Amazon.

2016a Herman Haeberlin Regained ~ Anthropology And Artifacts Of Puget Sound 1916-17, Amazon.

2016b Old Lukh ~ Native Puget Sound in Daily Life, Places, and Stories. Amazon.

2016c Pacific Plateau Portrayals ~ People, Places, Ponderings. Amazon.

2016d Leschi in Love ~ . Amazon.

2017a Minter Bay ~ Land, Lore, Loss, and Lucre in the South Salish Sea. Amazon.

2017b Native Met how ~ Improving Posterity. Amazon.

2017c George Gibbs Northwest Array ~ Full Reports, Place Names, Word List, Artifact Names, and Guide. Amazon.

2017d Herstory NW ~ Women Upholding Native Traditions

Miller, Jay, and Vi Hilbert

1993 Caring for Control: A Pivot of Salishan Language and Culture. pp. 237-239 in *American Indian Linguistics and Ethnography in Honor of Laurence C. Thompson*. University of Montana, Occasional Papers in Linguistics 10.

1996 Lushootseed Animal People: Mediation and Transformation from Myth to History. pp. 138-156 in *Monsters, Tricksters, and Sacred Cows*: Animal Tales and American Identities. A. James Arnold, ed. New World Studies. Charlottesville: University of Virginia Press.

Miller, Jay, with Warren Snyder

1999 Suquamish Traditions. *Northwest Anthropological Research Notes* 33 (1): 105-175.

Nelson, Charles

1990 Prehistory of the Puget Sound Region. pp. 481-484 in Suttles 1990.

Page, GA

1857 *HR Executive Documents* #37, 34th Congress, Third Session.

Ransom, Jay Ellis

1945   Notes On Duwamish Phonology and Morphology. *International Journal of American Linguistics* 11 (4): 204-210.

Riddell, E. E.

1932 History of Suquamish. Kitsap County Herald. Poulsbo, Washington. Friday, October 14.

Roberts, Helen, and Hermann Haeberlin

1918 Some Songs of the Puget Sound Salish. *Journal of American Folklore* 31 (122): 496-520.

Roblin, Charles

1919 M1343, Roll 6: Applications for Enrollment & Allotment – Washington Indians, 1911-9 Snoqualmie Squaxin Island Steilacoom Stillaguamish Suquamish Swinomish Tulalip-Spusam Wynookie {Originals in Box 7 NARA A1, DC}

1920   M1344   5 microfilmed reels, Records Concerning Applications for Adoption by the Quinaielt Indians, 1910–1919, Report of Special Agent [Charles] Roblin; Dr. Otis O. Benson, superintendent.

Ruby, Robert, and John A Brown
 1996 *John Slocum and the Indian Shaker Church*. Norman: University of Oklahoma Press.
Rygg, Lawrence Daniel
 1977 The Continuation of Upper Class Snohomish Coast Salish Attitudes and Deportment as seen through the Life History of a Snohomish Coast Salish Woman. Western Washington University: MA Thesis.
Sampson, Martin
 1938 The Swinomish Totem Pole, Tribal Legends. Told to Rosalie Whitney. Bellingham, Washington: Union Printing Company.
 1972 Indians of Skagit County. Mount Vernon, Washington: Skagit County Historical Society, Series 2.
Sercombe, Laurel
 2001 And Then it Rained: Power and Song in Western Washington Coast Salish Myth Narratives. PhD Dissertation, Department of Music, University of Washington, Seattle.
Sicade, Henry
 1940 XIX. The Indians' Side of the Story. pp. 490-503 in *Building A State. Washington, 1889-1939*. Charles Mills and O.B. Sperlin, eds. Tacoma: Washington State Historical Society.
Smith, Edgar
 1947 Indian Tribal Cases Decided in the Court of Claims of the United States, briefed and Compiled to 30 June 1947. General Accounting Office, Washington, DC.
Smith, Marian Wesley
 1940 *The Puyallup-Nisqually*. NY: Columbia University Contributions to Anthropology #32.
 1941 The Coast Salish of Puget Sound. *American Anthropologist* 43: 197-211.
Smith, Marian Wesley, ed.
 1949 *Indians of the Urban Northwest*. NY: Columbia University Contributions to Anthropology #36, New York.
Snyder, Warren
 1956 Archeological Sampling at "Old Man House" on Puget Sound. *Research Studies of the State College of Washington* #24 (1). Pullman, Washington.
 1968 Southern Puget Sound Salish 1: Phonology and Morphology. *Sacramento Anthropological Society, Paper #8*. 83pp.
 1968 Southern Puget Sound Salish 2: Texts, Place Names, and Dictionary. *Sacramento Anthropological Society, Paper #9*. 199pp.
Suquamish Museum
 1985 *Eyes of Chief Seattle*. Suquamish, WA.
Suttles, Wayne
 1951a The Early Diffusion of the Potatoe among the Coast Salish, *Southwest Journal of Anthropology* 7: 272-288.
 1951b Economic Life of the Coast Salish of Haro and Rosario Straits. PhD. Thesis, University of Washington, Seattle, Washington.
 1987 *Coast Salish Essays*. Seattle: University of Washington Press.
Suttles, Wayne, ed.
 1990 *Northwest Coast*. Handbook of North American Indians, Volume 7. Smithsonian Institution Press, Washington DC.

Suttles, Wayne, and William Elmendorf
 1963 Linguistic Evidence for Salish Prehistory: 41-52. *Symposium on Language and Culture*. Viola E Garfield and Wallace Chafe, eds. Proceedings of the 1962 Annual Spring Meeting of the American Ethnological Society. Seattle: University of Washington Press.

Suttles, Wayne, and Barbara Lane
 1990 Southern Coast Salish. Handbook of North American Indians. Wayne Suttles, ed. *Northwest Coast* Volume 7: 485-502. Smithsonian Institution Press, Washington, DC.

Suttles, Wayne, and Aldona Jonaitis
 1990 History of Research in Ethnology. Handbook of North American Indians. Wayne Suttles, ed. *Northwest Coast* Volume 7: 73-87. Smithsonian Institution Press, Washington DC.

Thrush, Coll-Peter
 2002 The Crossing-over Place: Urban and Indian Histories in Seattle. Ph.D. Dissertation, Department of History, University of Washington, Seattle
 2007 *Native Seattle* ~ Histories from the Crossing-Over Place. Seattle: University of Washington Press.

Tollefson, Kenneth Dean
 1982 Northwest Coast Village Adaptations: A Case Study. *Canadian Journal of Anthropology* 3 (1): 19-30.
 1987a Duwamish Cultural Continuity Study. Petition of Federal Acknowledgement.
 1987b The Snoqualmie: A Puget Sound Chiefdom. *Ethnology* 26 (2): 121-136.
 1989a Religious Transformation among the Snoqualmie Shakers. *Northwest Anthropological Research Notes* 23 (1): 97-102.
 1989b Political Organization of the Duwamish. *Ethnology* 28 (2): 135-149.
 1992 The Political Survival of Landless Puget Sound Tribes. *American Indian Quarterly*. Spring: 213-235.
 1995a Potlatching and Political Organization among the Northwest Coast Indians. *Ethnology* 34 (1): 53-73.
 1995b Duwamish Tribal Identity and Cultural Survival. *Northwest Anthropological Research Notes* 29 (1): 103-116.
 1996a In Defense of a Snoqualmie Political Chiefdom Model. *Ethnohistory* 43 (1): 145-171.
 1996b Tribal Estates: A Comparative And Case Study. *Ethnology* 35 (4): 321-338.
 1997 Tlingit: Chiefs and Present. *Portraits of Culture*. Ethnographical Originals. Melvin Ember, C Ember, D Levinson, eds. North America I: 267-292.
 2015a interview 7 January 2015, 2-3pm. TCP ~ National Register for Historic Preservation for Snoqualmie Falls. Conducted by Jay Miller.
 2015b Tribal Trio of the Northwest Coast. Jay Miller and Darby Stapp, eds. *Journal of Northwest Anthropology*, Memoir #10.

Tollefson, Kenneth, and Martin Abbott
 1993 From Fish Weir to Waterfall. *American Indian Quarterly* 17 (2): 209-225.
 1998 Snoqualmie Ethnicity: Community and Continuity. *American Indian Quarterly* 22 (4): 415-431.

Tweddell, Colin
 1950 The Snoqualmie-Duwamish Dialects of Puget Sound Salish. *University of Washington Publications in Anthropology* #12. Seattle.

1974 A Historical and Ethnological Study of the Snohomish Indian People. pp. 475-694 in Horr 1974.

1984 A Componential Analysis of the Criteria Defining an Indian "Tribe" in Western Washington. pp. 41-80 in *Western Washington Indian Socio-Economics:* Papers in Honor of Angelo Anastasio. Herbert Taylor and Garland Grabert, eds. Bellingham: Western Washington University.

US Court of Claims

1933 The Duwamish, Lummi, Whidby Island, Skagit, upper Skagit, Swinomish, Kikiallus, Snohomish, Snoqualmie, Stillaguamish, Suquamish, Samish, Puyallup, Squaxin, Skokomish, upper Chehalis, Muckleshoot, Nooksack, Chinook and San Juan Islands tribes of Indians, claimants, vs. the United States of America, defendant. Consolidated petition No. F-275. Seattle: Argus Press.

Walls, Robert

1987 *Bibliography of Washington State Folklore and Folklife.* Seattle: University of Washington Press. 301pp.

Waterman, Thomas T

c1920 Native Place Name in Puget Sound and Western Washington State. Microfilm #1864 on file, National Anthropological Archives, Washington, DC.

1922 The Geographical Names Used by the Indians of the Pacific Coast. *The Geographical Review* 12 (2): 175-194.

1924 The Shake Religion of Puget Sound. Smithsonian Report for 1922: 499-507. Smithsonian Institution Press, Washington DC.

1930 The Paraphernalia of the Duwamish 'Spirit-Canoe' Ceremony. *Indian Notes* 7 (2): 129-148, 295-3 12, 535-561. NY: Museum of the American Indian, Heye Foundation.

1973 Notes on the Ethnology of the Indians of Puget Sound. *Indian Notes and Monographs*, Miscellaneous Series 59. NY: Museum of the American Indian, Heye Foundation.

Waterman, Thomas T and Geraldine Coffin

1920 Types of Canoes on Puget Sound. *Indian Notes and Monographs*, Miscellaneous Series #5. NY: Museum of the American Indian, Heye Foundation.

Waterman, Thomas and Ruth Greiner

1921 Indian Houses of Puget Sound. *Indian Notes and Monographs*, Miscellaneous Series #9. NY: Museum of the American Indian, Heye Foundation.

Waterman, Thomas T and collaborators

1921 Native Houses of Western North America. *Indian Notes and Monographs*, Miscellaneous Series 11. NY: Museum of the American Indian, Heye Foundation.

Watson, Kenneth Greg, ed.

1996 The Legacy of Snoqualmie Falls. Special Issue. Snoqualmie Valley Historical Museum & *Snoqualmie Valley Reporter.* Wednesday, 28 February.

1999 *Mythology of Southern Puget Sound* by Arthur Ballard. Snoqualmie Valley Historical Museum, North Bend, Washington. Reprint

Watt, Roberta Frye

1931 *Four Wagons West*: The Story of Seattle. Portland: Metropolitan Press.

Webster, Lawrence
1982 Interview by Jay Miller. December. Transcript on file, Suquamish Tribal Archives, Suquamish, Washington.

White, Richard
1980 *Land Use, Environment, and Social Change: the Shaping of Island County, Washington.* Seattle: University of Washington Press.

Wickersham, James
1896 Pueblos on the Northwest Coast. *American Antiquarian* 18 (1): 21-24.
1898 Nisqually Mythology, Studies of the Washington Indians. *Overland Monthly* 32 (109): 345-351.
1899 Notes on the Indians of Washington. *American Antiquarian* 21 (6): 269-375.

Wike, Joyce A
1941 Modern Spirit Dancing of Northern Puget Sound. M.A. Thesis: University of Washington.
1952 The Role of the Dead in Northwest Coast Culture: 97-103. *Indian Tribes of Aboriginal America*. Sol Tax, ed. Proceedings of the 29th International Congress of Americanists. University of Chicago Press.

Wilkes. Charles
1858 *United States Exploring Expedition*, Atlas of Charts, Vol. II. Philadelphia.

Williams, Johnson
1916 Black Tamanous, the Secret Society of the Clallam Indians. *Washington Historical Quarterly* 7: 296-300.

Wingert, Paul
1949 American Indian Sculpture, A Study of the Northwest Coast. New York: J.J. Augustin Publisher.

Wright, Robin K, ed.
1991 *A Time of Gathering*: *Native Heritage of Washington State*. Seattle: University of Washington Press.

Yesler, Henry Leiter
1995 The Daughter of Old Chief Seattle: 11-23. *Images of Angeline*: Two Views of Chief Seattle's Daughter from the Nineteenth Century. Steve Heinzen, ed. Lowell Printing & Publishing, Everett WA. [Originally 1881]

Please help zap out typo-gnomes!